Now and Then

Reincarnation, Psychiatry and Daily Life

Also by Denys Kelsey

Many Lifetimes (with Joan Grant)

Now and Then
Reincarnation, Psychiatry and Daily Life

Dr D.E.R. Kelsey, MB, BChir, MRCP

ζ

Trencavel Press

First published in Great Britain in 2007
by the Trencavel Press, 3 Broadfield Court,
Broadfield Road, Folkestone, Kent CT20 2JT,
United Kingdom
www.trencavel.co.uk

© Machteld Kelsey

ISBN 978-0-9545786-2-6

Typeset by Trencavel Press
Printed by Hythe Printers Ltd.,
Pennypot Industrial Estate, Hythe, Kent

Contents

Note

In order to avoid the cumbersome 'he' and 'she' and their corresponding adjectives, the male pronouns and adjective are used exclusively but, unless the contrary is specifically indicated, they should always be assumed to include the female of the species.

Preface and Acknowledgements

Denys Kelsey passed away in October 2004 before he could write the acknowledgements for his book. We did, however, talk about them on various occasions, and he left a few notes. This is why I have been able to write them on his behalf.

For the purpose of clarification I should mention that I was closely associated with his work as from 1979. By then, Joan Grant's declining health had already, for quite some years, prevented her from taking any part in it. Joan died in January 1989, and Denys and I married later that year.

Denys wanted, first of all, to express his indebtness to his patients for the material they provided. He hoped that on reading his book they would be aware of his gratitude for what they had taught him; in particular those to whom his story relates.

Of almost equal importance for the book was Joan Grant, his wife of 28 years, who had a variety of psychic faculties. The most significant, in the present context, was her ability to recall details of a number of former lifetimes. Not only could she recall some former lifetimes of her own but she could also recall episodes from the former lifetimes of other people. In fact, he felt unable to do justice to the contribution she made.

As Cyril Drew said in his tribute to his great friend of Cambridge days, 'Denys had a unique understanding of human frailties and an outstanding gift for empathizing with those who sought his help. His devotion to his patients went well beyond the call of duty.' Denys brought the same dedication to his book, which he wrote over a long period of time. He much appreciated the encouragement he received from friends along the way. Two in particular should be mentioned for their thoughtful reading of the manuscript and the useful comments they made. They are Nick Halpin and Barry Maybury.

A final word of thanks goes to Margaret Anderson for her unfailing support of Denys, Joan and myself.

Machteld (Tilly) Kelsey   Gingins, Switzerland, 2006

We are grateful to the following for permission to reproduce material:

Egmont UK Ltd for 'A Song by Pooh' from *The Tao of Pooh* first published in Great Britain 1982 by Methuen Children's Books. Copyright © 1982, 1992, 1994, 1998 and 2002 by Benjamin Hoff.

Nicola Bennett-Reed for quotations from *Winged Pharaoh* by Joan Grant.

The BBC and Ian Stevenson for quotations from an interview by June Knox-Mawer with Ian Stevenson on Radio 4 on July 20, 1982.

Penguin Books Ltd. for quotations from *The Penguin Dictionary of Psychology* by A.S. and E.S. Reber.

Elsevier for quotation from *Dorland's Illustrated Medical Dictionary* (25th edition) edited by J.P. Friel.

Sacha van Rood-van Tuyll van Serooskerken for Renée van Tuyll's poem 'Each Life-Each Day'.

Introduction

I f it could be proved that we have all had previous lifetimes on this planet, I would not have felt it necessary to write this book. If I had decided to write it nevertheless, it would have been for a different reason. It would have been because, in the course of my career in psychiatry, two sets of circumstance provided me with experiences of kinds that do not fall to the lot of every specialist in this field. And I feel I should share them, and not only with fellow professionals.

First came the entirely accidental discovery, in 1948, that I had a facility for inducing the state of hypnosis. This discovery soon led me to become familiar with techniques of what is called 'hypnotic regression' which, in turn, paved my way to the verge of a belief in reincarnation. This set of circumstances, with its sequels, might justifiably be described as unusual. However, the second circumstance must be nearly unique.

It consisted of meeting and, for some twenty-eight years, being married to a psychic whose faculties included what she came to call 'Far Memory'. Her name was Joan Grant, and from her early childhood Joan had been accustomed to experiencing flashes of what she knew were memories of former lifetimes on this planet. Thus she had always looked upon reincarnation as a matter of course. Not until she was eleven years old did she fully realise that not everyone had similar experiences and viewed reincarnation in the same way. As an adult, she was sometimes able to see details of a former life of another person, a faculty that had proved crucial to the relief of more than one psychological problem long before we met.

Soon after we had started to work together, two patients, whom my best and prolonged efforts had failed to help, recovered immediately when, thanks to Joan, the origin of the problem in each case was discovered in events of a former lifetime. These two cases are described in *Many Lifetimes*, the book which Joan and I wrote together in 1967.

If, after my own work during the seven years before meeting Joan and then reading Joan's 'Far Memory' books, I had still needed justification for my belief in reincarnation, working with Joan on these two cases would have provided it.

This belief is similar, in a sense, to my belief that the sun will rise again tomorrow. I cannot prove that it will, therefore I cannot say that I *know* that it will, but I believe that it will so strongly that I would unhesitatingly stake my life upon it doing so.

Obviously, a belief in reincarnation offers extensions to the accepted framework of psychiatry. Above all, it compels us to recognise that a man must have a non-physical component because otherwise he would have nothing that could reincarnate! Once we accept that fact we can recognise that this earthly planet is not our permanent home. It can be thought of as a school from which we return home for the holidays. This home is obviously on a different, on a non-physical level of reality, and I usually refer to any or all of these levels as 'Upstairs'.

What is man supposed to learn during his 'terms', his lifetimes at 'school'?

Until he accepts that he has a spiritual component, he cannot know the real purpose of his life or have a true sense of direction. But once he has recognised that he has such a component, he will surely sense that what he has to learn must be the rules of daily living, which are conducive to and compatible with the sustained health of the individual and of the community. These rules would cover our relationships and behaviour towards one another in every aspect of life, and also our duties and responsibilities towards the maintenance of the very substance of the planet itself.

Currently our planet is sick. There are two very obvious symptoms. One of them consists of the wars that continue to erupt, like abscesses on the skin of a patient with blood poisoning. The other is poverty, which is spread over much of its surface like a rash. If reincarnation were universally accepted as a reality that meant as much to each of us as does our certainty that the sun will indeed rise again tomorrow, we could bring health to our planet.

It is impossible to prove reincarnation to the satisfaction of a materialist, if only because, for the resolute sceptic, the arm of coincidence can be of truly infinite length and can be invoked to explain any phenomenon. Because of this fact, I feel any evidence in support of reincarnation should be made available.

If a colleague happens upon this book, I hope he will find something of interest, but it is written for everyone who, at some time has asked himself: 'Why am I here? What am I supposed to be doing?' And: 'Is there any purpose in life?'

Part I

A Song by Pooh

A little something he just made up

How can you get very far,
If you don't know Who You Are?
How can you do what you ought,
If you don't know What You've Got?
And if you don't know Which to Do
Of all the things in front of you,
Then what you'll have when you are through
Is just a mess without a clue
Of all the best that can come true
If you know What and Which and Who.

1   *Some Personal History*

My belief in reincarnation really started as I was reading the opening paragraph of the book *Winged Pharaoh* by Joan Grant. The paragraph runs:

When the time came for me to return to Earth, a Messenger of the Great Overlords told me I should be re-born in Kam; and that the two who would fashion my body would welcome me, for we had been companions aforetime and the ties between us were of love and not of hatred, which are the two threads that bind men most closely together upon Earth; and for my brother I should have one with whom I had travelled long upon the great journey.

As I reached the end of that paragraph I knew that in reincarnation I would find the answer to the problem that had been perplexing me for several years. I knew it with the order of certainty that accompanies the knowledge that the word which has floated unbidden into one's mind, probably while doing something totally irrelevant, is the correct answer to the clue in a crossword that has been eluding one, maybe for days.

A week before the book came into my hands, I had learned from a chance acquaintance that a lady named Joan Grant had a faculty that she called 'Far Memory'. By dint of this faculty she was able to recall former lifetimes she had spent on this planet and she had written books about some of them, of which *Winged Pharaoh* was the first. My new acquaintance was obviously very well versed in extrasensory matters; moreover he knew Joan Grant personally. He had no doubt that the faculty she claimed was valid, and that what she called her 'Far Memory' books were indeed the valid accounts they appeared to be of some of her former lifetimes.

When *Winged Pharaoh* first appeared in 1937, the author had said nothing about how she had come to write it. She reserved that information for *Time Out of Mind* the autobiography of the first part of her present life, which she did not write until 1956. Thus, when I read the book in 1957, I had information about it which had been denied to its early readers and which must have contributed to the impact that its first paragraph made upon me.

I was forty years old when I read *Winged Pharaoh*. By then I had been a qualified doctor for fifteen years, for the last nine of them specialising in psychiatry. Without the somewhat unusual experiences that I encountered during those latter years, I'm sure I would not have recognised the significance of what Joan Grant had to offer. We started to live and work together in 1957, married in 1960, and remained married until her death, some twenty-eight years later.

We related some of our clinical experiences in *Many Lifetimes*, the book we wrote together, published in 1967. For the convenience of the multitude who have never read it or who have forgotten it, I will, here and there, recapitulate some of its salient points.

I cannot recall that I ever wanted to be anything but a doctor and for the first six years after I had qualified my work consisted of trying, in one way or another, to make people more comfortable in their bodies. In my first post I was the house surgeon in the orthopaedic department of a general hospital. In addition to the sprains, fractures, dislocations and arthritic problems that were the staple fare of that department, I gained considerable experience in dealing with injuries caused by enemy bombers.

My next posts were in departments of Internal Medicine, and included patients of all ages. Both the Army and the Navy thanked me for reminding them that I was now trained and at their disposal, but they said they had no need of my services at that time. It was in fact two years before I was summoned to the Royal Army Medical Corps and during that period I gained the postgraduate degree of Membership of the Royal College of Physicians. This is a coveted degree and it set my sights upon a career as a specialist in internal medicine as opposed, for instance, to surgery or obstetrics.

Once in the Army I was posted to Germany where I was first employed as, in effect, General Practitioner to the troops in the garrison town of Neumünster, just north of Hamburg, and later also to their families when they came to join them. After about a year in this capacity I was transferred to the large military hospital in Hamburg, where I was immediately allocated to the Department of Internal Medicine. It seemed that circumstances were indeed taking me towards an eventual career as a specialist in that field. However, an abrupt change of direction lay just ahead. As I described in *Many Lifetimes*, I discovered, entirely by accident, that I had an aptitude for inducing the state of hypnosis.

In 1947 the prevalent epidemic of influenza invaded the hospital and promptly felled two of the psychiatrists. Their department happened to be unusually busy and, though I knew nothing about psychiatry, I was asked to lend a hand there in any way I could.

During the first evening of this extension to my usual duties, I was summoned urgently to the ward because a patient had become 'violent'. I arrived to find the patient lying on his bed, being sat upon by two well-built orderlies. At my request they found somewhere else to sit, thus revealing a man in his late twenties who was holding his body so rigid that his limbs were quivering. He was in a state of acute panic.

I did what seemed the natural thing to do. I drew a chair up to the bedside and started to talk to him in what I hoped would be a soothing and reassuring voice. The ward was in darkness, except for a small blue light on the wall about a metre above his head. I asked him to try to concentrate on this light, thinking that if he could do so it would be more difficult for terrifying thoughts to enter his mind. Then I drew his attention to each of his limbs in turn, coaxing him to allow them to relax so that they lay on the bed as lifeless as logs. After perhaps fifteen minutes he was looking so peaceful that—quite casually—I said to him, 'Why not go off to sleep now?' At this suggestion, his eyeballs swivelled upwards and his eyelids snapped down in a curiously positive sort of way, and his breathing became quiet and regular. 'Good Heavens,' I thought, 'I've hypnotised him!'

I was astonished. I knew nothing whatever about hypnosis and had certainly had no intention of attempting to do anything of the sort. Indeed I know not why this thought came into my mind so promptly and so clearly.

The next morning I described what had happened to the senior psychiatrist in charge of the department. He had little doubt that I had indeed hypnotised the patient since I had unwittingly followed one of the classical methods of inducing the state. He asked me then to try to produce a similar effect upon another patient.

This patient was also a soldier, but one who was little more than a boy. He was suffering from symptoms that were a direct consequence of a gruesome motor accident for which he had been responsible a few weeks earlier, and in which his mate had been killed. When he was lying down I repeated, as closely as I could, the way I had spoken to the patient of the previous evening and, within minutes, this lad seemed to have reached a similar state. And then something else happened. Without anyone saying a word, without prompting of any kind, he seemed suddenly to be reliving the accident.

We saw the horror on his face as he realised that the crash was inevitable; and when he realised too that his mate was dead, there was an outpouring of grief and remorse that had not occurred before. For perhaps a quarter of an hour he wept. Then the weeping gradually turned to sobs. He became able to talk through his sobs and to tell us about the accident. When he had calmed down sufficiently we put him to bed in a side-room. The next morning his symptoms had vanished, though it was some days before he could talk to us without, at some point, almost breaking into sobs.

During the next weeks I had the opportunity to treat, under supervision, other patients in a similar way with some similarly dramatic results. I found this sort of work more rewarding than anything I had experienced hitherto and decided that instead of aiming at a career as an internist I would specialise henceforth in psychiatry. Accordingly, on being discharged from the Army I sought a junior post at Park Prewett Psychiatric Hospital, in Basingstoke, and was pleased to be accepted. During the next six years I gradually rose to becoming a member of the permanent senior staff.

In a psychiatric hospital housing some 1500 patients I encountered most kinds of psychiatric illnesses, but, without question, on account of my facility with hypnosis I had experiences of kinds that do not fall to the lot of every doctor. I was fortunate, too, in finding at the hospital a senior colleague who shared my interest in hypnosis, and we worked a lot together. I found it easier than he to induce the state, but he had more experience in making use of it.

Nowadays, it is common knowledge that there is a part of the mind that is called the 'unconscious'. It is an apt name because we do not know what it contains. We are able to know only as much about its contents as we are able to bring to consciousness. It happens that I share with many of my colleagues the belief that many cases of what are now called neurotic disorders are caused by material in the patient's unconscious. Hence, getting the relevant material from his unconscious into his consciousness is often a vital step in therapy. And this is where hypnosis can be exceedingly useful.

A particular feature of the hypnotic state is that it makes it much easier for a patient to regress. When a patient regresses, a part of his consciousness—sometimes all of his consciousness—leaves the present to merge with the memory of some past event that is locked in his unconscious. In a complete regression, the present time—for the patient—becomes the period to which he has regressed. I was soon familiar with observing adults reliving in this way experiences from their early childhood. It was this feature of hypnosis, used in the treatment of a particular patient, which opened for me the door to areas of mental activity hitherto unrecognised in contemporary psychiatry. As I also related in *Many Lifetimes*, this patient was a young woman of nineteen—I will call her Clare—

who was in a state of deep depression. She had recently been in another hospital, one that was famed for psychotherapy. The staff there had established that since Clare had reached adolescence her mood had never been normal. To use the technical jargon, she had always been either somewhat hypomanic or somewhat depressed. More colloquially, she had always been either a bit above the line or a bit below it. Since Clare's parents had always found her easier to manage when she was in the 'above the line' state, they had long regarded this state as normal. The doctors had concluded that the only treatment that might help her was a brain operation. (Let me remind readers at this point that the period we are concerned with was 1950. Much has changed since then!)

Clare's parents had rejected the idea of brain surgery for their daughter, had removed her from that hospital and arranged for her admission to Park Prewett, the psychiatric hospital that served their area. She happened to arrive on a day when I was responsible for admitting female patients, and our convention was that the doctor who admitted a patient remained responsible for the care of that patient. I mention this point to emphasise that it was for this reason alone, and for no other, that Clare became my patient.

If my training up to this point had been along more conventional lines, I'm sure I would have accepted the verdict of the famous names at that other hospital, which was, essentially, that nothing but brain surgery could be done for Clare. As it was, I decided to try hypnoanalysis and, mercifully, depressed though she was, Clare proved an excellent subject.

One day, after I had induced hypnosis, I started the session by asking Clare to tell me the first number that came into her head. Owing to her depressed state, every response had to be dragged out of her, but eventually she gave me the number five. 'Good,' I said, encouragingly. 'What can you think of in connection with the number five?' After a long pause she told me, 'Only that I've got five fingers.'

'Anything special about your fingers?'

After another long, long pause, 'I bite my nails'.

Since nail-biting can sometimes be of psychological significance, I told Clare that she would soon find herself in a situation that would throw light on her nail-biting. Within seconds, she found herself sitting in her pram, clad only in a sun hat, sucking her thumb. I asked her how old she was and she replied, unhesitatingly and quite firmly, 'Nine months'.

Nine months! This was already a regression to an earlier age than I had encountered before, but I sensed there was more to come. Suddenly, as she was lying on the couch, Clare became very red in the face, started to make violent sucking movements with her lips and furiously to pummel the wall. I asked her what was happening. She replied, angrily, 'My mother is holding me to her breast but there is no milk coming out.' A few moments later Clare gave a little start.

'What happened then?'

'She has put me over to the other side,' came the reply.

The pummelling was resumed until it was interrupted by another little start, accompanied this time by a little wail. Pitifully, Clare said through her tears, 'She has put me down and gone away!'

'Why has she gone away?'

'Because I was so angry...'

The infant Clare had genuinely believed that *it was her anger that had caused her mother to disappear.* This was a most interesting response because it supported one widely held theory of one cause of depression. I shall refer to it later in the book.

A week or two later I had the opportunity, with Clare's permission, to talk with her mother about this session. Her mother declared she had no doubt that Clare had indeed been reliving an incident that had really happened. She had always known she had no milk but, believing that an infant derived something magical simply from contact with the breast, she had always put her daughter to the breast *before putting her down and going to fetch her bottle.* Then, as if that confirmation of the validity of her daughter's regression were not interesting enough, she added, seemingly just as an afterthought, 'But I stopped doing this on the advice of my doctor when the baby was three weeks old'.

In that sentence Clare's mother had given me what I felt was conclusive evidence that, by the age of three weeks, her daughter had been able to appreciate a situation and, albeit mistakenly, to interpret it. I can understand that, unless one had witnessed these sessions, it was reasonable to judge me crazy for believing that the regression could have been valid because, at the time, around 1950, the almost universal view was that at three weeks the mind was not sufficiently developed to be capable of the activities I was attributing to it. And that was indeed the view of most of my colleagues. But it was impossible for me to deny the validity of what I had witnessed, and I became interested in trying to find out just when the mind began to function.

Clare's case was of the greatest importance to me. It prepared me for the case, about three months later, when, after a succession of regressions to ever earlier ages, a patient reached a scene from which the next step, if she were to regress any further, would be to find herself in the womb. And this is precisely what happened. I then brought her forward in time and—as I felt certain then and still do—*she relived the process of her birth.*

This case furthered my search for the answer to the question: 'Just when does the mind begin to function?' But it did more than that. It awakened my interest in the possibility that the precise circumstances of a person's birth might have lasting psychological effects. Indeed, I am sure that they can. In addition, as over the next two years regressions to birth and to ever earlier periods of life in the womb became a frequent occurrence, I came to believe that the prenatal period of our history was of paramount importance in the formation of character. Much later I came to realise that, while it can make an important contribution, it is very far from being the whole story.

This particular phase of my experience culminated in the case of a lady whom I will call Marilyn. To the best of my belief then—and still today—Marilyn, under hypnosis, relived an aspect of her conception. We shall be concerned with Marilyn again. For the moment I will say only that her case convinced me that we have consciousness from the very start of our life in the womb, and that even our conception is a relevant part of our psychological history.

It is fairly widely accepted now that a person is conscious in the womb, but this was not always so. In 1952 I wrote a paper on the subject. It was called 'Phantasies of birth and prenatal experiences recovered from patients undergoing hypnoanalysis'. Its publication in 1953 by what was then *The Journal of Mental Science* but is now *The British Journal of Psychiatry* was considered sufficiently newsworthy to be mentioned on the radio in the *Nine o'Clock News*. It was also reported in *Time* magazine. In the paper I stated my belief that what I had called 'Phantasies' were in fact a form of recall of genuine repressed memories. I would express that rather differently today, but I do believe they were, essentially, memories.

Professionally, these years of discovery were a lonely period because even my closest colleague and friend who had shared my interest in hypnosis found himself unable to accompany me on the path along which my work was taking me, while my colleagues in general thought I was crazy. Nevertheless, I could not help following that path; the succession of cases simply dragged me along it. And the thunderbolt of intuition that struck me after the session in which Marilyn relived her conception confirmed me in my belief that my interpretations of the material I had been receiving from my patients were correct.

The session in which Marilyn had relived her conception had occurred during the evening of the Saturday before Easter Day of 1952. After the session, back in my room at the hospital, I was musing upon the problem I had anticipated from the moment I believed that the material I was getting from my patients concerning experiences in the womb was the genuine memories they appeared to be. Hitherto I had avoided coming to grips with it, but the session with Marilyn had crystallised the problem and faced me with it inescapably. The problem was simply this: if Marilyn had in truth relived her conception, she must have perceived and recorded the event. But how? And with what? Obviously she had had no physical apparatus at the time that could have registered physical sensations, and recorded and interpreted them.

Suddenly I felt as if I had been struck by a thunderbolt: a thunderbolt of intuition. I sensed a voice almost shouting at me: 'Can't you SEE! This is the PROOF that in a human being there is a component that is not physical!!'

In fact, of course, that session was not proof of anything whatever; but reason could not resist the impact of that thunderbolt. For me personally the point had been proven. Irrefutably. As I remarked in *Many Lifetimes*, to have been told about the reality of the soul from various pulpits is one thing; to have been forced to the same conclusion by events in one's consulting-room is quite another. And though the thought never entered my head at the time, I had at least convinced myself of the reality of something that could reincarnate. At that point, in a state of suppressed excitement, I went to bed.

I don't know what had been going on in my head during the night, but I vividly recall that the next morning I positively exploded out of bed, exclaiming, 'Either I've gone crazy or I've got an idea.' I crossed the room to my desk on which my typewriter was standing, fed in paper and started to hammer away. I did not need to think. I heard no voice but as clearly as if someone were dictating to me, ideas just streamed into my mind, and then out through my fingers. To my great personal regret I have lost that essay, but I remember, word for word, how it began and how it ended. The opening sentence ran: 'You cannot bring peace simply by hammering an opponent to his knees. As soon as he feels strong enough, he will get up and attack you again. Peace will come only when the antagonists have undergone such changes of heart that they no longer wish to pit their energies against one another but to align them in the same direction.'

This was followed by the thought that here on Earth it was easy to recognise forces in opposition. There are the forces that tend to diminish the barriers between people, which I would designate as 'positive', and those that tend to increase those barriers, which I would designate as 'negative'. Love and fear are the most obvious examples of each category.

Next, the possibility occurred to me that those forces might be merely the 'down-here' form of forces that were in opposition on every level of the cosmos but which, on other levels, were in forms which we could no more understand than a dog could understand income tax. This notion was followed by the thought that perhaps each one of us, in his character, incorporates some of both forces of which, at least from a human point of view, one can be described as benign and the other as malign. If that were the case, then perhaps the fundamental task facing each of us during his lifetime, no matter what else he does— in the way of earning his living, for instance—is to change as much as he can of his malign into benign potentials. I found these ideas exciting and satisfying. They have not changed since they first came to mind in 1952, and indeed they have been a vital factor in the basis of my practice of psychotherapy.

It is from this point that the body of the essay has become lost, even to my memory; but the end remains fast in my mind. After some three hours I found myself typing: '...and this is love. But love is GOD! Therefore there must be a GOD!!!'

As those words appeared on the paper, the stream of ideas ceased, abruptly. But it was replaced immediately by a sensation of such joy as I had never experienced before and have not known again. It was ineffable. And it persisted for forty-eight hours.

The plethora of exclamation marks, which follows the words 'Therefore there must be a God', is an attempt to convey my astonishment at having written myself into believing in something I had never been able to believe in before. My previous 'non-belief' had been very serious. I was at one boarding school from seven to thirteen years of age, and at another from thirteen to seventeen. At each of these Church of England establishments there was at least one service every day in the school chapel and two services on Sundays, while at the latter school there were also House prayers every morning and evening. In addition, at both schools there was a weekly scripture lesson; and during the school holidays attendance with the family at the village church on Sundays was mandatory. With this degree of exposure I could hardly have escaped absorbing sizeable parts of the liturgy, including ideas, albeit hazy ones, of a 'World Without End' and 'Life Everlasting'.

However, I could not accept some of the basics of what I was asked to believe. I just could not have faith in something, which, with the arrogance of adolescence, I just knew could not be so. The Immaculate Conception—as I understood it—was one thing, and the resurrection of the physical body was another. Hence I felt very doubtful about the reality of God. No sound issued from my lips when the creed was recited during a service and I resisted all attempts to have me confirmed. Now, suddenly, in an instant, all the effects of my doubts had vanished. It was as if they had been magically swept away, to be replaced by an unshakeable certainty of the reality of a deity: of God.

In the same instant I understood Jesus Christ as a historical person who had really existed, who bore a special relationship to God and was therefore divine. If He had chosen to incarnate in some unusual way I had no doubt He could have arranged it, but whether He did or not seemed immaterial. I still did not— and do not—believe in the resurrection of the physical body, but that does not seem to matter either. What do matter are the two commandments He left us: 'Love God' and 'Love Thy Neighbour as Thyself'. The spread of our ability to render this planet uninhabitable makes them increasingly important—of this I become more firmly convinced every day. Of course, their source gives them added weight, but even if you choose to ignore the first of them, and to strip the second of all its religious connotations, experience suggests that failure at least to try to observe the latter is the essential causal factor of much of the world's unrest and of many individual psychological problems.

This realisation had a significant effect upon my approach to my work. It shifted the main focus of my interest from the stresses that had befallen the patient to the way in which the patient had reacted to them. In short, my approach to therapy became value-oriented. By this I mean I took it upon myself to judge whether any particular attitude was or was not conducive to the sustained health of the individual and the community. Repeatedly, my experience showed me that the nature of a patient's reaction to a stressful event or situation contained the clue to his problem. This topic occupies the second part of the book.

The next significant external event in my life occurred in 1957. This was the entry into my life of Joan Grant, to which I have already referred. Unfortunately, a certain incompatibility of temperament made it impossible for us to work together with a patient as a general rule, though Joan was always available for advice. It is largely with my professional experiences—and the thoughts arising from them—over the years that followed that we shall now be concerned.

2   *A Grey Motor Car*

While I was a member of the staff of Park Prewett Psychiatric Hospital, my private life was, for many months, the scene of an experience that became exceedingly useful in my work as a psychiatrist who specialized in psychotherapy. Since the story will enable me to introduce some technical terms and concepts quite painlessly, it will make a suitable point from which to start. At the heart of it all lies a grey motor car.

The single car we had was so frequently in demand for ferrying the children to and from various functions that an additional form of transport had become a necessity. Throughout a mild spring, summer and autumn a motor bicycle had been a delight to ride and had served me admirably; but on roads that featured ruts of frozen snow it had nothing to commend it. A second car was essential. All I needed—and all I could afford—was some elderly vehicle I could rely upon to take me to the hospital and back every day, only ten miles (sixteen kilometres) each way, and once a week to each of slightly more distant out-patient clinics for which I was responsible.

I told some local garages what I was looking for and a day or two later one of them telephoned to say that they had just the car for me. I hurried to see it and was confronted with a large, luxurious, second-hand limousine. It was totally unsuitable both for my purposes and my pocket and I said so, brusquely, because I was annoyed at the waste of my time. But I could not get that car out of my mind!

Starting from the misguided premise that a car of such quality would never go wrong, so money invested in the car would be as safe as in the bank, and more along similar lines, within forty-eight hours I had convinced myself that the only *sensible* course was to buy it. And the next day I did so, reducing my bank balance towards zero.

The following morning I set off on the ten-mile drive to the hospital with the petrol gauge showing that the sixteen-gallon (72 litres) tank was half full.

Within five miles I had run out of petrol. A faulty petrol gauge soon proved to be the least of my troubles. The car used nearly as much oil as it did petrol, and it was almost appropriate to reckon its consumption of the latter in gallons to the mile rather than by the more conventional standard. And I had possessed the car for only a few months when the price of petrol suddenly rocketed. Naturally, the value of such a mechanical monstrosity as I had acquired plummeted. The garage from whom I had bought it offered me just a quarter of what I had so recently paid for it.

There is no teacher like personal experience and so far I had merely been learning something about the hazards of buying a second-hand motor car. However, at this point a very personal lesson in psychiatry started.

I could no longer afford to drive the car, and any reasonable man would surely have said to himself: 'The petrol situation is not going to improve: accept that you were a complete idiot to buy the car and get rid of it, on the best terms you can.'

But I couldn't!

I bought an ancient Austin 7, the forerunner of all the Minis, to run around in; but I could not bring myself to part with the monster. My friends never stopped telling me I was crazy and, when I had a special shed built in the garden in which to house the car, even I had to admit there was more in my attachment to it than met the eye. But what was it! Any pride in ownership had long since evaporated and any idea along the line that I was competing with my father who had never owned such a limousine seemed ridiculous. Even the senior colleague who had been my friend and mentor since I arrived at the hospital was unable to help me to discover what was binding me to that wretched car.

At last, after about a year, there came the day!

I had driven to the hospital as usual in the Austin 7 and parked it outside the block that housed many of my patients. I was walking to my office with the lady with whom I was going to have the first session of the day when she happened to glance out of the window and see my little car. 'Oh,' she said, 'I see you have come in your pram, again!'

Her little joke had a most curious effect. I was able to continue with my work, for most of me remained anchored in the present; but part of me flashed back in time to the morning, when I was six years old, on which my mother had set off for a voyage to South America. And, though only a flash, it somehow included every detail of the occasion.

Ever since I had learned that my mother was going to cross the sea, I had spent hours looking at a large picture in our dining room of two fishermen in a dinghy who appeared to me, untutored as yet in the scriptures, about to be engulfed by a huge wave. This was the sort of boat in which I pictured my mother would be setting out across the ocean. I felt certain I should never see her again. Little wonder that on this morning of her departure I was clinging to her, begging her not to leave me. She was also hugging me and she was wearing at the time a grey fur coat. (I have since been able to confirm that her fur coat was indeed of grey squirrel.) Of course, I was unable to keep her with me and, as she vanished through the front door, I was left with a mental picture of my mother as something warm, soft and enveloping; infinitely desirable yet unretainable; and—above all—grey.

In that instant I understood the nature of my attachment to that car because it too was warm and soft and enveloping and—above all—it was grey! Even the woolly loose covers on the seats were grey. Suddenly, for the first time with all my mind, I saw the car only for what it was: a large vehicle that might conceivably be of some use to someone but was of no earthly good to me. My attachment to it dissolved instantly and the next day, without a pang, I changed both it and the mini for a car that really was suitable.

One might well ask how I could ever have come to confuse that mass of metal, glass, rubber and fabric with my mother, for this is what had been happening. That I did so illustrates the power that thoughts and feelings of which we are not aware can have upon our conscious feelings and behaviour. To explain how this material exerts this power I must start by drawing heavily upon ideas bequeathed to us by Dr Sigmund Freud.

Dr Sigmund Freud and the Unconscious

Dr Sigmund Freud—who is usually referred to simply as 'Freud'—was born in Vienna in 1856 and died in London in 1939. When the history of the last century, indeed of the millennium, comes to be written, Freud will surely rank among its most significant figures. He started his medical career as a physician, specialising in diseases of the physical nervous system. However, as many people are aware, while still a young man he spent some time working with Charcot in Paris, and became impressed with what could be achieved through hypnosis. Once back in Vienna he teamed up with another physician, one Joseph Breuer, who had already developed what he called 'the cathartic method'. It involved hypnotising the patient and then allowing him to talk, a technique that often resulted in the disappearance of the problem.

Freud noticed that much of the material, which emerged when the patient was hypnotised, seemed not to be available to him when he was in normal consciousness. On the basis of this observation, Freud presumed that there was an area of the mind that was unconscious, but the contents of which played an important part in influencing behaviour. He became particularly interested in the types of cases for which no physical cause could be found: patients who were suffering from what we now call neurotic disorders. On the foundation of his work with these patients, Freud developed a form of treatment that, without using hypnosis, centred upon exploring the contents of the unconscious area of the patient's mind. Freud called this treatment 'Psychoanalysis'.

The name became virtually Freud's copyright. In order to be called psychoanalysis, a treatment has to conform rigidly to certain features upon which Freud insisted, and to be based upon a precise philosophy. A discussion of these features would not be relevant to our theme, but part of the philosophy includes a concept of the geography of the mind and some of the ways in which the mind works. These are important to us.

Amongst a host of other ideas, Freud postulated three levels or areas of mental activity. First, there is the level that is often referred to as 'normal waking consciousness'. As its name implies, this is the level on which we are normally functioning when we are awake, and it contains only the thoughts and feelings and perceptions of which we are aware at each particular moment. Beneath this level of mental activity—in this context the prepositions 'beneath' or 'below' are as good as one another—there is the area which Freud called the 'preconscious'. In this area are stored all the memories which we can bring to our normal waking consciousness whenever we want them. For instance, the date of my birthday is seldom in my normal waking consciousness, but it is stored in my preconscious and I can bring it to my normal waking consciousness whenever I need it. Below the preconscious is the area Freud called the 'unconscious'.

Whenever we have an experience, which is so laden with unpleasant feelings of one kind or another that we do not wish the memory of it to be liable to return unbidden to our normal waking consciousness, we push it into our unconscious, though we are completely unaware that we are doing so. To use our first technical term, one that we shall encounter frequently, we 'repress' it. Thus to repress something simply means to push it into our unconscious.

The sight of my mother disappearing through the door and vanishing, as I believed for ever, evoked such sadness that I did not want to be reminded of it, and therefore I repressed its memory. It will prove useful later on if, at this point, we consider what exactly it was that I had repressed, for every repressed memory has essentially the same components.

Firstly, I had repressed a fragment of that part of my totality that enabled me to think of myself as 'I'. It was the part which, if someone had asked me why I was crying, would have enabled me to reply: '"I" am crying because "my" mother has gone away and "I" shall never see her again.' It was only the fragment of that part of my totality that was concerned with my mother and her departure that was repressed. The other parts, the parts that were related to my father, my sisters, my pony, my school—in short, all the other aspects of my life—were not involved.

This fragment of my totality, like any repressed fragment, embodied a wish, and this wish, like any wish, had three elements. Firstly, it had a mental picture of the situation as it was, which in this case was a picture of my mother disappearing through the door and vanishing—as I believed—for ever. Secondly, it had a picture of the situation into which I wished I could change it. This was probably less clearly defined but, in essence, it was a picture of my mother's continued presence.

If such pictures were the only features of a repressed memory, such a memory might be nothing more than a kind of immaterial dead weight; but there is also a third element which ensures that it can be anything but that. This element is *The Energy In the Wish* to change the first picture into the second: the situation as it was into the situation one wished it to be. Freud called a repressed memory with its several components a 'complex'. I propose to call it, instead, a 'ghost'. At this point, a word about such ghosts, and about symbols, a subject with which they are closely involved, will be appropriate.

About Ghosts and Symbols

Such a ghost always appears to be anchored, permanently, in a perpetual now. If it was formed during an individual's childhood, its fragment of 'I-ness' is a fragment of the totality of that child, and it remains at the age at which it was ghosted. It never grows up. A ghost, therefore, cannot evolve.

There are probably few of us who, without realizing it, are not carrying around in our unconscious one or more such ghosts, such fragments of the child that once we were. It is ultimately they who are responsible for many of our preferences and aversions. They are also responsible for a significant proportion of all emotional illnesses. In effect, a repressed fragment of 'I' remains very much alive and is constantly scanning the passing scene in which the individual finds himself, alert to discern therein some factor which it can see or, more accurately, interpret as repeating a feature of the situation of which the memory was repressed, resulting in the formation of the ghost.

I use the word 'interpret' because the 'I' of a ghost reacts to symbols, and while the 'I' of normal waking consciousness can always distinguish between a symbol and the reality, the 'I' of a ghost lacks this ability. An analogy may make the point clear.

At a picture exhibition one might find oneself looking at a portrait that reminded one, very vividly, of someone whom one had once loved dearly—and lost, but the memory of whom one had always cherished. One might even have been moved to buy the portrait. But if one did so, one would always be aware that one had, at best, only a symbol of one's lost love, not that lost love in reality.

But I had not cherished the memory of my mother, as I had perceived her hugging me that morning and then disappearing out of the door. I had repressed it, together with the longing for her return. Now, the 'I' of my normal waking consciousness and the 'I' of the ghost had seen the car at the same moment, but they had perceived it differently. The 'I' of my normal waking consciousness had seen it as a large, somewhat luxurious vehicle but one that was of no possible use to me. But let me stress again that a ghost lacks the ability to distinguish between a symbol and the reality. Hence, the features of 'cosy envelopingness' that the car suggested, combined with, above all, its greyness, were enough to cause the 'I' of the ghost to perceive it, not merely as a symbol of that mother who had vanished, but as that mother in reality who had returned! The fact that she had vanished some thirty years previously was irrelevant to the ghost. Ghosts seem to experience and measure time differently from the way we do.

In effect, the 'I' of the ghost had jumped for joy, exclaiming, 'Whoopee! Mama has come back and this time'—as I have explained already—'if I exert every effort I can keep her.' The energy in the ghost's desire to keep her surged into my consciousness and affected my subsequent behaviour. First it changed my feelings towards the car to such an extent that two days later I bought it. Having bought it, I could no more get rid of it than a small boy could be induced to throw his mother away until—thanks to my patient's little joke—I gained insight into the explanation of my attachment to it. It is perhaps only of personal interest that I have since realised that I have always avoided sadness that there was no need for me to feel. By this I mean that I would never choose a book or visit a play that I knew ended in tragedy. It seems to me that there is enough cause for sadness in real life.

In psychotherapy one finds that the matters that are symbolized are usually basic to life: sex, death, mothers, fathers, aggression, and gender by which I mean maleness or femaleness. It is, therefore appropriate to ask, 'What is the function of symbols?'

I think at least part of the answer is that they are a means of concealing a reality from ourselves or—perhaps and—the outside world. The reality may be the fact that within our totality we harbour certain feelings or ideas that we associate with guilt or fear or distress of some kind. Such a reality might be a wish to injure someone that is held in the unconscious of the individual so that at a conscious level he is unaware of it. In such a case, an object that is broken—entirely by accident, so far as the person responsible for the breakage is aware—might have been seen by the unconscious of that person as a symbol of the individual who is the object of the unconscious hostility.

An interesting example of symbolism was provided by the case of a young woman who suffered from attacks of shortness of breath. Her doctor rightly suspected that they were of psychological origin and referred her to my clinic.

She gave the impression of being a tightly buttoned-up person, but she always arrived carrying a capacious straw shopping basket, on one side of which was worked a very large, brilliantly coloured flower. On entering, she would cross my room and place her basket on the windowsill, which was the point furthest from the couch. She would then recross the room to the couch and settle herself upon it.

It was soon clear that, largely on account of the attitude of her parents towards anything remotely sexual, she had, throughout her life, tried to 'disown' her sexuality. But one's sexuality is an integral part of oneself. It is impossible totally to reject it. It will find expression somehow. What this lady had done, in effect, was to put her sexuality into her highly decorative shopping basket, and then place it as far away from herself as possible. That her efforts to suppress her sexuality were stifling her was revealed by the nature of her physical problem, the attacks of shortness of breath.

She came to see me once a week, and as her therapy progressed and she gained confidence that she could safely cast off all bonds to her restrictive parents, it was intriguing to see her unfolding like a flower. The day came when, unaware I am sure of the significance of what she was doing, she placed her basket beneath the couch. This event heralded the end of her therapy. Within two weeks, for the first time in her life, she was going out with a young man.

This is an appropriate note on which to close this chapter, but before doing so I want to make two points. The first is that young children are capable of understanding a great deal more than is often supposed. If the 'grown-ups' had shown me pictures of the sort of floating hotel in which my mother would be crossing the sea, I would still have felt sadness at her departure but I would have been spared the agonising sense of impending bereavement caused by the belief that she was disappearing for ever, which was what had caused me to repress the episode.

The second is that I have no sympathy with people who hold the view that to be described as a patient is humiliating, and hence insist upon the term 'client'. The word 'patient' is derived from the Latin verb 'patior', which means 'I suffer'. One consults a doctor—or healer who though medically unqualified may nevertheless be extremely effective—because one is suffering, and one is, therefore, in that context, a patient. Throughout this book, when it is appropriate, I shall refer to persons who have honoured me by seeking my help as 'patients'.

3   *Energy Problems*

O ne result of the Grey Car saga was that it led me, in due course, to
see that helping patients to rescue their ghosts was tantamount to
tackling problems caused by the energy from a repressed wish. 'But', I
wondered, 'what kind of energy is the energy in a wish? It is surely not any kind
of energy with which physicists are familiar.'

I could accept that for some time to come—perhaps forever—the nature
of this energy would be one of the Great Mysteries, like the Nature of God or,
for that matter, the nature of life. But I needed a concept, which would form a
working basis: a concept that would give me a picture of what I was trying to do.
And one day I discovered one.

Steam—and Fundamental Energy

I was contemplating the inch of clear space between the spout of a boiling
kettle and the cloud of water vapour it quickly became. I knew, of course, that
far from being empty, that inch of clear space contained what is rightly called
steam. It struck me then that this steam which, properly channelled, had the
power to move an ocean liner or a massive locomotive pulling fifty wagons,
could be transformed, not only into water vapour which, loosely, one could
think of as a gas, but also into water, a liquid, and into ice, a solid.

The thought then occurred to me that this steam could be taken to represent
Fundamental Energy. I was perfectly content to ascribe the origin of this
Fundamental Energy to God, and felt no need to pursue the question of its
origin any further! I conceived of this Fundamental Energy, in its original state,
as being without any fixed shape or form. But, thanks no doubt in some part
to the hours spent in chapel at school, I had no difficulty in imagining that it
could be transformed into everything, visible and invisible. It was then but a
step to accepting that it was not only every solid thing, be it animal, vegetable
or mineral, that consisted, in the final analysis, of this Fundamental Energy: it

could also become that form of energy we know as *Life*. Life is, of course, the essential form of this Fundamental Energy.

Certainly a plant gets energy from the sun; but without the energy of Life it can make no use of the energy from the sun. Without the energy of Life, all the sun will do is to dry the plant up or hasten its decomposition.

Certainly we get energy from food. But push food into a corpse by no matter what route, and the food will simply stay there until it—and the corpse—rots. The body needs the energy of Life to be able to perform the functions of digestion and metabolism that enable it to derive energy from the food. And, of course, the energy from food is required for all those functions that a body must perform in order to be able to continue to contain the energy that is Life.

The Fundamental Energy can also be converted into the 'substance', so to speak, of thoughts and emotions. I remember well a particular session with a man whose attitude to certain aspects of life was making him very unhappy indeed. Moreover, to the best of my belief, it was misguided. But despite everything I could think of saying to him, he found it absolutely impossible to change his attitude. I remember reflecting, after the session, 'At their own level, emotions can be as solid as an iron bar!' However, more immediately relevant, the Fundamental Energy that can be converted into Life can also become *the energy in a wish*.

So long as the energy in a wish can flow freely and bring about fulfilment of the wish, the individual will experience no problems, no symptoms arising from within himself—provided that the wish is benign. Of course, fulfilling even a benign wish may cause a person problems which originate outside himself: from the fist, for instance, of another person. But that is a different matter. Our concern is with what may happen within the individual if the flow of this energy is blocked; and it may be blocked in a variety of ways.

A Physical Block Causing a Physical Symptom

I was set thinking along these lines by a trivial incident that started with a dream. In the dream, someone was thrusting a smouldering straw beneath the nail of one of my toes. The pain woke me up, and it persisted after I was awake. Inspection immediately revealed the cause. A small septic blister had formed at the tip of the toe and was starting to burrow beneath the nail.

I was with the family at the seaside at the time, and I have no doubt that a grain of sand had worked its way into the skin. Its presence there had mobilised the mechanisms a body possesses to expel such intruders, and it was a form of that energy, Life, that enabled them to embark upon their job. However, the skin of the toe had been tough enough to resist their efforts. In other words, it had prevented the energy from flowing freely.

In my medical kit I had a sterile hypodermic needle. With it I pricked the blister, whereupon a bead of pus shot halfway across the room. The relief of pain which followed had three features which, taken together, were, and remain, significant. They are the reason I have dwelt at some length on this otherwise totally insignificant episode. The relief was immediate; it was complete; and it proved permanent. And the reason why these three features were significant is that, taken together, whilst still falling short of absolute proof, they constituted very strong evidence that my treatment had not only relieved the symptom but had also removed its cause.

The skin in that area, as well as being rather tough, is also firmly bound down to the underlying tissues, which makes it difficult for swelling to occur. Consequently the block to the flow of energy had caused pressure to build up, and it was this pressure that had caused the pain. Pricking the blister had removed the block, thus permitting the energy to flow again. The pressure was relieved, and, as would be expected, so was the pain.

A Physical Block Causing a Psychological Symptom

Let us now turn from the earthy reality of a blister on a toe into the more rarefied field of psychology. Here we are concerned with this 'energy that is Life' when it is in the form of the motive power of a wish. Suppose a telephone call has evoked an urgent wish to write a letter. The energy in that wish will be the power that sets in train and then fuels all the activities, mental and physical, that will result in the letter being composed, written and posted. If the materials and the opportunity are available so that the energy in the wish is able to flow freely, that is exactly what will happen. The energy will be converted into a letter, composed, written and posted. Once that has happened, I shall be free to turn my attention to other things.

But suppose I cannot find a pen!

The lack of a pen will block the flow of the energy, thus preventing the conversion from taking place. If the wish to write the letter persists, so also, of course, will the energy it contains, and the block will have two effects. Firstly, the blocked energy will build up pressure, which I shall experience as the sensation we call frustration. Secondly, it will deflect the energy from the original goal of writing the letter to searching for a pen. This might involve lying prone on the floor and looking under a large piece of furniture, an activity that, on the face of it, is far removed from writing a letter.

Let us suppose that at this point a friend enters the room, sees me burrowing under the cupboard and says, 'I don't know what you think you are doing but forget it and come and have a drink!' Let us further suppose that I accept his invitation, and in his cheerful company the feeling of frustration caused by the missing pen subsides. 'Is temporarily numbed' might be a more accurate description because when I am back in my office, of course it returns, proving—if proof were needed—that the interlude with my friend had been no more than a sort of psychological tablet or a painkiller.

However, if my friend had asked what I was doing and, on learning that I was searching for my pen, had almost immediately produced it from beneath a book where it had become hidden, this would have been an entirely different matter. The energy would have been enabled to flow again, thus instantly reducing the pressure and abolishing the feeling of frustration. The relief would have been immediate, complete and would have proved permanent, thus strongly suggesting, if not proving, that the cause of my distress had been correctly diagnosed and appropriately 'treated'.

Quantifying the Energy in an Emotion

Some years ago I had the idea of quantifying the intensity of emotion associated with some circumstance by ascribing to it, arbitrarily, a certain number of units. This number of units represented for me the amount of energy I estimated the emotion to contain. It then became a matter of judging whether the number of units of intensity of the emotion, be it one that I was experiencing myself or one that a patient was describing or displaying, was or was not justified by its apparent cause. If I judged the number to be too high, then, of course, an early aim in therapy would be a matter of discovering from where the excess of energy was coming.

I have put the word 'treated'—two paragraphs earlier—in inverted commas because, at least in a medical context, the word refers to the combating of an illness. In the case of the missing pen, though, there was nothing excessive about the intensity of my frustration. On the contrary. Assuming my feeling of urgency about writing the letter, or, to put it another way, that the number of units of energy in that feeling was appropriate to my understanding of the telephone call, my frustration was a perfectly normal, healthy reaction. It lay within the field of normal psychology rather than that of abnormal psychology or psychiatry.

By contrast, a prominent feature of many of the problems for which my help has been sought, indeed almost the outstanding feature of many emotional disorders is that the patient suffers from feelings of an intensity that is not appropriate. He might, for instance, be more depressed than his circumstances warrant, or more anxious, or more fearful. Or he might feel under pressure to behave repeatedly in a certain way, often a way that has no practical value. In short, under certain circumstances, his feelings contain a number of units of energy that is inappropriate. Or, if he has no abnormal thoughts or feelings, some part of his body may not be functioning normally.

A Psychological Block Causing a Physical Symptom

Before embarking upon this section I must clarify what it is that I am writing about or—more to the point perhaps—what I am not writing about. The need to do this arises because there is a growing body of opinion, not merely that every illness probably has a psychological component, but that the origin of *all* illnesses lies in the mind.

I can go along with this concept if, as I do, one believes that the mind has a non-physical component which arises from the soul. We shall be considering this topic later on. Here I will say only that a soul is shaped largely by the character traits it has acquired in the course of its history, and that its character traits will be one of the factors that determine the nature of its reaction to various kinds of stress; another factor may be external circumstances. This reaction may or may not be conducive to continued health. If it is not conducive to health, the nature of the reaction may determine on which part of the body the emphasis of the illness will fall. This point will be illustrated by cases later in the book. At the moment I am concerned with just two types of problem: firstly, so-called 'conversion symptoms'; secondly, a small section of what are regarded as psychosomatic illnesses.

The conversion symptoms are so called because they are the result of an emotional conflict of some kind being converted into a physical symptom. The symptom is usually one of impaired movement or impaired sensation, and it often turns out that the symptom provides what, at an unconscious level, the patient sees as an honourable escape route or protection from some unpleasant situation. In short, it has an *unconscious* motivation.

A case in point was Louise's finger.

Louise was eleven. The morning before consulting me she had woken up to find that the index finger of her left hand was rigidly fixed in the extended position. There was no pain or even discomfort, but she could not move it at all. Her family doctor had lost no time in referring her for psychiatric help.

'I hope it gets better quickly,' was Louise's opening gambit, 'because I want to get on with my music practice.' Considering that playing the piano was one activity that her rigid finger rendered almost impossible, this assertion caused bells to ring even in my—at that time—rather inexperienced ears. It came as no surprise when, under hypnosis, Louise revealed totally different feelings about her music practice. She detested it.

Louise's problem had arisen because she had won a prize at school for playing the piano. She believed that her mother, on the strength of this small achievement, wanted her to become a concert pianist. Hence there was a conflict in her mind between her desire never to have to touch a piano again and her wish not to hurt her mother's feelings by saying so. She had solved the problem by repressing most of her antipathy to the piano. Eventually, however, her unconscious had hit upon the idea that if she were to have a disability, which made it impossible for her to play, she could free herself from the instrument without hurting her mother's feelings. Hence she had formed the unconscious wish to lose the use of her left index finger, and there was enough energy in the wish to cause the finger to become, in effect, paralysed. A talk with her mother was clearly indicated, and was arranged.

Very quickly a different picture emerged. Louise's mother had been under the impression that, since winning that prize, a career as a concert pianist *had been the desire of Louise's heart*! From that point, a three-way conversation resulted in a more genuine and, therefore, far better relationship between mother and daughter, and Louise became disentangled from the piano without grief to anyone. After a face-saving session of physiotherapy, Louise's finger resumed normal function.

Rather as a leg may cease to function because it has been broken by too great a physical stress, an organ may cease to function properly because it has been damaged by too much emotional stress. Such a condition is often known as a 'psychosomatic condition', and it may be so severe as to threaten the patient's life. One day, the routine physical examination of a patient disclosed an alarmingly high blood pressure. So far the condition had caused no symptoms, but it was obviously a potential source of serious problems. I asked him, therefore, if he could think of any situation in his life, which might account for it. He had recently been disappointed over an expected promotion, but could think of nothing else. I said then that I would like to hypnotise him and see if anything else came to light.

He readily agreed and proved a good subject. I had sensed there might be more to his disappointment over the missed promotion than had so far found expression and asked him if he could explain why he had been passed over. It proved a profitable question. He was soon talking, vehemently and at length, about his father who, he felt, had repeatedly obstructed his progress in his business career. He saw being passed over for promotion as yet one more instance of his father's machinations. He had long wished to confront his father but had always been afraid of doing so.

In this case, the energy in the patient's wish to confront his father was blocked by the energy in the fear of doing so. He was unconsciously holding his body in a permanent state of readiness 'to fight or flee', a condition designed only for emergencies. Since he was now a man in his forties, it seemed reasonable to explore how far his fear was still justified. It soon became clear that his attitude towards his father was now largely a matter of habit. To my surprise, by the end of the session his blood pressure had fallen dramatically.

The two cases I have mentioned present a grossly over-simplified picture of the subject. Our knowledge of the precise way in which the soul—I do not apologise for stressing that the soul is the origin of the mind—relates to the body is still limited. Thus we cannot say precisely why a particular patient has reacted in the way that he has. In general terms we can say that the nature of the stresses and strains, the nature of the material upon which they are falling, and the circumstances involved are all factors that may play a part. My experience over the years has shown that in some cases the crucial factor may lie in a former lifetime.

I also think one can make one broad generalisation. Conversion symptoms are devised by the unconscious as a means to an end, while a psychosomatic condition is the result of stress. The precise nature of the stress may be an important factor in determining the nature of the illness. An individual may withstand immensely heavy and prolonged stress in an uncomplicated struggle for physical survival—after shipwreck, for instance. But if his struggle for his own survival were complicated by an underlying feeling of guilt that he had done less than he might to help someone else, this could predispose to, for example, a heart attack.

A Psychological Block Causing a Psychological Illness

A psychological block is probably the most common cause of such conditions as anxiety and depression.

Anxiety, for a psychiatrist, is a persistent state of irrational unease. It is the lack of an obvious cause that, for the psychiatrist, distinguishes anxiety from fear. Anxiety can be so severe as to warrant the term 'panic'. It is often due to feelings imprisoned in the unconscious, which are threatening to overwhelm any resistance and break through into consciousness. The nature of the imprisoned feelings may vary.

For instance, a patient may have, in his unconscious, an accumulation of aggressive feelings that he fears he would be unable to control if they were in his consciousness. Or he might, somehow, have acquired a wealth of guilt about having sexual feelings and has therefore imprisoned in his unconscious most, if not all, of his perfectly natural sexuality. The treatment of anxiety can be difficult, and we shall be returning to the topic in the second part of the book. It is one of the conditions to which reincarnation can sometimes make a useful contribution.

A memorable example of depression—which also provides an additional illustration of the power of symbolism—came to light during the session that really marked the successful conclusion of the case I referred to in the first chapter, *Some Personal History,* as the 'Breast-But-No-Milk' case. At a certain point it became appropriate to try to find out what had triggered the depression for which Clare had been admitted to the hospital she was in before she came to Park Prewett.

It transpired that Clare had been working in a smart dress shop in London and had managed to acquire some clothes which she prized particularly highly because they were off the ration, and those were still the days of post-war clothes rationing. But the day came when her father fell ill and she was needed to help at home. Her mother said she would come and fetch her in the car, and promised to bring some suitcases so that Clare could get her new clothes home uncrushed. To be fetched in the car was a luxury in itself since petrol rationing too was still very much in force; but what Clare was especially looking forward to was the promised suitcases.

On the appointed day her mother arrived, but late. Clare told me her mother tended to be late for everything and—who knows—she may well have been late with her daughter's feed on the occasion that had been the start of Clare's trouble. The infant might have been particularly hungry on that day and hence particularly incensed when the breast proved to have no milk. But be that as it may, the fact remains that when the car at length arrived, Clare rushed eagerly to fetch the promised suitcases—only to find that the car was empty. Her mother had forgotten them!

The car arriving late and containing no suitcases was a perfect symbolical repetition of the arrival of the breast—but no milk. Adult Clare's reaction had been to say—and to feel, 'Oh, it doesn't really matter.' But that night she was unable to sleep and a few days later a depression had fully developed.

At an unconscious level, grown-up Clare would have liked to pummel her mother for forgetting the suitcases, just as the infant Clare had pummelled her mother for having no milk. But, as the infant had understood it, her anger with her mother had caused her mother to disappear, and a mother who gave no milk was better than no mother at all. Hence the infant had become frightened of her anger, and thereafter fear had blocked anger from reaching Clare's consciousness.

This fear of her anger was the cardinal factor in Clare's illness. Put very simply, if someone has evoked anger within one, one would like, figuratively at least, to bop that person on the nose. But if the energy in the anger, and therefore also in the desire to bop the nose of the person who has evoked it, is blocked, the desire to bop a nose turns upon the nearest nose at hand which is, of course, one's own. Far more often than not, depression is the result of anger which, blocked from being felt at a conscious level and expressed against whomever or whatever has evoked it, has turned upon the angered one himself.

Clare's case illustrates three points very clearly.

Firstly, it shows how the energy in a wish, if it is blocked, can be the cause of a psychological illness.

Secondly, it illustrates that a repressed memory—or, as I call it, a ghost—is a reservoir of imprisoned energy.

Thirdly, it shows that since the ghost is the source of the energy that is being blocked, to rescue the ghost from its prison in the unconscious is, in many cases, the aim of therapy. But first, of course, one has to find the ghost.

I shall start the next chapter with a brief account of a period in my career that was unique but, alas, unrepeatable and hence unavailable for anyone else. Then, since I have found the use of hypnosis an invaluable aid in the search for a ghost, the rest of the chapter will be devoted to an account of how I, personally, induce and use the hypnotic state.

4   *Psychiatry in Arcady*

Part I: Collonges-la-Rouge

Before embarking on the subject of hypnosis, I must say something about the idyllic circumstances in which, over a period of some eight years, I learned much of what shaped my work as a therapist.

When Joan and I teamed up in 1957, she was engaged in fulfilling a contract to write a book about the area of France which centres upon the river Lot. The book appeared under the title of *A Lot to Remember*.

In the course of the year she had just spent in the region gathering material, she had come upon the little village of Collonges-la-Rouge. It had been a case of love at first sight. On one particular holiday from our practice in London, Joan took me to Collonges, and I too immediately came under its spell. For us, Collonges unquestionably possessed a certain benign magic.

The village lies cradled in a valley surrounded by heavily wooded high hills and is built entirely of a deep red stone. Joan, who had a nose for history, soon discovered that the nucleus of Collonges was a monastery, which had already been established for three hundred years when, in 1077, the Benedictines began building the present Romanesque church. Essentially, Collonges is a village of the twelfth century.

We stayed at the Relais St-Jacques-de-Compostelle, which was then a very simple hotel containing six plainly furnished rooms and offering an unpretentious but superb cuisine. We were intending to spend only two nights there, but Joan fell ill, and our stay extended to five weeks. During that period the village seemed to find us compatible, and we conceived the idea of buying a house there, to which we would bring groups of patients to stay with us for therapy. Within two years this seemingly rather unrealistic dream began to take shape.

We had stumbled upon a derelict farm labourer's cottage on the outskirts of the village. It was probably first occupied some three hundred years ago, and its last occupants had left some five years ago. The walls of the building were of red Collonges sandstone and sound—hardly surprising since they were a metre thick. And Joan had immediately spotted that the cottage stood less than a metre away from the pipe—only recently installed—that was bringing main water to the village. Snap!

The interior had to be completely gutted, redesigned and reconstructed. This work was soon in progress under the direction of Joan who, in addition to her psychic faculties, was no mean architect. The end result was a very comfortable, picturesque cottage in which it was possible to sleep ten in comfort and twelve at a bit of a pinch. We were not immediately inundated with patients but, little by little, they began to arrive.

We had been in Collonges a couple of years when Ian Stevenson, the Professor of Psychiatry at the University of Virginia and a long-standing friend of Joan's, visited us. He was engrossed in studying at first hand cases of children who insisted that they did not really belong to the family into which they were born but to a family who lived—maybe—some fifty kilometres away, and which was quite unknown to the child's parents. Enquiries would elicit the fact that this family had lost an offspring a year or so before the child who claimed to be one of them had been born. Eventually, the child would be taken to visit this family whereupon, to the astonishment of everyone, it immediately recognised many of its members, as well as toys that the deceased child used to play with and features of the neighbourhood.

Ian arranged for us to visit the USA to give some lectures, and this tour resulted at length in our book *Many Lifetimes*, and the start of a flow of patients from the States. We shall be encountering Ian's work again in the second part of the book.

Benefits of working at Collonges were soon apparent.

Even as a medical officer at Park Prewett I had always, whenever possible, organised my psychotherapy, which was predominantly hypnoanalysis and which, perforce, constituted only a fraction of my work load, into sessions of two hours, though it often meant starting early and finishing late. In Collonges there was no problem in continuing this practice, and a patient from those days who was recently kind enough to read a preliminary typescript of this book reminded me that more than once he had had two sessions of two hours in one day. Without exception, patients told me that they found the two-hour sessions infinitely more helpful than the more standard 'fifty-minute hour'. Far more often than not it meant that instead of work on a topic having to be interrupted because time had run out, it could be taken to its natural conclusion. I have no doubt that this practice made an important contribution to the speed with which many problems were resolved.

After a session, a patient was not pitchforked into the hazards of a busy city where to be thinking of anything but his immediate survival would have been to put that survival in jeopardy. Instead, he was free to reflect upon his session as he wandered off into a rustic paradise. According to the season, fields abounded with wild flowers, including a profusion of wild narcissi and varieties of wild orchids; hedges held quince trees and both yellow and purple wild figs; and there were fruit trees of many different kinds, cherries, plums, greengages, apples, peaches. There were also, of course, vines, but Collonges is not predominantly a wine-producing area. There were plantations of walnut trees—beautiful at any time of year—and of sweet chestnuts. And there were small birds which one seldom if ever saw in England, including a golden oriole, to say nothing of spectacular moths and butterflies. Swallowtails were not unusual, and I once saw a Camberwell beauty. Of course, guests were free to make friends with each other and might choose to go off on an 'explore'.

Mealtimes provided opportunities—which were usually taken—for the ventilation and discussion of endless more or less related topics. And the lighter sides of life were by no means forgotten, especially before and after supper. Our piano was hard-worked.

The patients lived with us virtually as family and shared every aspect of our lives, including shopping, excursions to one or other of the rivers for a swim, visits to local chateaux and so forth. Joan was in charge of the housekeeping, and it was also she who was the prime mover of any expedition. Joan and I did not often see a patient together, our methods were too incompatible, but she was always available for advice and help. Not many patients were with us for long enough for Joan and myself to become therapeutically significant symbolical parent figures, but occasionally it happened—with useful effect.

A factor of great significance for me was that, within a day or so, social veneers would have worn thin and the person beneath the veneer would have appeared. With experience, one became increasingly sensitive to nuances of attitude and of behaviour in the course of daily life that were often guides towards the origin, nature and relief of a patient's problem. Every feature which contributed to the speedy and satisfactory resolution of a patient's problem was important for at least one very mundane reason, particularly if the patient had come from America. Overseas patients were nearly always on a three-week ticket, which could be had at a significantly reduced price. This thought, constantly in the back of a patient's mind, could well have been a perpetual inducement to waste no time.

Towards the end of the 1960s we developed a routine of going to practise in New York in October, returning to Collonges in April. On account of being sponsored by Dr Robert Laidlaw, who was familiar with my work and was one of New York's most respected psychiatrists, the University of the State of New York licensed me to practise medicine and surgery in the State of New York, and I was made an active member of the Medical Society of the County of New York without being required to take any examinations.

For reasons outside the scope of this book we left Collonges in 1970 and returned to England, continuing our work in various rented houses. They all had a charm of their own. Nothing, however, could reproduce the atmosphere and magic of Collonges. I am not saying that Collonges as a site was unique. Other sites throughout the world have their own particular healing vibrations and sense of benign presence. But for the kind of work that I do and my general approach to psychiatry, Collonges combined the various facets I have mentioned into a highly congenial, effective and productive whole.

After that brief account of a most important period of my life, let us turn now to the subject of my use of hypnosis.

Part II: My Personal Use of Hypnosis

Hypnosis in General Medicine

In 1949, which was when my career in psychiatry really started, people as a whole tended to look askance at hypnosis and at anyone who professed to make use of it. It was as though hypnosis was considered to be closely allied to the Black Arts, and a hypnotist was assumed really to be interested only in getting people under his power. However, during the last twenty years acceptance and interest in hypnosis has grown and spread, to the benefit of medicine in general and of psychiatry in particular. Certain universities now offer courses in the subject and anything in the nature of a textbook chapter on the subject is totally unnecessary, but readers might be interested to have some idea of how I personally have used it.

Hypnosis is a state of altered consciousness and is useful mainly on account of one particular feature. In effect, it relaxes, to an extent that varies from one patient to another, the mechanisms which control the frontier between the conscious and the unconscious areas of the mind. As a result, the transfer of material from either of these areas to the other is greatly facilitated. In effect, a suggestion given to a person who is under hypnosis seems to fall straight into that person's unconscious, whereupon it functions like an unconscious wish, hence a large part of the value of hypnosis in general medicine.

We have already noted that an *unconscious* wish, if it is sufficiently strong, can produce an effect that is tantamount to a physical fact. This was vividly illustrated by a patient of mine whom I happened to encounter in the town one morning when one side of her face was swollen to the size of half a grapefruit. She told me that her appointment with her dentist was not until six o'clock that evening. As we happened to be outside a small shop of which I knew the owner, I took her inside and requested the loan for a few minutes of the room at the back. I had hypnotised this lady frequently in the course of her therapy, so there was no difficulty in 'shifting her level'—a phrase I prefer to anything akin to 'inducing hypnosis'—again. I told her then that as I snapped my fingers she would cease to feel any discomfort from her tooth until ten minutes before she was due at the dentist. I snapped them, and then brought her back to 'ground level'—another phrase I prefer to anything akin to 'bringing the patient back to normal consciousness' or 'terminating the hypnotic state'. When next we met, the lady told me that after my suggestion she had had a perfectly comfortable day until just before she was due at her dentist.

Agonising though toothache can be, a dental abscess ranks low in terms of gravity on the scale of conditions for which hypnosis can be used. Many hypnotherapists can relate similar experiences, and I personally have used it successfully to relieve the pain of severe chronic arthritis and of terminal cancer. Moreover I have found too that it can be used to allay anxiety before a surgical operation, and also to forestall pain after an operation upon the abdomen or the chest.

In *Many Lifetimes* I related how I once used it in plastic surgery. On that occasion the suggestions given when the patient was under hypnosis were directed towards enabling him to remain for a period of a month with the palm of his left hand 'glued' to the top of his right foot, as part of the process of transferring skin from a distant region of his body to repair an injury to the forepart of that foot. The result was all and more than could have been foreseen and desired. In effect, he never had to give a thought to his curious posture, which was maintained without any conscious effort, and, moreover, he developed almost a contortionist's agility in every joint he was free to move.

Another area of medicine in which hypnosis can be of the utmost value is childbirth. I hope and believe it is on the way to becoming a standard feature in the practice of obstetrics.

Hypnosis in Psychiatry

In psychiatry, the main value of hypnosis lies in the fact that it usually makes the egress of material from the unconscious into consciousness much easier than would otherwise have been the case. However, before going further, a few words of caution are, I feel, imperative.

Some Words of Caution on Using Hypnosis

We do not know what the factors are that cause a person to have an aptitude for inducing hypnosis or, on the other hand, to be very easily hypnotised; and herein lies potential danger. A person with no experience at all may choose to experiment, and may immediately find that he has an unusual aptitude for inducing the state. If he has chosen as a subject someone who, similarly, has no previous experience and happens to prove easily hypnotisable, the latter may reach a deep state almost at once, and the couple may find themselves in deep waters.

No matter for what reason one has attempted to shift a person's level, or a person is asking to be hypnotised, once the hypnotic state has been induced one simply does not know what will happen next.

There are three worrying circumstances, which can occur, and they all stem from the possibility of a spontaneous regression. As I described in the story of the grey motor car, when a person regresses, a larger or smaller part of his present day 'I' leaves the realities of the present moment and merges with the 'I' of a 'ghost' in his unconscious.

It might be that he regresses to a scene of his childhood when he spoke only his mother tongue, and this to the hypnotist might be an incomprehensible foreign language. In such a case, although the subject may be reliving some very unpleasant episode, he will be inaccessible to the hypnotist who will, therefore, be unable to help him.

Or the subject may regress to a situation of emotional complexity and find himself unable to return to the present day until the problem has been resolved— and its resolution may be difficult. In one such case of mine, the ghost initially appeared to be the victim in a traumatic situation, but no exploration of the episode from that point of view enabled the ghost to get free, or the regressed portion of the patient's present day 'I' to return to his normal waking consciousness. It was only when the patient and I realised that the ghost had in fact been the aggressor that resolution of the problem occurred. Return to normal waking consciousness then followed swiftly. In another case, we gained the initial impression that the ghost was male, and the situation was only resolved when at length we—that is, the patient and I—realised it was female.

Yet a third possibility is that the patient may regress to a situation of violence in which he mistakenly identifies the therapist as his opponent. In this kind of situation, temporary physical restraint may be needed, possibly in order for a sedative injection to be administered. To forestall such a situation, the 'safety device', which we shall come to shortly, is invaluable.

Briefly, anyone proposing to attempt to induce hypnosis is putting himself in a position akin to that of a surgeon who is about to perform an abdominal operation. Just as the surgeon needs to be justifiably confident of his ability to deal with whatever he finds inside his patient, a potential hypnotist needs to be justifiably confident of his ability to deal with anything that emerges from his patient. He must be prepared for any eventuality. This may include ensuring that both psychiatric and physical help are readily available, should the need for either of them arise.

These complications are not common, but they can and do occur. I am not mentioning them to discourage anyone from seeking help from a competent hypnotherapist but to discourage enthusiastic, inexperienced amateurs from having a go. In this connection I will stress that a cheerful party during which the bottles have been circulating freely is most emphatically *not* the time or place to experiment with hypnosis. I cannot forget the agonised voice of a lad who was telephoning me from a distant land. He had hypnotised his girl friend who had regressed spontaneously to a former lifetime, and he was finding himself unable to bring her back.

Induction of Hypnosis

An attempt to induce hypnosis usually arises for one of four reasons:

1. To relieve a physical problem, especially pain, as I described earlier in this chapter.

2. To aid psychotherapy, which will be the subject of the next chapter.

3. To satisfy curiosity.

4. In the hope of gaining a glimpse of a former lifetime.

However, I would not attempt to hypnotise someone for either of the last two reasons unless the inquirer was prepared to make an appointment on each of the next two days. The reason for this somewhat stringent condition is two-fold. Firstly, if the person accepts it, it is an indication that his interest is serious. Secondly—to express what I have already said in different words—inducing hypnosis is akin to opening a tin that has lost its label. One just does not know what may be inside! What emerges might prove to be completely innocuous, in which case I would probably feel there was no need for the patient to return even once. Or, it might prove disturbing, and he might need some help in integrating it.

Preparation for Induction

In every case the first step is to decide whether to induce hypnosis would really be in the best interests of the individual. For instance, except perhaps to aid psychotherapy, I would not attempt to induce hypnosis if there were any reason to suspect mental instability. Enquiry into general health, sleep, appetite and employment history, be it looking after a house and family or a job away from the house, will probably yield sufficient information.

However, if the person has come for a psychiatric consultation, this enquiry will of course be part of taking a detailed history of his life and his problem. It often happens that during this process something comes to light that poses a question to which the patient cannot find a satisfactory answer. I might then say that the answer could provide a useful clue towards a deeper understanding of his problem, and that hypnosis would probably help us to find the answer more quickly. This will become apparent in cases that I shall describe later. But whatever the reason may be for which the person is consulting me, once the possibility of using hypnosis has been raised, he will probably have some questions. The first is likely to be: 'Would you be able to hypnotise me against my will?'

'No. Certainly not!' would be my answer. 'It would be impossible to hypnotise you for the first time without your full attention and cooperation. And once you were hypnotised I would give you a suggestion that would make it impossible for anyone, including myself, to hypnotise you again, unless you first asked the hypnotist to do so, using a precise formula which I have chosen because it is so unlikely that it would ever be used unintentionally.'

Next might come: 'Would I be able to bring myself out of hypnosis any time I wanted to do so?' My answer would be: 'Almost certainly "yes". However, if you were having any difficulty, I would bring you out.' I might well choose this moment to mention what I call 'the safety device'.

The Safety Device

First I ask the patient to what name he answers most readily, for it might be a nickname. Let us assume that the name is Theo. I then tell Theo that if, in the course of a level shift, I were to address him firmly by that name, he would always hear it—under every possible circumstance—and the effect of hearing it would be to bring him out of whatever might have been occupying his mind and back to complete awareness of present realities. A safety curtain would then come down between the present realities and whatever he had been experiencing. I stress that while we are working this is a link that will never break.

Theo's next question may be: 'Will I be unconscious while I am under hypnosis?'

'No,' would be my reply. Hypnosis is often thought of as a kind of sleep, but this is a totally mistaken idea. When a person is under hypnosis, his sensory capacities are usually unchanged. Moreover he can talk and discuss and argue no less astutely than if he were in normal consciousness. However, by appropriate suggestions, it may be possible to make any of the senses of a person who is under hypnosis either more, or less, acute.

Another frequent question is: 'Will I have any memory of what happened while I was under hypnosis?' I find it impossible to answer this question with a categorical 'yes' or 'no'. Most patients do, some do not. Some patients are anxious for reassurance that they will remember everything, and one can assure these patients that one will see that they do so. Others are hoping for just the reverse. The problem here is that whilst one might be able to arrange that they will not remember anything, such a suggestion might negate the value of the session. But in this connection there is an important point. By specific suggestions one may be able to cause a patient to forget some specific part of a session. This can be useful as a means of ensuring that some unpleasant matter that has not been completely resolved does not bother the patient, in the interim before the next session.

Lastly may come the question: 'When I am under hypnosis, would you be able to make me do something I would not normally wish to do?'

My reply would be to the effect: 'The truthful answer is that it has been shown experimentally that such a thing is possible, if the hypnotist is prepared to go to the trouble of changing the subject's perception of reality.' I add that it would be an unfortunate patient who had chosen a therapist who would use the tools of his trade for nefarious ends.

When I have answered all the patient's questions, there is only one more step he has to take before we embark upon the process of progressive relaxation, and it is mandatory. This step is to the loo. There is no more certain block to a successful level shift than a bladder that is less than completely empty; nor, I may add, anything more exasperating for a therapist than a patient who, half way through the induction, says he thinks that perhaps after all it would have been better to have paid such a visit.

On his return, I invite the patient—Theo—to choose between lying down and sitting in an armchair. I personally prefer him to lie down, as in that posture it is easier for him to achieve complete physical relaxation. I cover him with a light blanket and ask him to fix his gaze upon a 'silver' ball—a relic of Christmas tree decorations—which is suspended about thirty centimetres above his head. Sometimes, even at this early stage, I introduce the 'safety device' for the first time, and I shall repeat it several times as the induction proceeds.

Then I emphasise that I have no wish to dominate him in any way. I explain that, in effect, I am trying to reinforce his own energy to get the channels of communication between the conscious and the unconscious part of his mind deepened and cleared so that communication between the two areas is made easier. I emphasise too that I have no wish to impose anything upon him, and that if I were to make a suggestion that he found unacceptable, he would be able to reject it completely and it would have no effect upon him whatever. I stress too that he has nothing to fight, because we are both on the same side—and nothing to fear. This is not a court of morals and he does not need to fear criticism or rejection or even that he might offend me. He has nothing to worry about: no past to worry about, no future to worry about, and no world outside this room, where he is perfectly safe.

The above remarks are interspersed between instructions to become aware of each part of his body in turn and to let that part relax. I usually start with the feet and work up to the trunk, the neck and then the head. If all has gone well, Theo's eyes will probably have closed spontaneously by this time, and his breathing will be perfectly regular, signs that his level has indeed shifted. However, rather than do any kind of test, I shall assume that this is the case and tell him that I am now going to bring him back to ground level by counting slowly from twenty down to one. Having reached one, I shall ask him if he feels OK, and if he answers that he does, I shall tell him that I am going to shift his level again by counting slowly to twenty. By the time I reach ten his eyes will probably have closed and by the time I reach twenty he will have reached a deeper state of level shift even than before.

Then I shall say to Theo something like: 'I am going to bring you back now and end this session. But before I do so I am going to give you two suggestions. They will be what are known as post-hypnotic suggestions, which means that they will take effect only after the present session has ended, in response to some specific stimulus or circumstance. The first of them concerns the formula I mentioned earlier. Henceforth, even if you want a particular person to hypnotise you, he will be absolutely unable to do so unless you first ask him, using these precise words: 'Please shift my level'. This suggestion applies to me as well as to anyone else.

The second suggestion is that once you have uttered those words it will be necessary for you only to lie down on the couch and look at the silver ball or some similar object, and for me—or any other therapist—to count to twenty, for you to reach a deep degree of level shift.

If, at this session or any future session, there has been any regression, I shall first bring Theo back to the present day. Only when I am satisfied that he is truly back entirely in the present will I bring him back to ground level by counting from twenty down to one, several times if I feel it is necessary. Patients vary in respect of the ease with which they return to ground level, and I shall chat with Theo until I am confident that he really is back in normal waking consciousness.

The work during this first meeting with Theo, of learning his problem, taking his history, explaining the value of hypnosis, answering his questions about it, inducing the state and finally ensuring that he is back in normal waking consciousness will have occupied the two hours I allow for a session. The ground will now have been so prepared that at the next session work on Theo's problem can begin without delay.

5   *Hypnosis in Hypnoanalysis*

In the terms to which I have become accustomed, the aim of any form of so-called 'analytical therapy' is to help a patient to rescue the ghost whose energy is causing his problem. In terms that are more familiar to most people, and certainly to my colleagues, this means raising to the patient's consciousness material he has been carrying around in his unconscious.

The value of hypnosis in this task lies in a feature I remarked upon in the previous chapter, that of facilitating the movement of material in both directions, between the conscious and the unconscious areas of the mind. A case, which illustrates this feature in its simplest form, is that of a young lady of twenty whom I saw only once, but whom, on account of her diminutive stature, I always think of as Midge.

Interpreting a Dream

Eighteen months before Midge consulted me, her father had been killed when the aeroplane in which he was a passenger crashed into a mountain. Ever since then her sleep had been severely disturbed by a recurring dream. She would be on a mountain, searching for the plane. She would find it and approach it, but would be unable to bring herself to open the door and look inside, because she could not bear the thought of seeing her father's dead body. At that point she would wake up.

I explained to Midge that a dream often has a hidden meaning which, psychologically, is far more important and informative than the dream as we dreamed it, and that with the help of hypnosis it was often possible, quite quickly, to bring the hidden meaning to light. Midge readily agreed to allow me to hypnotise her and proved an excellent subject.

Once her level had shifted, I told Midge that when I snapped my fingers the dream would start, just as if she were in bed at home. This time, however, she would find she was able to open the door and look inside the plane. I snapped my fingers and the dream started. Midge was on a mountain, searching for the plane. She found it and approached it. And this time she did open the door and look inside. Her father was indeed there, but he was not dead! To her dismay, he was very much alive. I brought her back to ground level and the explanation of her dream quickly emerged.

Her father's work had involved constant travelling and much as she genuinely loved him, she loved even more sharing her mother's bed when he was away. This was the truth she had repressed. Midge was carrying around a ghost that was pleased that her father would not return so that she would not have to leave her mother's bed. Midge was able to accept this truth and a month later I had a letter from her. The dream had ceased—and of her own accord she had returned to her own bed.

Of course, I do not know how long Midge's therapy might have taken if she had not been a good hypnotic subject. But there was an occasion when a classical Freudian analyst asked me if he could have some hypnoanalytic sessions with me, just for the experience. We agreed to have four sessions. Fortunately he proved an excellent hypnotic subject and at the end of our last session he declared with astonishment that in four sessions I had got further with him than he would expect to get with a patient in two years. He went on to say that if I embarked upon an analysis with him, he would want to see me five times each week for about five years!

Why does classical psychoanalysis take so long and why does hypnosis tend to shorten the period required so dramatically?

In the course of the chapter about the grey motor car, I described Freud's concept of the geography—perhaps 'anatomy' would be a better word—of the mind. However, I omitted to mention one extremely important feature. This is a sort of frontier post at the transition point between the conscious and the unconscious. The function of the officers at this post is to prevent material from the unconscious from entering normal waking consciousness. It is because these officers are so skilled at their job that it can take a long time to overcome their resistance. Though a person under hypnosis is emphatically not asleep, the frontier guards are very relaxed and the hypnotic state makes a variety of techniques available for slipping material past them. It happened that, under hypnosis, Midge's frontier guards virtually went off duty, so that there was no resistance at all. Hence in Midge's case we were able to start analytical work with the barest minimum of introduction and solve her problem in a single session. While somewhat unusual, such a success in one day is not unique.

Preparation for Hypnoanalysis

If the person arriving for his second session is seeking help for a purely physical reason, such, for instance, as the hope of forestalling pain following surgery, the post-hypnotic suggestion I gave him during the first session will allow us to start work with a similar minimum of preliminaries.

However, if the person is consulting me for a psychiatric problem, some introduction is needed. The precise form that this takes will vary from one patient to another, but it usually includes an explanation of the formation of a ghost, and an explanation too of how the energy from the ghost is the cause of the problem. If we can find the ghost and bring it to the patient's consciousness, it will no longer be in a position from which its energy can cause problems. Hence we are setting out to find the ghost.

Let us assume that Theo, the hypothetical patient upon whom I described a technique for inducing hypnosis, has arrived for his second session. In the course of his first visit, I learned that he is seeking help for his depression. Hence I will probably explain my view that depression is usually the result of anger that is imprisoned in one's unconscious turning upon oneself. What we probably need to do for a start, therefore, is to find whether indeed he has an unconscious store of anger. This is the first step in which hypnosis can help us.

We dealt with Theo's questions about hypnosis in the first session, and unless further queries have occurred to him, I shall just remind him of the necessary preliminaries, culminating in his saying to me, 'Please shift my level'. I shall start to count slowly to twenty, pausing at an early stage to repeat the safety device which I described in the previous chapter. By the time I have reached twenty, Theo's level will have shifted and before anything else I shall repeat the safety device yet again. Then I shall probably say to Theo something like: 'I am going to count slowly to ten, and as I am counting something will be bubbling up to your consciousness, and whatever it is it will take us a step towards finding if there is a store of anger in your unconscious.' Whatever it may be, my first suggestion is akin to the opening move in a game of chess. Theo's response will influence the subsequent course of events, and of course I cannot know what that response will be. I cannot therefore predict the future course of his therapy, so we will leave Theo at this point.

Regression

The most useful phenomenon that hypnosis contributes to hypnoanalysis is unquestionably regression. This is the phenomenon above all that shortens the time needed for even a radical analysis. I personally seldom try to induce a regression. However, if I sense that an experience a patient is describing is symbolically repeating some earlier occurrence, I will first try to crystallise in my mind the emotional essence of the scene he is describing. Then I may say to him: 'I wonder if you have experienced anything like this before. If you have, perhaps you will go back to that experience now.'

For instance, a patient was describing the occasion when, as a child, although he was in no danger whatever, he was terrified when he saw a steamroller on the road coming towards him. In the light of what seemed to me to be the emotional essence of the situation, I said to him: 'I wonder if there was some earlier occasion when you felt you were about to be crushed by something much larger than yourself. If there was, perhaps you will find yourself back in that situation now.' I was not surprised when he regressed to a scene in which, with some justification, he was terrified of his father.

I feel that, in effect, I *open the door* to a regression, and the patient may or may not go through it. I do not apply any pressure.

It can happen that the instant a person is under hypnosis he undergoes a spontaneous regression. It does not happen very often, but one needs to be prepared for the possibility, for it can be dramatic. My practice of taking care to install the safety device as early as possible is due to an experience with a patient I shall call Jim, when I had installed it early only as an unusual precaution.

The Importance of the Safety Device

Jim and the Bottle Torture

Jim was a very strong, wiry man in his early forties. I would never have betted on myself in any trial of strength against him. At his first visit he positively exploded into my consulting-room. Even before he had sat down he was demanding that I hypnotise him to enable him to control his furious temper. I replied that I felt it was essential that we had some talks first in order to get him a bit more relaxed. 'Damn it, I AM relaxed!' Jim shouted, bashing the arms of the chair with his fists. Nevertheless, he agreed to have some preliminary talks, and in the course of them I learned that his temper had indeed caused him more trouble than enough, by way of both loss of jobs and social embarrassment. At the end of each talk he would seek assurance that at the next session I would hypnotise him.

The day came when I said I would try to do so. He was still so tense that I felt sure there was no possibility of his level shifting and that it would really be only a matter of going through the motions of inducing the state. Nevertheless,

I bade him remove his shoes, loosen any tight clothing and lie down on the couch. Next, I installed the safety device.

Within seconds I had cause to be thankful that the device was already in place, because the initial words of the induction process were scarcely out of my mouth before Jim's level had shifted and his back had arched to such an extent that he was supporting himself on his heels and the back of his head. Moreover, horrendous noises were issuing from his throat. His posture seemed to be the result of a violent, uncontrollable spasm. I feared that he might injure a vertebra, so I called him, firmly, by his name.

The safety device did not fail. Within moments Jim was sitting up and was accessible to conversation. However, his face was brick red and, as he seemed to be having difficulty breathing, I moved to open the window.

'Don't do that,' Jim croaked. 'I could jump straight through it!' If he had been determined to do so, I am by no means sure I could have restrained him. We were away from home at the time and as I was working in our apartment on the sixth floor of a hotel, his exit by that route would have excited comment. However, he was soon calm enough to discuss the significance of his posture.

One possibility, which had occurred to me, was that he had regressed to a moment immediately after his birth, and someone was trying to aspirate mucus from his throat through a metal catheter. However, this notion rang no bell with Jim at all and, as he was unable to contribute anything himself, he was soon imploring me to shift his level again. Since the safety device had worked so well, I agreed to do so.

Again his level shifted almost immediately and he resumed the same posture as before—if anything, even more vigorously. I feared for his back even more acutely, and I soon addressed him again, firmly, by his name. Once more he responded and was soon sitting up. This time, however, he had a strangely menacing expression. His first words were: 'I feel I'm a wild animal on the prairie. I want to climb to a high place and be the lord of all I survey.' This was disconcerting enough, but then, flexing his fingers, he declared: 'And now I should like to strangle somebody.'

In retrospect, Jim was clearly not right back to ground level and, if I had called him firmly by his name once more, this would almost certainly have completed the process. However, I felt it would be wise, first, to take some precautionary measures. I slipped into the room next door where Joan was talking with a patient and, very hurriedly, said, 'Joan, phone the reception desk and ask them to send their most robust elevator man to stand outside my door; it is possible we have a problem.'

As I might have predicted, Joan did nothing of the sort. Instead, she came straight into my room, took one look at the figure sitting on the couch and sat down beside him. 'Hello Love,' she said, 'you are very frightened.'—a possibility that I confess had not occurred to me—'What's the trouble?' At that, Jim flung his arms round her, seeming to cling to her in an extremity of desperation. In a few moments, as if by magic, he began to calm down. Suddenly Joan exclaimed: 'I know what happened to you! You were captured outside Carcassonne and subjected to the bottle torture!'

'Carcassonne!' Jim bellowed in fury. 'I could never get into the place!' And gradually the story unfolded.

It appeared that Jim had been a member of forces laying siege to Carcassonne in the Middle Ages. Carcassonne, I will mention, for those unfamiliar with the region, is a fortified town in southern France, some one hundred kilometres south east of Toulouse. It rises from a wide plain, which might possibly explain Jim's announcement that he felt like a wild beast on a prairie. But be that as it may, during this siege the defenders captured him. The bottle torture consisted of the spout of a leather funnel being forced down the victim's gullet, whereupon water was cascaded into his stomach. This would fully account for the posture Jim had assumed so quickly and for the noise he was making in his throat. Very soon he and Joan were chatting together like two old war veterans.

Within half an hour one of the other reasons that hypnosis is such a very useful agent became apparent. Despite the fact that he had been reliving a truly horrific experience, Jim was so firmly back on ground level that I had no qualms about letting him get into his car and drive himself home. This could not possibly have been the case if I had been using one of the so-called truth drugs.

Without Joan's help I do not know what the outcome of that session might have been, and not every therapist can call upon an assistant with the faculties that Joan possessed. I never hypnotised Jim again except under hospital conditions, but, as it happened, he seemed to have lost all his excess steam. I think the explanation of this remarkable result must be along the following lines.

Jim had died under the torture and had left a ghost behind. This ghost contained a vivid memory of the torture, and feelings of intense frustration at being unable to get into Carcassonne, frustration that included feelings of ungovernable rage. In his present life, the slightest frustration resonated to this ghost and called out some of the ghost's feelings of frustration and fury. However, if one is harbouring fury against one person, one does not gain lasting relief by knocking the stuffing out of someone else! And Jim could not possibly have known who or what was the real object of his fury since it lay in another lifetime. That possibility had not even occurred to me and, but for Joan's intervention, I think Jim would have gained little from that session. Who knows if he and I alone, without Joan's help, would ever have managed to discover the circumstances leading to his alarming posture and hence his rage. It happens sometimes that the psyche, as a whole, will just not allow the memory of certain traumatic circumstances to reach the individual's normal waking consciousness. Though Jim's case ended happily, it was that experience which made me careful henceforth, even with the apparently most placid patient, to ensure that the safety device was implanted at the earliest possible stage.

A Regression in a Compulsive Disorder

Regression was instrumental in resolving quickly an unusual problem that was presented by a lady whom I will call Odile. She wrote to me from her home on the continent, saying she could only come for four sessions, but was hoping I would be able to relieve her of her compulsion to keep thinking about and looking for a certain man. I replied that I was willing to try.

When Odile arrived, I learned that she was in her mid-twenties. She was happily married and was content with her life. She had university degrees in history and archaeology, and worked for a magazine. Odile then revealed the astonishing fact that the man she was looking for was dead!

The focus of her compulsion was an actor whom we may call Paul Wren. Odile had first seen him in a play on television that had left her totally indifferent. She had given neither the play nor Paul Wren another thought until, some months later, by which time she knew his name, she happened to see him mentioned in a magazine and learned that he had died of a heart attack. Thereafter she found herself compelled to think about him, whether she wanted to or not, to such an extent that it was difficult for her to do anything else. She had a sense that he needed something and, although she knew he was dead, she was always looking for him. She recognised that this was stupid because she wanted nothing to do with him. For a year before consulting me, she had seen several psychologists and psychiatrists, but to no avail.

Her level shifted easily, whereupon I asked her to see Paul Wren in front of her. She soon saw a man, but he was too far away for her to be able to describe him. I suggested that as I snapped my fingers he would come closer. I snapped them, but instead of the man coming closer she found herself looking at a horse race. It was not a present-day event—the clothes of both the jockeys and the people belonged to the period of 1840 to 1850. And though in the scene the horses were running, she observed that they were not moving. In fact everything was still. She realised that she was looking at a picture.

I asked her then to become very aware of the person who was looking at the picture. Immediately she identified with a girl who was crying. I asked her why she was crying. There was a long pause, and at length I asked, 'Are they tears of joy, for instance?'

'No! I'm sad.'

'Why?'

'Because I have quarrelled with my husband.'

If I asked Odile what the girl was doing, she spoke as though she were observing the girl and would speak of her as 'she'. However, if I asked, 'What are *you* doing?' her answer would always be in the first person. Little by little, partly in response to my questions, we learned that the girl's parents had died when she was young. The man who later became her husband adopted her. He took her to live in his château and, when she was sixteen, he married her. This event happened only a few months before the episode with which we were to become concerned. One day she thought she saw her husband with another woman. In jealous fury she cut up the picture of the horse race. She knew he loved it very much and was very proud of it because he had painted it

When her husband discovered what she had done, he was shattered. She tried to seek his forgiveness but he rejected her. Later on, she found him with a blonde and beautiful woman in his arms. This time, again in jealous fury, she went into the cellar and swallowed some rat poison. She did not mean to kill herself, only to frighten her husband. But then, terrified of dying, she rushed to him for help. He ran to fetch the doctor, while her brother, who had witnessed the whole scene, stayed by her side. On his way to the doctor her husband had a heart attack and died. On hearing the news, her brother looked at her with a horrible expression in his eyes and said, 'You have killed your husband!' The girl felt she had indeed killed him, as surely as if she had stabbed him, and she experienced the most profound feelings of guilt and remorse.

I suspected that we had reached a crucial point in the story, and I took her through it several times. I have no doubt at all that her feelings of grief and guilt and remorse were absolutely genuine.

Now comes the strange part of the story.

Odile herself said, 'I was half mad'. In a sense this was true. She knew her husband was dead and she spent hours beside his grave in the cemetery. At the same time she was constantly asking everyone, 'Where is my husband?' She genuinely believed he was somewhere around and would come back to her. Thus, after seven years, unable to bear her burden any longer, she took her own life, by throwing herself from the wall that surrounded the château. She admitted she had never forgiven herself.

I very gently explained to Odile that the girl she had been had effectively cut her mind into two. It was as though she had become two people. One of them was always going to the cemetery, having realised that her husband had indeed died. The other was constantly asking people where her husband was, being unable to accept the reality of his death, thereby avoiding the pain and the guilt.

To my understanding, this meant that the girl had died, leaving behind as a ghost the part of her that was still wishing for the return of her husband. This ghost was still part of Odile's totality.

We know that an unconscious wish, if it has sufficient energy, can have the effect of a real fact. When Odile had learnt that Paul Wren had died, the ghost resonated vigorously to this news. Its energy broke free, burst through into Odile's consciousness and became focussed upon the actor. What it was about the actor that had this effect never became clear.

When, in her regressed state, Odile had identified with the girl, I explained to her that it was essential that she heal the split in her mind. It was essential that the part of her mind, which accepted the reality of her husband's death, should persuade the other part to accept it too. In an effort to make the situation a little easier for her, I reminded her that she had intended only to frighten her husband, and that her intention had been born out of jealousy. 'Jealousy,' I said, 'is admittedly not an emotion to be proud of, but it is a very human emotion. Very few human beings can honestly claim to be without a capacity for jealousy.' So what it really came down to was that she had to forgive herself for being human! I added that, incidentally, it would give her former husband no pleasure to feel that on his account she had become mad!

We learned next day that this session had enabled her to free herself completely from Paul Wren, and on her last morning—the fourth session—she was a thoroughly cheerful, happy lady. And two further points came to light, one amusing, and the other gratifying.

The former stemmed from the fact that her husband in her earlier life had been enthusiastic about horseracing while her present husband had had no interest whatever in the sport. As part of her search for something that in her present life simply did not exist, she had persuaded her present husband to take her to some race meetings. As a result, while she had remained indifferent, he had now become addicted to them!

The interesting point was that she used to have a fear of heights, but on this last morning she had found that it had completely vanished. I am sure the fear had stemmed from the way she had ended that former life. Its disappearance was, I feel, an indication that we really had completed the job.

Projection Techniques

When a patient does not regress spontaneously to the ghost whose energy is causing his problems, and nothing has come to his mind at the count of ten' I may decide to use one of the projection techniques which the hypnotic state makes available. There are as many varieties of these as the mind of the therapist can devise, but the principle behind all of them is the same. Essentially, the patient is told that he will see in front of him some form of blank space upon which the unconscious part of his mind will project images. Since they are coming from his unconscious, he will not know what is going to appear, but once it has appeared he will be able to read or to describe it. Patients vary in respect of the particular variety of screen they work with best. I often start with the crystal ball. If the patient sees nothing in it, I usually next try the schoolroom blackboard variation. I tell the patient that he will find himself standing before an ordinary school blackboard with a stick of chalk in his hand. At a certain signal—usually reaching the count of ten or a snap of my fingers—his hand will write a word on the blackboard.

I remind him that since it will be his unconscious that moves his hand, he will not know what word will appear. Though the word may mean nothing to the patient, it may give me a hunch, whereupon I may say to him: 'I may be right or I may be absolutely wrong, but I have a hunch that the significance of that word is so and so.' The patient may respond: 'Oh NO! I don't think that is right'. Stressing that he will not know what answer is coming, I will tell him then that as I snap my fingers he will write on the board either the word 'right' or the word 'wrong'. Very often it is, after all, the word 'right' that appears, and it usually becomes clear quite soon that we are indeed on the right track.

If the word 'wrong' appears, it may be that my hunch was indeed mistaken or that we are up against resistance by the frontier guards who are trying to save the patient any distress that might follow his realising that my hunch was right. The therapist has to do some swift thinking.

A Short White Linen Coat

It may also happen that neither the patient nor the therapist can see any significance in the first word that appears. This occurred one day in respect of the word 'white'. I therefore asked for a second word. This time it was 'linen'. Still no bells rang, so I asked for yet one more. This time the word was 'coat', and this word unlocked a flood of memory that was loaded with feeling.

The patient's ambition had long been to become a doctor, and his father could well have provided him with the means to undertake the training, but he had refused to do so. This was the source of a wealth of resentment against his father. Some of it was conscious but still more was unconscious, and proved to be a significant factor in the origin of his agoraphobia, the condition that had driven him to seek my help.

Yet another variation is the cinema screen. I tell the patient that at the count of ten he will find himself looking at a blank screen, just as though he were in a cinema, waiting for the show to begin. If he finds he can see the screen clearly, I tell him that this time, as I reach ten, the unconscious part of his mind will start to work like a film projector and throw pictures on the screen. Once the film starts, he will be able to give me a running commentary upon it. An example of the screen technique will appear in a later chapter.

A projection technique often produces material that is invaluable in its own right, but the material may also have the effect of precipitating a regression. On one occasion this occurred when, instead of a cinema screen, we were using the empty stage of a theatre. The problem was recurrent attacks of nausea.

Recurrent Attacks of Nausea

The patient was an attractive married woman in her late twenties. Since childhood she had suffered from recurrent and unpredictable attacks of nausea. When telling me about them, she added in a tone that suggested it was a point of honour, 'I never vomit!'

Her entire alimentary tract had been investigated on numerous occasions and nothing had ever been found amiss. Similarly, psychiatric interviews had proved fruitless. No pattern could be found to which the attacks conformed. They might occur if she was anxious—before an examination, for instance—but equally during a film she was thoroughly enjoying, or a date with a boyfriend that she had been anticipating with pleasure.

The lady proved a good hypnotic subject. She could see the stage clearly and a play soon started. It concerned a young woman who had become pregnant out of wedlock, and this at a time and in a place where it brought great shame upon the entire family. In contrast to the young man whose hopes of becoming a doctor *in his present life* had been frustrated and who had merely remembered the 'white coat' episode, this patient almost instantly regressed to a former lifetime and identified completely with the young woman on the stage. There had been a furious family row and the girl had been sent away to have the baby.

The baby was adopted and the girl returned home. Then, instead of becoming the sort of person whom young women in a similar plight could approach, confident of a sympathetic ear and helping hand, she became prudish and censorious. As that fact emerged, the explanation of her problem became clear. In that past life she had become pregnant because she had allowed herself to be carried away by the intensity of her feelings. Her pride had refused to allow her to forgive herself for this weakness, with the result that a ghost had been left behind. Nausea and vomiting had been the first signs of her pregnancy, the penalty for losing her control of herself.

In the present life, whenever she was experiencing a feeling or an emotion of more than 'x' units of intensity, the ghost was stimulated and its energy caused her to have the sensation of nausea. This sensation not only acted as a warning but also effectively reduced the intensity of her feelings in the current situation. She had taken pride in never vomiting because, though of course she had not been conscious of the reason, the fact that she had not vomited meant that she had not lost control of herself.

The reason that no pattern had been discerned to which the attacks of nausea conformed was that the *nature* of the feelings or emotion was irrelevant. They could be feelings of anxiety, as I suggested earlier, perhaps about a forthcoming examination; or of pleasurable anticipation, or of enjoyment or of dismay. All that mattered was their *intensity*. It was their *intensity* that triggered the ghost into releasing the energy, which caused the nausea.

With this understanding she was able to accept once more as part of herself the ghost of that young woman whose only sin, really, had been that of being all too human; and the attacks of nausea ceased.

In this chapter I have been aiming at two targets. I have tried to show how I set about attempting to rescue what I call ghosts, which is one important aspect of my work. And I have tried to show how speedily and efficiently hypnosis seems able, in effect, to clear a path straight down to the ghost in question. This seems to be no less true when the ghost is anchored in a former lifetime. Indeed, it has become increasingly clear how important it is that one recognises just when material a patient is producing in fact pertains to a former lifetime.

It is time now to say something about the factor that is involved in every psychological problem: the soul. The next three chapters form a trilogy on the subject.

6   *Conception*

In the previous chapter we looked at three cases in which the success of the treatment was in large part due to acceptance of reincarnation. At the heart of any belief in reincarnation is the soul, and this would seem an appropriate time to reflect upon this intangible entity. Such reflections will form the substance of this and the following two chapters. In this chapter we shall be concerned with the subject of conception since there is more to this process than we were taught as medical students! In the next chapter we shall consider the soul's contribution to consciousness, and in the last of the three we will look at what might be called the anatomy and physiology of the soul.

For much of what I have to offer on the subject of conception I am indebted to the patient whom I call Marilyn. Although I described her case in the book *Many Lifetimes* and mentioned it briefly in the first chapter of this book, I will repeat the essence of her case here, partly for the convenience of that majority of readers who will never have heard of *Many Lifetimes,* or who, if they have, will have long since forgotten it; and partly because I wish now to go into its aftermath in more detail.

Marilyn's Conception; Before and After

Marilyn was twenty-six, of working class origin, married and the mother of two small children. When she came under my care, she had been suffering from a depression for two years.

Only after several weeks of hypnoanalysis, the main feature of which was details of her disastrous relationship with her mother, was she able to tell me that her most distressing problem was such a fear of sex that she even had to leave a conversation if it turned upon sexual matters. Sexual intercourse with her husband, which occurred very rarely, was agony for her. Almost in the same breath she said that she also had a horror of injections. The proximity of these admissions made me wonder if, for her, an injection had some symbolical meaning.

Two significant sessions preceded the final and crucial one. In the first of these, Marilyn regressed under hypnosis to the moments immediately following her birth. She was conscious of something tight round her neck that was choking her, and of a man injecting something into her arm. She interpreted both the constriction round her neck and the injection as attempts on the part of her mother to get rid of her.

Marilyn started the next session by declaring that she felt she would not be able to get better until she had discovered the origin of her idea that her mother did not want her. Under hypnosis she declared she was certain that this idea had originated before her birth. I enabled her to regress to the intrauterine state and at once she appeared to be in great distress, moaning, 'I'm burning, I'm burning.' She told me that the pain was in her stomach. I asked her to see something that would tell us how long she had been inside her mother. She saw a figure 'seven' and then the word 'months'. She was certain that the burning was due to something her mother was doing to try to get rid of her.

I told Marilyn then that if she had ever felt anything like this pain before, she would now go back to that experience. I counted up to ten and again she moaned that she was burning. This time she was equally clear that the pain was in her head. I asked her how big she was. In a very faint voice she replied, 'Very tiny.' She told me that her arms and legs were only buds. Again I asked her to see something that would indicate how long she had been inside her mother. This time she saw a 'six', which she knew referred to six weeks. Again she was quite certain that the burning was due to an attempt by her mother to get rid of her.

I suggested to Marilyn then that she come forward in time to the event of leaving her mother. At a certain point she began to look worried. She felt there was something round her neck. In answer to my question, she said she had been inside her mother for five months. I mention this point only because another patient, regressed to the intrauterine period, also gave five months as the period he had been in the womb when he too had become aware of something round his neck—and was born with the cord round his neck.

I suggested that Marilyn continue to move on in time. Minutes later she became very distressed indeed. She felt she was in a tunnel and that her struggles to get out of it were proving futile. 'Then someone grabbed my legs and pulled them out, and then something hard and painful got hold of my head and began to twist it.' Next, she was lying on something white and felt she was choking from something round her neck. She was aware of a man and a woman, both dressed in white, and someone shrieking, 'I don't want her! I don't want her!'

At this point I brought Marilyn back to the present day and out of hypnosis. She recalled all that she had been through and insisted that it was as real as the memory of her breakfast. She realised clearly that it was her birth she had experienced but had no idea what it was that had been round her neck.

At the next session, which proved to be the last, Marilyn greeted me with: 'Do you know, Doctor, I feel somehow it was my fault that my mother did not want me, and that I shall not be well until I know what it was I did wrong.'

Since I believed she had already been back to the time when she had been inside her mother for only six weeks, her assertion prompted me, once she was under hypnosis, to ask a question I had never asked a patient before. In a voice as level and non-committal as I could make it, I asked, 'This thing you did wrong: did it happen before you started to grow inside your mother or after? Was it after or before?' Without hesitation and without any sign of emotion but absolutely calmly came the reply: 'Before.'

'Is it possible for you to recover this event?'

'Yes.'

'How can I help you to recover it?'

'By counting to a hundred.'

So I counted quietly to a hundred and asked her what she could tell me about herself. In a barely audible whisper she said, 'I'm a tiny spot'. She could tell me no more about herself except that she was in a small place. Then she suddenly announced that she had moved to a larger place, and she knew she had to touch something. 'But it keeps moving away from me.'

I sat waiting. Suddenly, she clapped her hand to her forehead, gasped with pain and exclaimed, 'I've touched it...! And OH! THE PAIN! And NOW I know what it was I did wrong. I should never have touched the thing that was moving!'

Marilyn repeated this phrase over and over again: 'I should never have touched the thing that was moving!' After some minutes I interrupted and told her that I was going to bring her back to the present day; that I would count from a hundred down to one and that as I was counting she would be coming forward in time to the present moment. She came back to normal waking consciousness uneventfully, whereupon she announced: 'I know all that was real, but would you kindly tell me what it all means?'

I could not and did not doubt that she had been reliving her conception and her subsequent life in the womb. However, rather than tell her this I tried, with appropriate questions, to lead her to realise the answer for herself. My efforts only brought to light an apparent fact that astonished me. I was aware that

Marilyn had had only a very limited formal education that probably did not include much biology, but I did not expect what appeared to be her literally total ignorance of the biological facts of life. She did know that if you wanted a lady rabbit to have babies you would have to get a mister rabbit too, but she had no idea of the precise role each played in reproduction. She seemed never to have heard of spermatozoa and ova; and despite the fact that she had borne two children, she had no idea of even the existence of the umbilical cord. To her, the navel was 'something that happens when you are born.'

Marilyn was of good average intelligence and I do not think a wish to deceive me was a content of any part of her mind, conscious or unconscious. It is possible that when younger she had known all these things but for some psychological reason had repressed the knowledge, but I do not think this is the case. I believe her fear of sex had been present from the very start of her life and had had the effect of stifling all curiosity about anything to do with the subject. As she had been under an anaesthetic when her children were born, it is possible that she had never seen an umbilical cord. It's just conceivable, though I did not ask about this, that she never saw either of her children naked until the stump of the cord had fallen off, in which case she could have remained ignorant of the significance of the navel. Be that as it may, the most leading of questions failed to bring her nearer to any understanding, and eventually I offered to tell her what I believed she had been reliving.

Up to this time, Marilyn's condition had not changed from its state prior to the start of treatment. She had seldom appeared severely depressed, but she was completely listless. Her expression was wooden. She seldom smiled. She would always do anything that was asked of her, but never showed any interest in or enthusiasm for what she was doing. However, as I began to tell her about the physiology of conception, a look of enlightenment started to dawn on her face that was profoundly moving.

She had not the slightest doubt that her experience as a tiny spot was a reliving of the period immediately *before* conception, and that 'touching the thing that was moving' was the moment of conception itself. She exclaimed, 'Now I know what it was I did that was wrong! I was never meant to be born! That explains why I have never felt there was a place for me in the world.'

She paused for a moment, looking thoughtful. Then, with a truly joyous note she went on, 'But what does it matter that my mother never loved me! My husband does and so do my children. I have all the love any woman could want!'

On that note we ended the session. It had started at about half past eight in the evening of the Saturday before Easter Day of 1951. When it ended, at about half past ten, Marilyn was one radiantly happy lady. At about ten o'clock next morning I looked in on her in her side room. She was still in bed but she opened one eye. It had a glint of which I would never have thought her capable as she said, 'I want my husband.'

He was working in a different part of the country and could not reach her until the next day. Ten days later they went off together. Upon her return, she called in to see me. After eight years of marriage and two children they had been having their first real honeymoon, and she looked a different woman. Some weeks later she wrote to tell me that she had just had several teeth out under local anaesthetic and the injection had not worried her in the least. I did not see Marilyn again but she kept in touch with members of the nursing staff. Two years later I received the sad news that she had been killed in a motor accident.

Shortly after Marilyn had left the hospital her mother came to see me. She confirmed the details of Marilyn's birth, as Marilyn had relived them in sessions. These included being delivered as a breech ('...then I felt someone grab my legs and pull them out, and then something hard and painful grasped my head and began to twist it. The next thing I knew I was lying on something white and choking from something round my neck...'), and Marilyn was indeed born with the cord round her neck. Her mother denied ever trying to get rid of the child, but went on to tell me something which interested me at least as much as any admission of attempts at abortion would have done. Her husband's mother had been so fanatically jealous of her as to threaten her with physical violence if ever she became pregnant. Hence her pregnancy had been a period of chronic fear, punctuated by more than one moment of panic when her mother-in-law had had to be physically restrained from trying to carry out her threats.

From this, one may surely assume that Marilyn's mother was at least in two minds about being pregnant; and one may wonder if Marilyn, whilst inside her, was not constantly aware of these feelings telepathically. Moreover, the moments of acute panic would have caused surges of adrenalin into her mother's blood stream, and they might surely have been responsible for the sensations of burning which Marilyn experienced.

When that final, momentous session with Marilyn had ended, I was confronted, inescapably, with a question that hitherto I had managed to keep right at the back of my mind, and it was this: If Marilyn had indeed relived her conception—and I could not doubt that this is what she had done—she must have perceived and recorded the event. But *how? And with what?* She certainly had

had no physical apparatus that could have played a part. It was whilst musing on this question that I experienced the thunderbolt of intuition: 'Can't you see? This is the PROOF that in a human being there is a component that is not physical!'

In truth, the session was not proof of anything whatever, but reason could not resist the impact of that thunderbolt. For me, the case was proven. That was the point at which what one might call 'Marilyn's contribution' ended. It has been of vital importance for me, but it left me with the question: 'What is the origin of this non-physical component?'

I was anchored in the mistaken assumption that since the physical body arose from a contribution from each parent, the same must be true of the non-physical component. Hence, for a satisfying answer to that question I had to wait for six years—until Joan Grant came into my life.

Two Stages to Conception

Almost the first question I asked Joan was how she understood the process of conception. Her reply was essentially as follows: 'There are two stages in the process of conception of which the physical event, the penetration of the ovum by the sperm, is only the first. The sperm and the ovum each contain energy and, when they meet, their combined energy is sufficient to initiate the process of cell division by which that single cell, dividing first into two, then into four and so on, gives rise to the billions of cells which constitute the body of a baby. However, that cell, or rather, the small ball of cells that it quickly becomes, will die unless, within about forty-eight hours, an *incoming soul* has attached itself to it. The soul will then be the immediate recipient of the continuous flow of Life that will enable the development of the embryo, and, of course, the life of the person the embryo will become, to continue.'

This reply was delivered in the calm assured tone of a teacher explaining an established fact to a student. There was no suggestion of any 'I believe that...' or 'My view is that...' And to me it rang true.

It was through Joan's books, which I had read only weeks before meeting her, that I had begun to think of an incoming soul as a 'person' who was temporarily without a physical body; and the explanation of conception Joan gave me made it clear that I had completely overlooked an essential point of that last session with Marilyn. Whether, as I had previously assumed, Marilyn had regressed to the meeting of the sperm with the ovum or, as I was now convinced was really the case, to the attachment of her incoming soul to the ovum that had already been fertilised, was immaterial. The essential point, the one which I had missed completely, was that Marilyn herself had said that the awareness of herself as a tiny spot, knowing she had to touch 'something which kept moving away', was a reliving of an experience which had immediately *preceded* the completion of her conception. It was when her incoming soul succeeded in touching that something that the process of her conception was completed. Marilyn had, in fact, regressed to identifying with her incoming soul *before it had acquired even the first element of a physical body.*

The idea that she could have regressed to her soul-to-be may seem preposterous; but if one believes, as I most emphatically do, that sometimes a person can merge with split-off parts of former selves, which is what he has done when he relives details of former lifetimes, there is surely no reason why he (or 'she' of course!) should not relive the moments just before his soul enters what will become his next physical body.

That Marilyn's incoming soul knew that it had to touch something, which kept moving away from her, indicates that the incoming soul had both an order of consciousness and a sense of individuality, of 'I-ness'. And that brief period of identification with the incoming soul tends to substantiate Joan's account of the second stage of conception. Moreover, Marilyn's flash of insight: 'I was never meant to be born: that explains why I have never felt there was a place for me in this world' tends to support my certainty that, while the brain is obviously the physical element in consciousness, the non-physical element derives from the order of consciousness of the incoming soul.

Incidentally, I have wondered if the fact that the 'thing' the incoming soul of Marilyn knew it had to touch kept moving away from her was related to her mother's ambivalence about becoming pregnant. That ambivalence might also, surely, have been responsible for the pain Marilyn felt upon touching it.

In Chapter 3 I asserted, in effect, that if a specific incident in the course of therapy is followed instantly by relief of a symptom that is complete and proves permanent, that relief suggests very strongly that the cause of the symptom has been found and appropriately dealt with. If that belief is justified, Marilyn was not the only patient, in my own experience, to have regressed to, or at least to have got in touch with her conception. Julia, a patient who arrived shortly after Marilyn had left the hospital, seemed to do much the same thing with an equally gratifying result. Hers proved to be one of the most curious cases I ever encountered. For a reason that will become apparent, I think of it as 'Julia and the Mermaid Fantasy'.

Julia and the Mermaid Fantasy

Julia was in her mid-twenties, married, and the mother of two sons. She was admitted to the ward in a kind of sleep from which she could not be roused. However, examination revealed no physical problems, so I decided upon a policy of wait and see. By the next morning she had regained consciousness and her story began to unfold.

Julia was the daughter of a merchant seaman who had vanished from the scene before she was born, and of a lady who supplemented her earnings as a waitress in a small seaside restaurant by entertaining selected clients in her flat. On these occasions, Julia and her still younger sister were *almost* always sent out into the street to play. I stress 'almost' because Julia had witnessed enough at an early age to give her the idea that a sure way to her mother's arms seemed to be the possession of a single organ below the waist. The significance of this observation will appear in due course.

On one of the occasions when the two little girls had been sent out of the flat, they had strayed beyond the end of their road into the town and become lost. Eventually, exhausted, they had sunk to the pavement and fallen asleep. At a later stage in the therapy, it became clear that the state, which had necessitated Julia's admission to hospital, had been a spontaneous regression to this sleep. A policeman had come upon the two little babes in the street and, since they bore no form of identification, had arranged their admission for the night to the local orphanage.

The next morning, Julia awoke to find that in the cot next to hers was a child who had webbed fingers, a condition in which the fold of skin that normally joins adjacent fingers only at their bases extends a considerable distance towards their tips. The sight caused Julia to develop such a certainty that if ever her two *legs* were to touch skin to skin they would stick together that she was never able thereafter to sleep unless she was wearing pyjama trousers! This was the first hint I had of the significance, for Julia, of a single protuberant organ below the waist.

The next relevant point to emerge was that Julia could not bear the idea of her legs being seen naked. It was as impossible for her to expose her legs in public as for most women it still is to expose their breasts. When, during World War II, she joined a Women's Branch of the Armed Services, her idiosyncrasy was respected and she was excused PT (physical training) because she could not bring herself to appear in the standard costume in which, of course, the legs were bare. For the same reason she had never been able to bring herself to sunbathe, wearing just a swimsuit. It was clear that—to use the technical jargon—she had sexualised her legs.

One day, very hesitantly, Julia told me that during sex with her husband she preferred always to be on top, and she was anxious to know if this meant that she was homosexual. At that time her husband weighed about 115 kilograms or 252 pounds, and I felt justified, therefore, in assuring her that there was no need to leap to that conclusion. However, since the possibility was worrying her, I suggested that we explore it.

Quite soon, under hypnosis, Julia was recalling the fact that as a very small child she could not tolerate anything *that kept her legs apart!* Nothing would induce her to keep her knickers on. At any opportunity she would take them off and hide them—in the coal scuttle, up the chimney—anywhere she could reach. This interesting information suggested strongly that for the first year or two of her life she had wished, in full consciousness, that her legs *were* stuck together, thus providing her with that apparent key to her mother's arms, a single organ below the waist. In due course this wish became unconscious, whereupon it became the source of the *conscious fear* that made it impossible for Julia to sleep unless she was wearing pyjama trousers.

In view of the experience of the 'Breast-But-No-Milk' case, together with that of all the patients who had regressed to the period in the womb, I felt we should try to discover when and why this wish for fused legs had really been formed.

Under hypnosis, Julia soon regressed to her period in the womb and, like Marilyn, experienced pains that she felt sure were due to efforts her mother was making to get rid of her. Since her father had disappeared shortly after her conception, Julia's interpretation of her sensations could well have been correct.

At the next session, Julia regressed again to the prenatal period, this time to the moment when she became aware that she had two legs. She was extremely distressed at this discovery! Then, to my astonishment, she said she could feel herself, as a foetus, *doing her utmost in fantasy to fuse those legs into a single limb!*

Julia started the next session by reporting a dream. She had dreamed that she was 'something like a tadpole'. She was swimming along when she struck a rock with her head, whereupon her tail dropped off!

This dream intrigued me because Julia's education had been scarcely less rudimentary than had Marilyn's. Even if she had known what a spermatozoon looked like, it is extremely improbable that she would have known that shortly after fertilising an ovum its tail drops off! On this account I felt the more sure that her dream truly derived from a hidden memory of her conception and, with appropriate explanation, this was the interpretation I offered to Julia. Without a split second's pause for reflection, but absolutely instantly, she 'knew' it was correct. She had not the slightest doubt about it. And the next day she told me that as soon as our session was over she had rushed to catch the bus into the town to buy a swimsuit. Then, for the first time in her life, she had spent a happy afternoon sunbathing with her friends. But that is not the end of the story.

Julia's husband had a job that sometimes entailed his spending periods of several months or a year or two in different parts of the world. If Julia did not accompany him to each new locale, she always followed, as soon as possible, with her two sons. A couple of years after leaving the hospital Julia sent me a snapshot of the family playing happily on some tropical beach, with Julia clad only in a bikini. The relief of her symptom concerning her legs had not only been immediate and complete but could surely also be considered permanent.

At the time that I was working with Julia, the notion of reincarnation had not entered my head. Hence it is only in retrospect that I have wished I had tried to discover just why Julia had brought in with her, into her present life, such a very strong desire to be male, for I feel sure this is what she had done. The activities of her mother, which she had sometimes witnessed, could then have reinforced a desire that was already there.

I do not claim to understand Julia's case completely. It is almost beyond all credibility that under some circumstances the loss of the tail of the sperm could have an effect upon the incoming soul, but...? At the least, I feel that Julia's case in no way undermines my certainty, based upon the case of Marilyn, that we are aware of the emotional circumstances surrounding our conception; that this awareness becomes part of our total experience, and that it can affect the rest of our life.

In the next chapter we shall consider the contribution the soul makes to consciousness.

7   *Consciousness: Discarnate and Incarnate*

Scientists have long held the view that consciousness is produced by the brain, or that the brain is responsible for consciousness. This view cannot be more than half correct. It is tantamount to saying that this book is the product of my word-processor, or that the word-processor is responsible for this book.

Any computer is a complex piece of apparatus but, unless it is receiving energy in the form of electricity, it is inert. And even if it is receiving electricity, it cannot do anything unless someone is operating it.

Much the same is true of the brain. Without energy in the form of Life, the brain is a lifeless lump of extraordinarily complex meat. And even if it is receiving this energy, it cannot do anything beyond organising those functions of the body of which we are normally not conscious, unless it has an operator. Without an operator, there is no consciousness, and that operator is, ultimately, the soul. The consciousness of an individual starts, therefore, with the consciousness of his soul.

Various experiences—starting with the case of Marilyn that I described in the previous chapter—have made it impossible for me not to believe that the soul has consciousness. For instance, another patient of mine relived a fragment of her life during the Second World War when, with a host of other children, she was being evacuated by train from a city to the country. At a certain moment one of the children, looking out of the window, exclaimed, 'Ooh look! There's an aeroplane!' And indeed there was an aeroplane, a German one, and it bombed the line. The train stopped, so abruptly that passengers were thrown all over their compartments. My patient recalled making her way through a heap of bodies to the corridor and thence to the door of the carriage, which she managed to open.

She jumped out and found herself between the tracks. She walked to the rear end of the train and had just started to cross the line behind it when it moved backwards, just far enough to knock her over and pinion her by one leg to the rail. She lay there, drifting in and out of consciousness, until the rescue team reached her. The only way they could free her was by amputating the pinioned leg.

She relived the journey by ambulance to the hospital. She wanted only to die, but the efforts of the doctors and nurses to keep her alive—in particular, the energy in their wishes that she should survive—made it the more difficult for her to get out of her body. However, at last she succeeded. She then became aware of herself hovering above her body, looking down upon it and upon the staff who were still working on it. She kept trying to tell them they could stop their efforts because she was FREE; and she could recall her frustration at being unable to make them hear. She was not yet aware even that she had died, and she had not had time to realise she was now functioning on an order of consciousness which was different to that of people who were still encumbered with bodies. But there is no possibility of doubt that she had consciousness.

A Celestial Consultant

Communications with Someone Who had Recently Died

Readers of *Many Lifetimes* may just possibly recall the final chapter. It was about the last weeks of the life of our friend Ray, who was dying of cancer. A few days before she died she told us that she had found our work with her so helpful that after she had passed on she would help us in every way she could. Most assuredly, she has kept her promise.

I sense that the first thing Ray did for me was somehow to make it possible for me to communicate with her in a way that I have never been able to communicate with anyone else who has died.

During the last weeks of her life Joan and I were her constant companions and came to know some of her close friends, who also became friends of ours. Shortly after her death, two of these friends, a married couple whom I will call Max and Sophia, visited us for a weekend in France, where we were then living. The evening before they were due, Joan and I were having supper when I suddenly became aware that Ray had joined us with an urgent message for me.

Joan took a notebook and pencil from her bag but they were not needed, the message was so brief. Ray 'told me' that Sophia and Max had a problem and that she—Ray—wanted me to help them to resolve it. She went on to describe the problem, the nature of which was so bizarre that it would never have occurred to me spontaneously. The moment Ray had delivered her message I was as conscious of her leaving as I had been of her arrival.

The next day, as expected, Sophia and Max arrived. Joan went to bed soon after supper, leaving us chatting. At what seemed an appropriate moment I said to them, 'Look, tell me to mind my own business if you like, but have you by any chance a problem of this nature?' And I relayed to them what Ray had told me. They were astonished. 'Indeed we have', Sophia exclaimed. 'And we were longing to talk to you about it but we did not like to take advantage of a social visit to seek your professional help. But how in the world did you know about it?' I told them then about Ray's visit the previous evening, which they took as a perfectly normal occurrence. Max added, 'I think she was the only person outside ourselves who knew of the problem.' A brief discussion sufficed to clear the matter up.

It seems to me that there are only two ways in which I could have learned of their problem. One is by direct thought-transference from Sophia or Max. That is a possibility, especially since, by their own admission, the problem had been very much on their minds; but if that were the case, why should the message have seemed, so very clearly, to come from Ray? I would hardly have been more aware of her if she had been physically in the room talking to me. The other—and I think the more likely explanation—is that it was indeed a direct communication from Ray. Either way, my reception of the message suggested a faculty I never knew I had.

The two-way communication with her, which Ray has made possible, has enabled me to adopt her as, in effect, a 'celestial' second opinion whom I can consult when I feel in doubt about the next step to take during a session. A striking example of the value of her help in this capacity occurred when I was treating a man who suffered from attacks of a strange form of agoraphobia. He is, incidentally, the patient I mentioned in Chapter 5 who recalled the white linen coat episode.

A Strange Case of Agoraphobia

The literal translation of agoraphobia is 'fear of the market place', but in psychiatry it has come to mean a fear of open spaces. Usually, when and while a person is afflicted with this fear, it is a constant feature of his life. With my patient Brian, however, the pattern was different. He used to suffer from irregularly spaced attacks of a condition that rendered him absolutely incapable of *venturing more than a mile from his bed*. It mattered not where this bed was. It could even be the bed he had reserved but not yet seen in a hotel in a town, which he was about to visit on business. All that mattered was that it was *his* bed.

Even under hypnosis Brian had been unable to contribute anything to account for his curious symptom and, wracking my own brains having proved fruitless, I asked Ray for help.

The reply came—and no one who had been in my skin could, I feel sure, have doubted that it came from her—as clearly and as quickly as if she were telephoning from a house across the road: 'Ask him if dying with his boots on means anything to him.'

Obediently I did so, and the response was dramatic. 'My word it does!' my patient exclaimed. 'Where I was brought up we were taught that it mattered not what a rascal you had been all your life, so long as you died in your bed you went straight to heaven. But if you died out of your bed, then no matter how virtuous your life had been, you went in the other direction.'

Later in the session—he was not under hypnosis—Brian suddenly declared: 'Doctor, I feel absolutely certain that I once committed a crime of violence and bolted into a monastery for sanctuary. In order that the monks could work in the fields, the area of sanctuary in that monastery extended for a mile from the altar. My bed symbolises that altar.'

This information dovetailed with a fact that had already come to light. If a public bench bore a WET PAINT sign, it was impossible for Brian to pass it without touching it to ensure that it really was wet, such was his determination that no one should ever make a fool of him. One can be sure that this determination covered an unconscious fear that people *would try* to make a fool of him, a fear that was almost certainly a rebound of an aggressive streak in his own character of which he was completely unconscious.

This unconscious streak was hinted at by the immediacy of his reply: 'Physical violence', when I had asked him what he would consider the most serious form of crime. Some talks along this line brought to light the fact that his attacks of agoraphobia tended to occur after some circumstance had made him angrier than, at the time, he had realised. This understanding ended the attacks.

The Embodied Soul

When a soul has attached itself to a fertilised ovum, I'm sure it immediately endows that ovum with the order of consciousness it has brought with it. This order of consciousness, which I call 'Discarnate Consciousness', functions, of course, without any physical apparatus. It perceives without the aid of sense organs and communicates by what we would call thought-transference. In short, it operates by what are known as psi faculties. It has been shown conclusively that the foetus is sensitive to the mother's feelings about being pregnant, and in the very early days this can surely be only by means of its discarnate consciousness.

Furthermore, I have found that a patient regressed to the prenatal period can always tell me how long he has been in the womb. Since the stage of her pregnancy is seldom out of the mother's mind, in the early days at least, the foetus presumably acquires the information through its discarnate consciousness.

Just how extensive is the range of the discarnate consciousness of the very early embryo we have yet to learn. I would not be surprised if, in due course, virtually irrefutable evidence emerges that it is able to pick up the feelings, not only of the mother but also of people who are emotionally important to her, and even of people to whom its presence is of material significance.

However, development of the physical body proceeds apace. By the end of the fifth week of the embryo's life, the foundations of all the essential structures, internal and external, have been laid, and by the end of the eighth week the embryo has a recognisably human appearance and is henceforth referred to as a foetus. It seems that the physical body loses no time in starting to envelop the soul and, as it is doing so, the discarnate consciousness comes to work more and more through the developing physical structures of the nervous system. Thus, in effect, incarnate consciousness—taking that term to mean all the levels of consciousness described by Freud—comes to overlay the discarnate consciousness. This, I think, explains why the majority of people have relatively little in the way of extrasensory faculties. Instead of the boundless range of clairvoyance, what the individual sees is limited to what his eyes permit. Instead of clairaudience, he can hear only what his physical auditory apparatus can pick up. Communication, instead of being by thought transference in which case the distance between the people concerned seems to be irrelevant, is limited to what can be conveyed and received by physical means.

Obviously, there is a great deal to be learned about the process by which the incarnate consciousness comes to overlay the discarnate consciousness. The extent to which it occurs seems to vary from one person to another. In some people, it seems to have been complete. In others, who have always had marked extrasensory faculties, it seems to have ceased early in life. In still others, it would seem that at least certain of these faculties have been regained in the course of a lifetime.

The relationship of discarnate consciousness to incarnate consciousness awaits clarification. For instance, is it the discarnate consciousness that holds the memory of former lifetimes? Shall we become more adept at gaining access to the discarnate consciousness? What is the relationship between the discarnate consciousness and ghosts of former lifetimes? What part does discarnate consciousness play in intuition? Once the reality of discarnate consciousness has become as generally accepted as Freud's concept of the unconscious, a vast new area of understanding of ourselves will be available.

In any event, I am sure the process by which incarnate consciousness overlays discarnate consciousness is never complete at birth but continues for several years. This would account for some of the characteristics of childhood thinking.

For instance, a child can believe that his thoughts and wishes are responsible for events in his surroundings—the so-called magical thinking of childhood. Allied to this is a child's ready acceptance of fairy stories.

From mediums and others who claim to have knowledge of such matters, we learn that the magic on which such stories are often based echo conditions of existence on the level which the child has so recently left and of which he retains memories, just below, if not side by side, with his developing incarnate consciousness. For instance, we are told that on those immaterial levels of reality which I usually refer to as 'Upstairs', wishes really do come true, a fact which could underlie the magic wands which are standard equipment for all self-respecting Fairy Godmothers.

On our level we are familiar with stories of frogs turning into Princes Charming and, of course, with the effect a glass slipper can have upon a girl whose foot it happens to fit perfectly. I learned from Joan who, I am quite certain, had genuine knowledge of existence 'Upstairs' that on that level changes of form are commonplace, especially in the case of those 'people' whose job it is to rescue ghosts who are stuck 'down-here'. They may have to assume the form of someone whom the ghost knew and trusts and to whom he will listen.

Other patients, who have appeared to be recalling or reliving periods between lifetimes in a physical body, have told me that the wish to be in a particular place is enough to transport one there. This could surely underlie the stories involving magic carpets or seven-league boots, which certainly take the hassle out of travel.

Such information makes me wonder whether economics and an urge for power are *really* the principal drives behind the advances of technology. In one of its forms, the aim of technology seems to be to produce ever bigger results from ever lighter pressure upon ever smaller buttons. Is this a progression towards making wishes come true?

The development of an aeroplane which could be scheduled to permit one to have breakfast in London, mid-morning coffee with a friend in New York and be back in London for tea could be seen as movement towards the mere wish to be somewhere else being enough to get one there. It could also be seen as a step towards being in two places at once, which—I am told—is another feature of life 'Upstairs'.

Are we, in fact, trying to bring 'Upstairs' conditions down-here—if not quite in the sense that the author of The Lord's Prayer had in mind?

But no matter how completely incarnate consciousness may appear to depend upon the brain and the nervous system, these physical structures are, in effect, simply the tools of the soul. Tools that the soul is compelled to use when animating a physical body. However, the presence of the soul is the sine qua non for consciousness.

Suppose I am looking at a tree. Light rays from the tree stimulate the light-sensitive cells at the back of my eye in the retina. From these cells a chain of nerve fibres carry impulses that induce changes in cells in a certain area of my brain. But in no way whatever do these changes in the cells resemble a tree. In effect, the tree is represented in these cells by a code, and it is the soul that cracks this code so that I am aware I am looking at a tree.

We are familiar with one form of energy being transformed into another. In the telephone, for instance, the voice is transformed into electrical impulses that travel along wires to another telephone that turns them back into sound. But what is the mechanism by which changes in physical nerve cells are converted into the psychological reality of awareness?

Equally mysterious is the way in which the energy in a wish, which is a psychological and hence an immaterial reality, is able to initiate the chain of chemical reactions which result in the contraction of a muscle. This question was brought to mind by a passage in *Winged Pharaoh*. The reader will recall that *Winged Pharaoh* was the first of the books written by Joan, and it was written by dint of her faculty of Far Memory. The book could be described as the posthumous autobiography of Sekeeta, which was her name in one of her lives in the First Dynasty of Egypt when she was the daughter of the Pharaoh.

One day, when she was still a child, she had wandered into her father's study where he happened to be showing her brother an anatomical drawing of a man. Sekeeta joined them and I cannot do better than quote her account of the incident:

> *I was still looking at the picture and I saw that in the top of the head there was a tiny man, delicately drawn. I pointed to it and said: "Have we really got a copy of ourselves inside our heads, or is it just a way of writing?" And Father said: "Yes, all animals have it. It is through this that the commands of the spirit are translated to the body. It cannot be seen except by a*

seer. If Ptah-Kefer looked with the eyes of his spirit at this part of a man who was about to raise his arm, then a flash of time before the earth arm was raised he would see it being done by the arm of what is called the 'ka ibis'.

"Do you remember the soldier from the garrison of Na-Kish who was brought here from the temple? His captain sent him down in one of the grain boats. He had seen his wife seized and killed by a crocodile. The shock was so terrible that he became dumb, and he was sent here to see if we could cure him. Now this is what had happened to him: so great had been his fear and horror that the force of his emotions had injured his ka ibis. Just as a man whose shoulder muscles are torn cannot throw a spear, the ka ibis could not translate the orders of this man's spirit to the speaking muscles of his throat, and he became dumb. But when Ptah Kefer saw what was wrong, the ka ibis was strengthened with healing, until it was once more able to obey its orders."

I believe that the above is essentially a true account of what happened, of the words that were exchanged, in the study of Sekeeta's father some three thousand years ago. I find it a fascinating story.

Ptah Kefer was a seer who was held in the highest esteem by Pharaoh himself. We can assume, therefore, that he was neither deluded nor a charlatan. If he saw a non-physical something that was called the ka ibis, the existence of which was widely accepted, then I think we have to assume that this non-physical something really did exist. And if it existed as recently as three thousand years ago, it must surely still exist today.

I wonder: could what was called the ka ibis be the bridge—or one of the bridges—between the immaterial and the physical? Could it be the agent that transforms the immaterial energy in a wish into the form that starts the chemical processes that result in nerve cells sending those impulses down nerve fibres which cause muscles to work? If this possibility were established, it would form another category of functional disorders that have a psychological cause.

When I read the story I found myself reflecting that today, three millennia later, we could not effectively improve upon either the diagnosis or the treatment of that Egyptian soldier.

I like to think that this chapter consists largely of inferences drawn from events that I have experienced or observed—or read about! I am sure the Egyptians who lived several thousands of years ago had a great deal of knowledge concerning consciousness and extra-sensory matters, which has been lost. Is it coming slowly back to light?

8   The Origin of a Soul —
Supra-Physical Body and Psyche

At the heart of any belief in reincarnation lies the soul.
As a physician, I am obviously interested in health, the health of the
body as well as the health of the mind. However, as a psychiatrist, it is in
the health of the mind that I have specialised. But, as I have declared repeatedly,
I believe the mind to be *the product of aspects of the soul, working through or in
combination with the brain.* Hence, I think of myself as trying to heal the soul.

'Aspects' of the soul?

Yes. When orthodox medicine recognises, as I'm sure one day it will, that a
human being has a soul which, though intangible, is no less a reality than are
his liver and kidneys, it will have advanced into a new area. We can anticipate
that one consequence of this step will be a rapid increase in our knowledge of
this entity; of its different parts and their functions; of what we might call its
anatomy and physiology. This will lead, not only to recognising still more of
the conditions in which the essential problem lies within the soul, but also to
recognising *within which part of the soul it lies.* This in turn could lead to more
precise diagnosis and more effective therapy.

The Origin of a Soul

On this subject, as on the subject of conception, I find what Joan told me to
be satisfying. Her view was that the soul starts as the particle of energy, derived
from God, which organises the different parts of an atom. Doing this job it
gains experience and, since experience is at least part of the substance of the
soul, it grows larger. It becomes the organising element of, first, a simple mol-
ecule and then, growing larger with experience all the time, of more complex
molecules. In due course it evolves to becoming *the animating element* of the
smallest physical particle we would describe as living.

Thus it starts its long climb up its evolutionary ladder as it becomes the animating element, or as I prefer to call it, the 'non-physical component' of ever

more complex physical forms, first of plants and then of animals. During this period, the whole of this non-physical component is either in a physical body or out of a physical body. Eventually the time comes when it has accumulated so much experience that it is able to become the non-physical component of the most complex organism we know of: a human being.

In this capacity it soon gains so much experience and becomes so large that no longer can the whole of it be contained within a single physical body. Instead, only an extract of it becomes the non-physical component or, as I now refer to it, the 'soul' of the next human individual. The entire non-physical mass, from which the soul is an extract, is what I think of as the 'Spirit'. An individual's lifetime ends when his soul leaves his physical body and returns to the spirit whence it came. In due course, another soul will emerge from that spirit, taking with it a selection of the experiences that the spirit has accumulated from the succession of souls to which it has given rise.

In *Many Lifetimes,* Joan, using different terminology, likened what I call the spirit to an orange, of which the soul is a segment. The juice that, of course, is common to both the orange and the segment, represents the character. The principal purpose of each lifetime is to give the individual an opportunity to further the evolution of his character or, more accurately perhaps, the character of his soul. To the extent that he has achieved this, when the individual's soul returns to the spirit, the character of the spirit will be modified. When, as a result of the modifications brought about by each returning soul, the character of the spirit requires no further modification, that spirit will not need to send further souls into incarnation. It will continue its evolution on other levels of reality.

But let us descend from speculation upon these ethereal matters to a consideration of the amoeba, a microscopic speck of pond life.

The Amoeba

The amoeba must be a relatively early physical form. Its body consists merely of a nucleus embedded in a blob of jelly that is encased in a very flexible membrane. But, like every other organism, an amoeba is alive only so long as it is incorporating a non-physical component. The amoeba is able to move about, to engulf food particles and to reproduce. The last is a complex process that involves the amoeba splitting itself into two, each half having the appropriate number of chromosomes. But whatever part of an amoeba's totality organises this operation, the amoeba must be harbouring a non-physical component, or it would have no life.

But even my imagination boggles at the thought of an amoeba saying to itself as the sun goes down, 'I have been a very good amoeba today', or, for that matter, 'a very naughty one'. I would attribute the ability to deal with such matters as right and wrong to a part of the non-physical component for which I would reserve the term the 'Psyche'. I am sure the psyche requires a brain of a minimal degree of complexity before it can function. This is something that the amoeba, surely, does not possess. Hence I feel we are compelled to assume that a non-physical component has at least two parts. I call one of them the *psyche*, and the other the *supra-physical body*. (I have italicised those terms only to emphasise what I personally mean by them, because I know that other workers and indeed readers might already attach different meanings to them.)

The Supra-Physical Body

I think that the psyche and the supra-physical body are both features of the same entity, but that they appear at different times. For a long period, from an evolutionary point of view, the psyche is in a dormant or latent state. At just what later stage of evolution the brain is sufficiently complex to serve the psyche is not precisely known, but I do not think it is a matter that need concern us.

I believe one function of the supra-physical body is to be the immediate recipient of the constant beam from the spirit of that special form of energy we call Life. It then converts this energy into the different forms required by the various organs whose activities keep the body alive and functioning, both physically and mentally. As I remarked elsewhere, in one of its forms this energy is the substance of the emotions.

It is when the supra-physical body has finally left an organism that the organism has died. When a patient is in coma, for instance, injury to the brain may have rendered it unable to serve the psyche, but the supra-physical body will keep the vital functions going. It is only when the supra-physical body has withdrawn from the physical body that the individual is dead.

It is logical to suppose that the supra-physical body has a sense of individuality, of 'I-ness'. In a brief talk with Dr Lyle Watson, the author of *Supernature I* and *Supernature II* amongst other books, he made the interesting point that the most primitive organism that preyed upon others must have had a sense of identity which enabled it to distinguish itself from everything else. Otherwise, when it had worked up an appetite, there would have been nothing to stop it from making a quick snack of itself! And if it has a sense of identity, it must have a rudimentary consciousness. It may be possible to challenge this notion but I find it very useful.

With that notion in mind, it becomes reasonable also to ascribe certain intelligence to the supra-physical body.

Intelligence, essentially, is the ability to make use of experience. For instance, it is surely reasonable to suppose that the ability to judge speeds and distances, acquired through experience during prehuman incarnations, contributes to a motorist's ability to judge whether or not he has time to overtake the car in front of him in the face of the car that is approaching. One can assume that his psyche has little to do with his decision since he reaches it before the most expert mathematician, presented with the problem on paper, would have had time even to read all the data!

To anyone who would claim that such an ability is just a reflex action' I would suggest that it is the non-physical component, and specifically the supra-physical body, which makes these reflexes possible. And let me repeat, without the non-physical component the organism would have no life.

One duty of the supra-physical body is to ensure that the structure and chemistry of the body are maintained within very narrow limits. This is accomplished by mechanisms of which we are largely unaware, such as those of digestion and of metabolism, and of the healing of unnoticed wounds. However, if a situation gets beyond the power of the supra-physical body to rectify unaided, then a symptom is experienced which, in the human being, brings the psyche into play. For instance, if a feeling of breathlessness is not relieved by automatically slowing down, the supra-physical body, in effect, tells the psyche to do something. The psyche will know about measures for getting more air, even to the extent of summoning a doctor who could bring a cylinder of oxygen. In species in which activity of the psyche is minimal, the supra-physical body will make use of the knowledge we call 'instinctual'; if that does not help, the plight of the organism may indeed be desperate.

As I said in *Many Lifetimes* I see the supra-physical body, in one of its functions, as analogous to a magnet placed beneath a sheet of paper that has been covered with iron filings, which represent the cells of the body. The lines of force between the two poles of the magnet will draw the iron filings into a pattern and hold them there. If something—the point of a pencil, for example—disrupts this pattern, the lines of force will restore it. In a living organism, if illness or accident disrupts the pattern, it is ultimately the supra-physical body that is responsible for directing an extra supply of the Life energy it receives to the healing mechanisms which work to restore it. This analogy provides a rationale for supra-physical healing which, one may presume, works through reinforcing this energy. However, as I also described in *Many Lifetimes*, there is a point at which this analogy of the magnet and the iron filings breaks down. No matter how much you disturb the pattern of the real iron filings, this will have no effect upon the underlying magnet. But if an illness or injury to a real physical body is sufficiently severe, and especially if it is associated with strong emotion, it may also damage the supra-physical body.

I have not the slightest doubt that any injury to a supra-physical body can be healed between lifetimes, but I think that, for various reasons, such healing may not occur. One of these is that the injury to the supra-physical body may be a feature of a ghost that was left behind and so never reached the level where such healing could take place. My understanding of this possibility arose out of the case of Anne who for many years had suffered from pain in her back. However, this pain was not the problem about which she was consulting me.

Healing the Supra-Physical Body

Anne of the Injured Back

Anne was a young married woman who was referred to me on account of a psychological problem: her fear of anything to do with having a baby. It was entirely incidental that her therapy freed her of the physical symptom which, in fact, she had not even mentioned to me. However, it happened that in a particular session Anne was experiencing herself, in an earlier lifetime, as a young woman who was bathing her baby. The baby slipped through her grasp, fell on its head and soon died. This was distressing enough, but Anne felt that there was a still earlier life in which there had been a tragedy connected with a baby, which she also needed to relive. This remark was followed by a silence that was broken only when, after many minutes, I asked her if she could tell me what was happening. In an entirely different voice, one of utter weariness, she almost moaned, 'It's sooo...HOT...'

I asked her what she could tell me about herself. Sometimes she seemed hardly to be speaking to me as she continued, '...so hot...so hot...got to keep walking...I can see miles ahead...a line of people...going across the desert... stretches for many miles...the sky is very blue...bright dazzling blue...hurts the eyes...we have to keep our heads covered.'

I asked her what sort of head covering she had. 'It's long and white and all one piece...you wind it round and cover your head against the sun and the sand...And at night it's terribly cold.'

Little by little it transpired that she was a young girl, perhaps ten years old, ...that the people had been forced to take this trek...

'It was a terrible journey...the HEAT...no water...and if you drink it, it does not quench your thirst...you have to keep going, you can't sit down...you don't know where you're going...and you're supposed to have faith...'

In the hope of identifying this exodus I asked some questions and learned that they were going towards the sun in the morning, and were walking on sand that was hard so long as you kept to the track, but off the track it became soft. It's colour was 'rather white'—which was why it was so difficult in the sun...so glaring...

To begin with they had had some animals—goats and donkeys—but they had long since died or been eaten. No one had enough strength to help those who could no longer keep up, so they were killed. They could not be left behind...

One evening her group had camped by a well from which they were warned not to drink because the water was probably poisoned. The child had decided she could endure no more and would kill herself. During the night she managed to drag herself to the well and drink. As Anne lay on the couch, she started to writhe in pain, clasping her abdomen. I had no doubt that she was reliving the intense abdominal pain, which ended with her death. As I felt there was no point in letting the distress continue, I intervened and asked her what had been the final straw that had caused her to decide to kill herself.

'It was the pain in my back.'

'What was causing that?'

'Something in my pack...a cooking pot...'

I succeeded then in persuading her to go to sleep.

Those last words had seemed entirely plausible. I could imagine that on such a trek a family would rate a cooking pot as one of its most treasured possessions. I therefore slipped one hand beneath her back, between her shoulder blades, and placed the other at the same level in the centre of her chest. I made a mental picture of the damage a heavy iron pot would do to the skin and the muscles of the back of an emaciated small girl and visualised energy flowing between my hands, bringing the tissues back to normal. After some minutes I sensed that I had done all I could and withdrew my hands.

This session had taken place at my house and, as my next appointment was not for a couple of hours, I turned to my desk and dealt with some letters, leaving Anne to go on sleeping.

After half an hour she stirred. A few moments later she sat up, as bright and chirpy as could be. Then she looked puzzled. 'It's funny', she said, 'something seems to have happened to my back. I did not think of mentioning it, but it never feels quite right and sometimes it is really bad. I have been in hospital on traction for it once, but no one really seems to know what is the matter with it...now, all of a sudden, it seems perfectly well!'

Soon after this session, Anne spent a holiday on a farm, helping with the harvest. It had been heavy work, just the kind of thing she would have expected to cause her back to give her pain. However, it had given her no trouble at all.

Twenty years elapsed before I met Anne again. I was delighted to learn that her back had remained trouble-free, and that she and her husband had a teenage child. Since Anne never referred again to anything that might have befallen another baby, I wonder if the fate of this young girl was in fact the earlier experience she had felt she needed to recover.

I am sure this case is an example of an injury to the physical body that also affected the supra-physical body because it had occurred under conditions of such emotional distress. If the psyche was involved at all, it was only to a minimal extent because there was no guilt or shame about any aspect of the episode. In this respect, Anne's case differed from that of Robert, which I will describe now.

Robert's therapy required only two sessions, both of which I recorded. The result of the therapy was so dramatic that I feel the story merits being related in some detail. We shall then be in a position to compare the two cases.

Healing the Supra-Physical Body and also the Psyche

Robert of the Painful Legs

Again we are concerned with a physical symptom, but the origin of this one is rather more involved than was the pain in Anne's back.

Robert was a professional man in his mid forties. He was comfortably placed from every point of view: financial, social, professional, and he had a happy family life. He was consulting me rather as a last resort, on account of the severe pain and sometimes weakness which could affect any area of the front or the back of either leg. He had suffered from these symptoms ever since an incident, some twenty years previously, which he assumed was responsible for it.

With a crowd of boys and girls he had been playing on the edge of a swimming pool. Simply to show off he had dived in at the shallow end—and he had hit his head on the bottom. He was not knocked out but he fractured two vertebrae and for a short time he was paralysed. X-rays taken at intervals since the accident had shown there was still residual damage to his spine, but not enough to account for the severity of his symptoms. I suggested to Robert that he allow me to hypnotise him because it might then be easier for us to discover the cause of his pain. He readily agreed and quickly reached a deep state of hypnosis. He was soon reliving the swimming pool episode, which seemed to have been the source of so much trouble, and it became clear that he had indeed made this dive for no other reason than to show off. Rather ruefully he said, 'It was a stupid thing to do.'

I asked Robert to get a very clear picture in his mind of the pain. This he was able to do without any difficulty.

Then, a sudden strong hunch prompted me to say to him, 'I don't think this is the first time you have had this sort of pain. I think you have had a pain very similar to this before. If I am right, as I'm counting to twenty, something will be coming to your awareness that will help us to understand when and where it was.'

As I reached twenty Robert said, 'I've got a picture of a man standing in a courtyard...on cobblestones...he's a blacksmith standing over a brazier, with horseshoes...there are turrets all round him... It's more a general awareness than an acute picture in detail...but it's not imagination because it's staying too long... I'm not having to hold it...it's just there... There are diamond-shaped holes in the brazier and he's got long tongs in his hands...' Robert says he feels completely disinterested in this blacksmith so I tell him that as I am counting to ten something will be bubbling up to his awareness that will tell us why, out of all the millions of pictures that might have come to his mind, there came this picture of the blacksmith. A few moments after I reach ten he becomes aware of pain in his legs. I sense that what is about to happen may be very distressing, so I decide to use the 'screen technique'.

I tell Robert that he will soon see in front of him a blank white screen on which the unconscious part of his mind, working like a cinema projector, will be able to throw pictures. I stress that because it is from the unconscious part of his mind that the pictures are coming, he will not know what is going to appear on the screen, but when it is there he will be able to tell me about it. It will be as though he is watching a film and giving me a running commentary upon it. I tell him that I am going to start by asking a question to which he will project the answer on the screen.

I have got so far as, 'Is there a link between the forge and...?' when Robert bursts out, 'Good Heavens! I'm wearing ARMOUR! My legs are heavy with armour and I can see on your screen a picture of a knight...he is on a horse and riding up to the front of the screen and raising his visor...just like in a film.'

There is a pause, and then, 'Straps...there are straps round my thighs...my legs feel so heavy...something is digging into my back...' Personal memories prompt me to ask him how long he has been on the horse. 'I'm not on a horse,' he replies. 'I don't know whether I'm standing up or lying down...it's just that my legs are so heavy; it's as though I've got weights like armour on—on my thighs, particularly.'

I ask Robert to tell me anything more that he can about this person whose legs are so heavy. For instance, is the person male or female?

Little by little we learn that the person is definitely male and about the age that Robert is now. He does not know why his legs are so heavy, but he cannot move them. With personal memories in mind once more, I ask him if perhaps he has been on a horse which has fallen and has fallen across him, pinioning his legs. That idea does not seem to be right either. Several more suggestions are similarly rejected. At length I ask Robert to describe the pain to me again.

'It is an ache,' he says, 'not necessarily a sharp pain, though this comes occasionally...but it is an ache...and my heels hurt. They are very sore...'

Now comes a spontaneous contribution: 'Now I have a picture of a man lying on cobblestones, trying to move his legs...and he can't do it...and he's in armour.'

'Why is he lying there?' I ask.

After a long pause, Robert says, 'I can't say it's me...it's as though I'm looking down on somebody...he hasn't got a helmet on...and he's supporting himself on his left hand and using his right hand to try and drag his legs along.'

I ask Robert if there are other people around.

'Yes...but I can't see who they are. I'm just aware there is somebody...to the right hand side...and he's trying to pull himself backward...out of their way... He's got long fair hair...no helmet...and he's got his mouth open as though he's shouting...and he's got gauntlets on—I can see those.'

'Is he in pain?'

Yes...and he's very angry. I can't hear what he is saying but his mouth is open as if he is shouting very violently.' At this point Robert says, 'I'm sorry...I'm in a lot of pain and I need to go to the toilet.'

'OK,' I reply. 'I'll snap my fingers and you will be able to cope perfectly adequately.' I do so and Robert gets up and goes out.

This is proving a good example of the value of a special use of the screen technique. To begin with it is as though the patient were watching somebody else. There is a degree of remoteness which makes recall of an unpleasant experience easier. Now, however, as I hoped would happen, Robert is beginning to identify with the character on the screen.

His mission accomplished, Robert returns and is instantly back to where he was before the interruption.

Resuming, I say to him, 'It sounds as if your legs are broken, and possibly your pelvis too.'

He responds, 'It's broken and at an angle...and I'm wearing pointed shoes ... they're riding things...and I feel my right leg is bent... I'm pretty sure that means it's broken...about four inches above the knee. I don't think my left leg is broken but certainly my pelvis is cracked...it goes up...towards my right hip...and I'm trying to push myself backward with my left arm and I...can't...do...it...and I'm howling with pain.'

At this point I ask Robert, 'What do you feel about having got yourself injured like this?'

'Cross...frustrated ...very angry that I should have let it happen.'

'Very angry that I should have let it happen.' I repeated his words to him, emphasising them. 'What happened?'

'I think I fell off a horse. I don't think anyone did anything to me.'

'Why did you fall off it?'

'I think I was showing off...that came straight to my mind when I was looking for a reason.'

'O.K....what exactly were you doing by way of showing off?'

'I don't know...'

'I think you do', I said. 'I think you know very well... Now...what was it you were doing?'

'I couldn't have been standing on the saddle, surely? But that is the picture that came to mind...but that's bloody silly...can't be right... No! I honestly don't know.'

'I think you do,' I insist. 'I think you know very well and that you are extremely ashamed about it. I may be wrong, but that is the feeling I get—very strongly. There is not only great pain but also a lot of shame associated with it. As I'm counting to ten, something will appear on the screen to show whether I'm right about that or wrong.' I count to ten.

'Yes! I think I've fallen off a horse but I've got an image of...you know...the things they used to put the knights up on their horses. They put a rope round their waists or something like that and pulled on a rope and they used to go up...a sort of crane...and I've fallen off... That's what I've done! And I've fallen on my left bottom...a thud...and it's dead...what a bloody silly thing to do...but why is my right leg broken? ...I could be wrong...I can almost feel a distinct line across my pelvis going up to my right hip, where it's broken. It feels so distinct. My right leg has got the heel down in the dirt...it's bent and numb...and I'm trying to push the palm of my left hand down in the dirt to drag myself backwards...

NO!! The gear broke!! As you wound the handle there was like a piece of metal that stopped you from falling...'

'A sort of ratchet?'

'A ratchet! That's right! ...A long ratchet sitting in between two stays, and that broke and that's why I fell down...and I think my back hurt because the armour hurt it...and there is a sharp point going into my back where I fell...and I'm cross because they are all going off without me...I can see horses going from left to right...men and women on them...just going off to have fun...'

There is a long silence, which I break by telling Robert that I think we have done enough for today. I bring him back to the present and to ground level.

Once back in normal consciousness Robert comments, 'That was more than sheer imagination! There was something absolutely tangible and definite about it...as you were talking I felt my whole body twisting to the left...absolutely mis-shapen. How incredible! I had broken my pelvis from here to here'—he draws an imaginary line with his finger—'my right leg was broken about there'—point-ing—'and I was trying to pull myself...like that...'—demonstrating—'and as I'm doing so, that is *exactly* the sort of pain I get.'

I share with Robert my impression that the session was indeed a valid reliv-ing of an experience, and point out that showing off was a factor common both to the accident in the present life and the one in that earlier life.

The next session took place four days later. Robert starts by telling me that he has been wondering if he imagined everything in the last session. 'But the fact is,' he continues, 'that since then I have been almost entirely free from pain. This is remarkable because, while I am accustomed to an occasional pain-free day, most of the time the pain is continuous.'

I ask Robert to lie down, and help him to shift his level. When he has reached a deep state, I ask him if he recalls the events of the previous session. He does, and he has no doubt that they are part of his total experience. I ask how long he lived after the accident. He knows he died quite soon afterwards, but not immediately because he is experiencing himself on a bed in a room with a win-dow, where a woman is looking after him. He is in great pain, but also in a state of great shame for having sustained the accident. 'I was trying to be funny...as he wound the handle I was kicking my feet about like a child...and the thing broke...and I fell...down on my left side.' Robert repeats the story that emerged at the last session.

Then I ask him: 'Had you got over the *shame* that you felt about the accident before you died?'

'No,' Robert replies. 'I can never get over the humiliation of it. I should not be on this bed.'

'Did you,' I ask, 'come to see the pain of it almost as a just punishment for being so stupid?'

'Yes,' Robert replies, 'as a penance. I don't know if I was a knight...but I was married...the woman looking after me is my wife and I am ashamed for her...'

'Did you forgive yourself before you died?'

'I can never forgive myself.'

I'm sure that this reply indicates an attitude that has caused a ghost to be left behind, and unless Robert rescues the ghost by accepting it back into himself, I'm sure he will continue to have pain in his legs. I feel sufficiently certain of my ground to explain this to Robert. I explain too that his problem is basically one of false pride. The fact that he had been so stupid was too humiliating for him to accept.

I then offer Robert the thought that humiliation is the feeling we experience when some circumstance has forced us to accept that in some respect or other we are not as big as we had chosen to believe that we were. The circumstance has punctured an illusion; it has knocked a brick out of the edifice of our false pride, and that is always painful. Finally, I remind Robert that while he may indeed have acted rather stupidly, we are all prone to moments of stupidity, especially when young, as he had been at the time of the swimming pool accident.

Robert is silent for several minutes. Then he says, 'You are right. I was too proud to accept that I could have been so stupid. Of course I can accept that man as part of me.'

I ask Robert then how his body is feeling.

'A bit battered and bruised,' comes the reply.

I tell him I am going to beam 'healing energy' on him and that he is going to use it to heal the man on the bed. And I remind him that there is no need for him, Robert, to suffer any more pain on account of the accident in the swimming pool. Then I repeat, in essence, the technique I used on Anne. When I feel I have done all I can in that respect, I ask Robert to come back to the present in his own time. After a few minutes he opens his eyes and declares he is feeling fine. I count him back to normal waking consciousness, stressing as I do so that on no account will he slip back into a state of level shift.

I did not hear from Robert again until, some three years later, I telephoned him to ask how he was. He replied that he had remained absolutely free of pain. This was a happy state of affairs for him and gratifying news for me because, he told me, for the previous *twenty years* he had been making the rounds of all the surgeons and hospitals in the country who specialised in orthopaedics, but to no avail.

Let us now have a further look at ghosts, and especially the ghosts of Anne and Robert.

Comparing Ghosts

As I have explained, an essential part of the substance of a soul is experience. In this context, the word 'experience' includes not only what happens to us and what we do, but also our thoughts and intentions and feelings. As I have also explained, if an experience is so heavily loaded with unpleasant feelings that we do not wish to be reminded of it, we repress it. We split it off from the main body of our experiences and push it into our unconscious. But in splitting a particular experience off from the main body of our experience we are splitting off a part of our soul. If that part of our soul is still split off when we die, it will become a ghost, and will be anchored in time in the situation that led to it being split off.

The unpleasant feelings may arise from circumstances that are predominantly *outside* ourselves or *inside* ourselves, and they may concern predominantly either the supra-physical body or the psyche. In the case of Anne, what she had split off was predominantly the experience of that ghastly trek, culminating in the unbearable pain which carrying the cooking pot had caused in her back. The general distress of the trek plus the pain in her back had affected her physical body so severely that they had affected also her supra-physical body. Her psyche might have been involved in the feelings of hopelessness resulting from the lack of any sense of destination, and finally in making the decision to take her life by drinking from the poisoned well. But there was no evidence of any feelings of guilt or shame about taking her own life, or about leaving the cooking pot to be carried by someone else. There were, in fact, no feelings arising from the psyche that were keeping the ghost imprisoned. Hence what needed to be rescued was predominantly the injured portion of her supra-physical body.

Robert's case was very different. The injuries sustained by his fall were obviously extremely painful and had involved his supra-physical as well as his physical body. But, as Robert himself admitted, what he could not tolerate were the feelings of shame and humiliation of being responsible for the accident by showing off. This inability was a manifestation of his false pride, which was a feature of his psyche. It was a significant part of his problem because it was the main cause of the ghost being left. Hence, no less than his supra-physical body his psyche was also in need of help to accept that ghost back into himself. It would seem that my remarks about humiliation and about the tendency of young people sometimes to be stupid had been all that was necessary to enable him to do this. Had he not been able to do it, then I think it is very probable that he would have continued to punish himself by having pain in his legs.

A feeling of guilt is always an indication that a soul is trying to reject an experience that is part of itself. If one accepts one has done whatever it is about which one feels guilty; if one genuinely regrets it; if one has tried to make such amends as one can; and if one can resolve at least to try not to repeat the offence, then, I think, it is usually only false pride that can stop one forgiving oneself.

There is another reason why an injury to the supra-physical body may not be healed 'Upstairs', and this, strangely enough, does not concern a ghost.

Suppose a devout worshipper had spent upon her knees an amount of time that most of us might consider grossly exaggerated. When she died, no matter how much physical damage—perhaps in the form of arthritis—her knees had sustained over the years, and no matter how much discomfort they might have been causing her, she would have been proud of her symptoms as evidence of her devotion.

When she died, there would have been no part of her devotional activities that she would have wanted to disown and hence no ghost would have been left. BUT, her pride in any damage to her supra-physical body as evidence of her devotion might have caused her to refuse to accept any healing. In this event, any future body that the relevant part of that soul animated might have a 'constitutional' weakness of the knees. In fact, the effect would be similar to the pain in Anne's back, though the reason for it would be different.

In the next chapter we will take a broader look at psychiatric treatment in the light of a belief in reincarnation.

9   *Reincarnation and Psychiatric Treatments*

At different times in the long course of history up to the middle of the 18th century, mental afflictions had been variously attributed to possession by evil spirits, punishment by the Gods, a sacred gift of the power of prophecy, imbalance of what were held to be the four bodily humours: blood, yellow bile, black bile and phlegm; and witchcraft. The last named came to be seen as conspiracy with the devil to destroy the Church. Methods of treatment had ranged from making holes in the skull to allow the evil spirits to escape, to every imaginable form of torture designed to make the body too uncomfortable for an evil spirit to want to live in it.

It was not until the end of the 19th century and the beginning of the twentieth that psychotherapy was established, largely by Freud, as a means of treating psychological problems.

Just what is psychotherapy? Psychotherapy is just one form of psychiatric treatment. *Dorland's Illustrated Medical Dictionary*, 25th edition, tells us that: *'Psychotherapy is treatment designed to produce a response by mental rather than physical effects, including the use of suggestion, persuasion, re-education, reassurance and support, as well as techniques of hypnosis, abreaction and psychoanalysis, which are employed in so-called 'deep psychotherapy'.'* To avoid confusion later, I will clarify the expression 'deep psychotherapy'.

Freud had worked with Charcot in Paris and had been impressed with what could be achieved through hypnosis. Once back in Vienna he teamed up with another physician, Joseph Breuer, who had already developed what he called the 'cathartic method'. It involved hypnotising the patient and then allowing him to talk, a technique that often resulted in the disappearance of the problem. Freud noticed that much of the material, which emerged when the patient was hypnotised, seemed not to be available to him when he was in normal consciousness. This led Freud to presume that there was an area of the mind that was unconscious but the contents of which played an important part in influencing behaviour. On this foundation Freud developed a form of treatment that, without using hypnosis, centred upon exploring the contents of the unconscious area of the patient's mind. Freud called this treatment 'Psychoanalysis'. The name became virtually Freud's copyright. In order to be described as psychoanalysis a treatment has to conform rigidly to certain features upon which Freud insisted, and to be based upon a precise philosophy. A discussion of these features would not be relevant to our theme.

Whatever the virtues of orthodox psychoanalysis may be, it has certain very practical drawbacks. One of them, as I explained in Chapter 5, is that the time it requires puts it beyond the reach of most people. However, many psychiatrists, of whom I am one, believe that exploring a patient's unconscious and enabling him to become aware of hidden aspects of himself is often an indispensable part of treatment. Consequently, deviations from classical Freudian analysis have arisen, including hypnoanalysis, which is my specialty. However, they all derive from Freud's original work. They are correctly referred to, collectively and individually, as *analytically oriented psychotherapy*. But, since the unconscious can be thought of as lying deeper in the mind than normal waking consciousness, they all tend also to be referred to as 'deep psychotherapy'. In these terms, Freudian or classical psychoanalysis is the original 'deep psychotherapy'.

Most people would regard psychotherapy as a way of treating the mind. However, as I have frequently remarked, I believe the mind to be the product of the soul, working in combination with or through the physical brain. Hence, as I see it, psychotherapy also treats the soul. Since it is the soul that reincarnates, I believe that any form of psychotherapy should—though it may not be—thought of as treating the soul. I will enlarge upon this view in the second part of the book.

It is to deep therapy that belief in reincarnation makes its most obvious contributions but, before we discuss that topic further, let us look at two prominent forms of therapy which pay little heed to the unconscious. These are the so-called Humanistic or Existential Therapies, and Behaviourism.

Existential or Humanistic Therapies

The names best known in connection with these therapies are probably Carl Rogers, Rolo May, 'Fritz' Perls, and Abraham Maslow. These therapies recognise that a person's upbringing during childhood plays an important part in shaping the sort of person he becomes, but in therapy they do not dwell upon the patient's past. They focus upon him as he is in the here and now, aiming to help him to become all he might be. In short, a more mature person. They are at their best with people who sense they have potentials that they are not realising; but the therapies have wide applications.

For instance, consider someone who has been suddenly afflicted with extremely severe abdominal pain. A surgeon diagnoses a perforated duodenal ulcer, an ulcer so deep that it has actually made a hole in the wall of the gut. Clearly, it is the person's body that is in immediate need of attention, in the form of surgery; but the cause of the ulcer may lie in the patient's mind. To restrict the aim of treatment simply to healing the ulcer would, therefore, be to leave the less urgent but possibly more important problem untouched.

The existential therapist would, I'm sure, like to know if the patient has been feeling under constant stress and keeping his body permanently in the state that was designed only for emergencies. If he has been and still is feeling under constant stress, is the feeling justifiable? If it is, can he be helped to react to the situation in a healthier way? In this context, I see each individual as the pilot of his own personal aircraft. It matters not how long he has been flying on a mistaken compass point, that is, behaving in an inappropriate way, because he is free at any moment to change his direction and fly straight towards his intended destination. However, difficulties can arise if something is blocking the steering mechanism.

For instance, he may be a chronic worrier. If this is the case, his tendency to perpetual worrying may be a character trait. At least in some instances, it may be beyond the capacity of the existential therapist to help the patient to change the trait. If all other measures, including for instance group therapy, have proved unsuccessful, some form of analytically oriented therapy might be indicated. And if the cause of the worrying is unfinished business from a former life, which the patient's soul has brought with it into the present life, even this form of therapy may be unsuccessful unless the therapist believes in reincarnation.

Experience suggests that, especially with the aid of hypnosis, it may be possible to enable the patient to recall that former life situation and free himself from it. This would obviously be a more satisfactory solution than a lifetime of careful dieting and an endless regime of pills to regulate his digestive juices and more pills to modify his anxiety. As I have said, we shall be returning to this subject later.

I frequently use an existential approach myself, but, as with all forms of therapy, it is important to recognise its limitations. No form of therapy is suited to every patient.

Let us look now at a school of therapy which has no interest in the reason for a symptom, Behaviourism.

Behaviourism

The Behaviourists are interested only in how a person behaves. They see inappropriate behaviour as, essentially, a bad habit. They assume that at some time the patient has responded unsuitably to some situation, and that this response has become reinforced. However, they are not interested in the situation or the circumstances that have led to the behaviour. They concentrate simply upon changing the behaviour in the here and now. They have a variety of techniques for achieving their end.

For instance, it is impossible to feel anxious and to be relaxed at the same time. Hence one technique starts with teaching the patient to become completely relaxed. When he has achieved this step, he is gradually introduced to the situation that evokes anxiety, while being urged to remain completely relaxed for as long as he can. With practice he is able to come nearer and nearer to the situation while still being relaxed, and hence free of anxiety. Other techniques feature more or less subtle schemes of rewards and penalties.

For me, however, the word 'Behaviourism' always brings instantly to mind the case of Sylvia.

Sylvia and Pastry Shops

Sylvia, in her mid-twenties, slim, attractive, happily married, and the mother of a five-year-old son, had a problem. Whenever she happened to pass a pastry shop, the aromas wafting through the door would evoke an irresistible compulsion to go in and, to use her own words, gorge like a pig. She resented being at the mercy of a compulsion that was foreign to her fastidious nature.

She had fought the compulsion in every imaginable practical way but to no avail. At last she had sought the help of psychotherapy. Several months of work with a very competent therapist had succeeded in modifying her antagonism towards her mother and her rivalry with her sister, but had failed to affect the compulsion. Then her therapist happened to learn of my belief that the source of a neurotic condition was sometimes to be found in a former lifetime of the patient, and she brought Sylvia to see me.

After hearing Sylvia tell her story, I explained to her that while it was normal for the aromas from a pastry shop to awaken some desire in anyone, in her particular case it seemed to release energy from a source that was hidden in her unconscious. This energy would invade her consciousness and so strongly reinforce her natural desire that it became an irresistible compulsion. What we needed to do, therefore, was to find this hidden source of energy, because once it was brought to her awareness the energy would lose its power. I explained too that the task would be easier if she would allow me to hypnotise her. Sylvia readily agreed to this course, proved an excellent subject and quickly reached a deep state of level shift.

I told her then, that as I was counting to ten, something would be bubbling up to her consciousness and that it would take us a step towards the object of our search. As I reached ten, Sylvia was experiencing herself as a boy of nineteen standing in snow on skis. That scene was swiftly replaced by a scene of the boy's home, which turned out to be in Vienna. The boy recalled that the family would visit one of the pastry shops for which, of course, Vienna was renowned, whenever there was a cause for celebration.

The next scene was a displaced persons' camp, for it was wartime. Rations in the camp were sparse and the boy spent much time day-dreaming about the pastry shops of Vienna. He had also joined a small group of friends who had agreed that if one of them were to come upon any form of food—even a potato long past its best—he would share it with the others.

One day a Red Cross parcel arrived at the camp for this boy. Amongst other things it contained a tin of condensed milk. In view of their agreement he should, of course, have shared it with his friends. But the longings springing from his sweet tooth were too strong for him. He managed to hide it and when he was alone he drank it. All of it.

Immediately, he was appalled at what he had done. He wanted only to find his friends, confess his crime, assure them that he really did love them and beg their forgiveness. But before he could find them, an air raid started and, after a terrifying half-hour of crashes and flashes, the bomb fell which killed him. At this point I brought Sylvia, still under hypnosis, back to the present day and explained what I believed had happened.

I explained first that every experience becomes a part of the substance of our soul, and that a feeling of guilt means that one part of our soul is wishing it could disown another part of our soul. If it should happen that we die while feeling such guilt, then, if the feeling is strong enough, the part of the soul that is being rejected will indeed be split off from the rest and be left behind as what I call a ghost. I said I felt sure that something like this had happened in the case of the young man from Vienna. As he died he had been wishing most fervently that he had not cheated his friends, and also that he had not had the sweet tooth that had driven him to do so. Consequently, all that part of his soul which had been involved in the incident had become split off and stuck in this way, and it included his craving for the pastries of pre-war days.

In the present day, the aromas from pastry shops in Sylvia's nostrils resonated to this ghost, whereupon the energy in the ghost's cravings was stimulated and released and invaded Sylvia's normal waking consciousness. Once there, it reinforced any perfectly normal longings Sylvia might have for such delicacies so powerfully that they became irresistible.

However, it was only so long as that part of the young man's soul remained stuck as a ghost that the aromas from a pastry shop could have this effect. Therefore, the next step Sylvia needed to take was to recognise that the ghost of this young man was a part of her totality and to become reconciled with him; in effect, to accept him back into herself.

'But that would be impossible!' Sylvia retorted. 'What he did was unforgivable!'

I asked Sylvia then, 'If you had been one of the friends whom the boy had cheated, would you have been able to forgive him?'

'Of course I would,' came the instant reply.

'Do you think you were more generously minded than those friends?'

'Of course not,' came the reply, equally promptly.

'Then we can safely assume that his friends forgave the boy long ago. And we can be equally sure that God has forgiven him, because he truly regretted what he did. And when you come right down to it, what he did was simply to give way to a very human weakness. I wonder why *you* cannot forgive him. Could the truth of the matter really be that you are simply too proud to forgive yourself for being merely human?'

'H'm,' Sylvia responded. 'You must let me think about that.'

A long silence followed. It ended with: 'You can bring me back now. I know that my compulsion is finished.'

Back in normal waking consciousness, Sylvia repeated, 'I know that compulsion is finished, and now I also understand two other things I never thought of mentioning to you. One is my terror of thunder, which I'm sure resonates to the air raid in which I was killed. The other is the strange urge I sometimes get to rush round to all my friends and assure them I really do love them.'

I am not a behaviourist and therefore cannot speak with authority. But I can imagine that a behaviourist might have considered treating Sylvia's problem with aversion therapy. The aim of this form of therapy is to cause the unsuitable thing or activity, which the patient finds irresistibly attractive, to become linked in his mind with something he finds repulsive. I can imagine that this form of therapy might have successfully squelched Sylvia's compulsion, but to be satisfied with that result would be to be satisfied with doing less for the patient than might be done. Moreover, if one were to block the outlet that the energy in the compulsion had chosen, one knows not where it might try to find egress next. In short, it might cause a new symptom and—who knows—possibly one that was even more distressing.

In a sense, any symptom that is caused by energy coming from a ghost can be understood as the cry of the ghost to be rescued. It is important to hear and to heed such a cry because, as I have said, a ghost is anchored in a perpetual 'now' and hence cannot evolve. And since a person's ghosts are a part of his totality, the existence of a ghost is a brake upon that person's freedom to evolve.

Nevertheless, I can envisage circumstances in which, even after the real cause has been dealt with by other techniques, a symptom might persist and a behaviourist technique might be just what was required to clear it up. Consider, for instance, the case of Gregory.

Gregory

Gregory was a boy of fifteen and he was at a boarding school. His problem was what he called his 'rocking'. From his infancy onwards, he told me, as soon as he was in bed he would have an urge to lie on his left side, draw his knees up and then, over and over again, twist the upper part of his body onto his back, at the same time flinging his right arm over his head. This would continue even while he was asleep, and it was incurring the displeasure of other boys in his school dormitory. We decided to search for the origin of this rocking.

Under hypnosis, Gregory immediately found himself watching a man climbing a high, steep rock-face in a snowstorm. He commented that to be climbing at all in such weather was very dangerous, and to be doing so alone was crazy. Then: 'There! It had to happen. He has fallen. He cannot move his legs—I think because they are covered with debris. A moment before he fell he saw some men just rounding a bend on the path below.'

I asked Gregory how the man came to be on that rock-face.

I'm sure Gregory was not aware of the change, but this question appeared to cause him to move from a position as an observer to one of being an active participant. In effect, he *became* the man on the rock face.

He told me that he was an aerial photographer. He had been taking photographs for military purposes somewhere in Southern France. It was obviously World War II. He and the pilot were on their way home to England, flying along the northern edge of the Pyrenees, when they were attacked and shot down by an enemy aircraft. The pilot managed to land the plane and Gregory scrambled out, clutching his precious box of photographs. He made straight for nearby woods but soon found he was being pursued by what he called 'The Little Green Men', who were in fact Spanish border guards.

Trying to evade them he turned into what proved to be a cul-de-sac, and they captured him. They took him to the local police station where he was searched, care being taken not to discover his pistol and ammunition. Then he was put into a cell on the ground floor. Over the window there were bars, one of which was loose. After darkness had fallen, he heard a low whistle from outside, to which he responded. He was told to remove the loose bar and climb out. His benefactor took him to his house and gave him a good meal. He then provided Gregory with a map and some suitable clothes, and set him on a path through the mountains.

Before long Gregory again found himself being pursued, and this time by a posse of Germans—a very different matter to the friendly Spanish border guards. He decided his best hope lay in taking advantage of a big bend to leave the path he was following by scaling the rock face which bordered it on one side. He was some way up this when, looking down, he saw that the German patrol was rounding the bend. At this point he fell.

On the ground, he found himself on his left side with his legs so heavily covered with debris that he could not possibly move them. His spare ammunition was in his haversack, the straps of which had broken during his fall. It had come to lie beyond his head, just out of reach. He was repeatedly twisting the upper part of his body and flinging out his arm in a desperate attempt to reach it when the patrol, realising the situation, came up and shot him.

Glimpses of still earlier lifetimes as well as episodes of his present life had revealed that Gregory had an extraordinarily courageous and determined soul. The aerial photographer was of the same fabric. He was so determined to get his photographs back to England that he refused to believe he was dead. As a result, part of Gregory's soul was still anchored in the scene as a ghost, still trying in vain to reach the haversack that contained his ammunition.

I set about convincing the ghost that the war was over, that his side had won and that he had done everything that could possibly have been expected of him. Once he—the ghost—had accepted these facts, I think I managed to reconcile him with his former pursuers. After all, there had been no reason for *personal* animosity between them. My next step was to send an urgent message to Ray, asking her to come and rescue Gregory's ghost. I felt so certain that she would do so that I told the ghost that a very friendly blonde lady would soon approach him and invite him to go with her, which he was free to do. After a few minutes, speaking through Gregory, the ghost announced that just such a lady was approaching and holding out her hand to him, and that he was going to go away with her.

Of course my suggestions concerning Ray were totally unscientific. There is no possible way of proving that Ray really did arrive and that the ghost of Gregory really did go with her. I have simply related what happened. I then brought Gregory back to the present day and to ground level.

Rather like Anne, the patient who, as a small girl in a former life, had died on that trek through the desert, Gregory's first words were: 'Something has happened to my back!' He continued: 'I've had pains in my back for years. People have blamed them on a fall from my pony, but I never felt that was right, and anyway, no one has known quite what was wrong with my back, but it suddenly feels alright!' And I learned, some twenty-five years later, that his back had never troubled him since that session. But the rocking had continued! At the same time, I also learned that, sadly, Gregory had recently died.

Does not the fact that the rocking continued mean that the story of the aerial photographer was not a valid regression to a former life but only a fantasy?

No. I think not. The assumption that the story of the aerial photographer was valid far-memory is supported by the fact that the pain in Gregory's back, which no one had succeeded in either satisfactorily explaining or relieving, was precisely what one might have expected from such a fall. The intensely emotional circumstances surrounding the fall were precisely the kind of conditions under which I would expect an injury to the physical body to have affected the supra-physical body also. The injury to the supra-physical body would have been a feature of the ghost, and the fact that following the session Gregory had no more pain in his back surely indicates that we were successful in freeing at least part of the ghost. Gregory's fall from the pony might well have resonated to the injury the aerial photographer sustained to his back when he fell.

I think there are at least three possible explanations for the persistence of the rocking.

One is that I had indeed failed to free *all* of the ghost. I had failed to bring *all* of the energy in the photographer's wish to reach his haversack to Gregory's normal waking consciousness. If that were the case, part of the ghost would still be there, trying to reach it. I personally think this is not the correct explanation because, before asking Ray to rescue the ghost, I feel I had not only helped the ghost to realise that the war was over, that his side had won and that he had done everything that could possibly have been expected of him; I am sure I had also helped him to become most happily reconciled with his former pursuers.

The second explanation, which I think is far more probable, I can best explain by means of an analogy. The energy causing a symptom that has no physical basis can be likened to a river by the time it reaches the sea. The river may have started from a single spring, in the shape of a single traumatic event, but by the time it reaches the sea it will have received contributions in the form of the energy in emotions from many tributaries, that is to say other, quite unconnected traumatic circumstances. Thus, even if one could eradicate the original spring, this would not produce a dry riverbed. In other words, the energy still causing Gregory's rocking might well have been coming from sources totally unconnected with the aerial photographer's ghost.

A third possibility is that the energy which had caused the rocking every night since Gregory was an infant had, in effect, worn a groove from his soul down to those cells in his brain that were responsible for causing the muscles that produced the rocking movements to work. Even if the spring and all possible tributaries had been dealt with, the groove might have remained. In the present life, whenever an emotion of any kind—not only a negative one like anger or grief or fear, but even a positive one like enthusiasm, or pleasurable anticipation or joy—*exceeded a certain intensity*, it would overflow, so to speak, down the groove and induce the rocking. I know of no experimental work that might substantiate this notion, but to give such a hypothetical groove time to heal, it would seem essential to deflect the energy into some more appropriate form of expression. This, I can imagine, is where a behaviourist approach would be exactly what was needed.

We will now temporarily leave the subject of psychotherapy to consider another form of psychiatric treatment: Psychopharmacology.

Psychopharmacology

Over recent years a great deal has been learned about the chemical processes that occur in the brain and about drugs which can influence them. In some instances, a disorder of the brain's chemistry may be the essential problem and treatment with one or other of these drugs may be precisely what is genuinely needed; but we must be careful that we do not deceive ourselves.

To take again the analogy of a motor car and its driver as a unit: if the unit were constantly travelling dangerously fast, one could possibly prevent this behaviour by some device which limited the extent to which the accelerator could be depressed—which would be analogous to a tranquilliser—and this might be the best that time and circumstances permitted one to do. But quite apart from possible undesirable side effects, this would not be tackling the real problem, if this lay in the answer to the question: 'Why does the driver habitually drive too fast?'

A single conversation might be enough to reveal that the answer was, for instance, an attitude to life that was needlessly competitive, and then to convince the individual that he could change this attitude and would be far happier if he were to do so. Or it might require so-called deep psychotherapy to discover the reason for his attitude and make it possible for him to change it. Yet a third possibility is that the driving too fast might, in terms of this analogy, represent a chronically slightly above-the-line state of a manic-depressive illness, or bipolar condition, as it is called nowadays. In this case the ideal treatment might be a combination of drugs and psychotherapy.

We have reason to be grateful for psychopharmacology. Even by doing no more than ameliorating symptoms, it enables many car/driver units to stay on the road. So long as we do not confuse relieving a symptom with solving the real problem, it is a great blessing.

With psychopharmacology I would link electroconvulsive therapy or ECT. Its use is highly controversial, but its results can be dramatic with minimal side effects. I shall never forget a certain elderly lady who was brought into my consulting room by her daughter with whom she was staying. She was able just to shuffle along a few inches at a time. Her face wore a pitiful expression of misery. She was ceaselessly wringing her hands and whimpering, 'Oh dear, oh dear! Oh dear, oh dear!' Conversation with her was impossible.

Physical examination obviously revealed that she was frail but did not disclose any physical illness. I advised her daughter to take her home and said that I would visit the house the next day, with an anaesthetist, and give her mother an ECT. This plan was carried out without a hitch and repeated on half a dozen occasions at intervals of a few days. Within weeks the lady was back in her own home, living on her own, which was what she preferred, and looking after herself perfectly competently. I heard later that her favourite treat was to be taken by her son-in-law for a trip in his private aeroplane!

I can believe that every change in mood is related to a change in the microchemistry of the brain, and that the mood cannot change unless the chemistry changes. Far more often than not, the change occurs spontaneously without any obvious cause. On the other hand, it may be brought about by any circumstance which changes a sad 'Oh dear, the glass is already half empty!' into a 'Whoopee, the glass is still half full!' Such things happen in real life. A persisting view of life that is unjustifiably gloomy may be due to inappropriate patterns of thinking. A form of treatment that specifically addresses this problem is known as 'Cognitive Therapy'.

In my experience, depression occurring in people under forty has usually responded to psychotherapy. I have occasionally encountered a patient in whom the factors causing the depression seemed perfectly clear, but working through them has, nevertheless, brought no relief at all. Eventually, albeit reluctantly because one could not guarantee there would be no impairment of memory afterwards, I have advised a short course of ECT. This was in the days before the advent of anti-depressive drugs. In each case, after three treatments, the picture had completely changed. And, happily, there was no impairment of memory. I cannot escape the impression that the ECT had some effect that enabled the patient to make use of the psychotherapy, which, previously, he had been unable to do. For this reason I have linked ECT with psychopharmacology.

However, these cases occurred long before I had come to believe in reincarnation. Now, with cases like that of Robert of the painful legs and Anne of the painful back in mind, both of which we encountered in the previous chapter, I wonder if the present day events which had appeared to cause the intractable depressions had not been *symbolical repetitions* of events from a former life. Mention of such possibilities brings us back to the whole question of freeing or rescuing ghosts.

Analytically Oriented or Deep Psychotherapy

A fundamental aim of deep psychotherapy can be seen as helping the patient to rescue his ghosts. This is true, whether the therapist believes in reincarnation or not, because a ghost is a split-off part of the soul, and it may just as well have been split off earlier in the current life as in a former one. Belief in reincarnation extends a therapist's notion of the unconscious. It may lead a therapist to open up valid and helpful areas of enquiry that would not occur to someone who did not hold that belief.

For instance, an attractive lady of thirty had never been able to enjoy a sexual experience. It was as though she had an in-built thermostat, and whenever she reached a certain pitch of arousal, a mechanism would cut in that completely dowsed the fire. Her history revealed that her parents were so rigid and restrictive in all sexual matters, and so frightening when they were angry that one might have felt that being brought up in such an atmosphere would be enough to account for her problems. However, my belief in reincarnation prompted me to ask, 'I wonder why you *chose* those particular parents.'

Not surprisingly, this was a question that had never occurred to her. Under hypnosis it became clear that her parents were only the most recent of a succession of restrictive factors. The start of her problems—as we learned in due course—was a tragedy in a long-past life, which she had brought about through sexual jealousy. In a state of profound remorse she had entered a convent. There she had been taught that real virtue lay in having no relationships with human beings but only with God. And, of course, above all, no sexual relationships. In her state of remorse she had been intensely suggestible and had embraced this doctrine wholeheartedly. She spent the rest of her life in that convent, sternly repressing all sexual feeling. She died as its Mother Superior, still imbued with the notion that true virtue lay in the renunciation of all sexual feelings. Henceforth she chose parents whose attitudes would reinforce her own unconscious efforts to keep all such feelings repressed. This was a patient whose problems, I am convinced, could never have been resolved within the framework of just her present lifetime.

With increasing experience of therapy involving earlier lifetimes, we shall no doubt become more adept at recognising energy that is coming from a ghost stuck in a former lifetime. As it is there are certain clues, though none of them are infallible.

For instance, one such clue is the appearance of a symptom at a very early age—like Gregory's rocking.

Another is a frequently recurring dream during childhood. The episode I mentioned in an earlier chapter of the small girl in the train that was bombed came to light when we were exploring a dream which had often recurred during her childhood. In the dream she would find herself in what seemed to her to be a vast shed for manufacturing bicycles. This shed proved to be the dream version of the railway station—pertaining to a former lifetime—in which the children who were to be evacuated to the country had foregathered.

Unusual Rescues of Ghosts

Joan was insistent that the main task of some souls between lifetimes in physical bodies is to rescue ghosts who are anchored on earth, and this seems to me very probable. On earth, there are living individuals who are able to see the ghosts of people who have died, either recently or long ago, and who can sometimes set them free.

But can a therapist rescue a ghost of someone who is living if the person is not physically present during the operation? I have two experiences that bear on this question, but as the therapist in each case was Joan, who was a psychic with a variety of faculties, they can hardly be taken as the basis of a general answer.

A Fear of Noise

The pile of telegrams we found on our return to our home in France after one of our sojourns in New York heralded the first of these experiences.

At the bottom of the pile was one from Japan, and the others were from points east—the last being from London. They were all from the same person who was urgently seeking an appointment with us, though the reason was not stated. We arranged for him to visit us two weeks later.

An express train from the Gare d'Austerlitz in Paris used to deposit many of our visitors at our local station, Brive-la-Gaillarde, at about nine-thirty in the evening. At around seven-thirty on the day our patient was due we were having a peaceful, uneventful supper when Joan abruptly left the table. Some minutes later I followed her, as I usually did, to make sure all was well with her. I found her huddled in a corner of our bedroom in a state of terror. It was some minutes before I could make enough contact with her to learn what was happening. As she was telling me, she gradually came back to 'ground level'.

She said, 'The man in the train who is on his way to us was thinking of us, and spookwise he was shining like a beacon. I could not help being drawn into him, and then I found myself at the bottom of a shell hole. It must have been the First World War. A dead man was in there with me, and overhead the most horrific bombardment was going on...and on...and on.' Her final words were: 'We don't know why this man is coming, but I would bet my life his problem is something to do with *noise*.'

I rejoined the company downstairs. At about ten o'clock our visitor, whom I will call Hugo, arrived. He was a polished, cultured, thoroughly composed business executive in his mid-forties. It was obviously too late for a session, so after greetings and some coffee we all repaired to bed.

The next morning I had a session with Hugo. 'My problem,' he said, 'is noise. Loud bangs fill me with terror. As long as I can remember I have been terrified of thunderstorms. As an adult, with the aid of a stiff drink I can just about cope, but as a child I would cower under the table or the stairs. People thought it was all very funny but I assure you it was—and is—not.' I nodded my understanding. 'The reason I am seeking your help now,' Hugo went on, 'is that I have been offered a job in the Far East that I would very much like to accept, but out there fireworks are a part of life and I am not sure I could stand it.'

Hugo accepted my suggestion that he allow me to attempt to induce hypnosis so that we might the more easily discover the origin of his fear. However, my best efforts proved in vain. Eventually I decided that the only thing to do was to tell him of Joan's experience while he was on his way here, which I did. Hugo's response was understandable: 'It sounds very plausible—and very remarkable—but obviously I cannot say "yea or nay".' However, all this happened some twenty-five years ago and in that time no noise has been loud enough to bother him. I feel we are entitled to say that the cure was immediate, complete and bids fair to prove permanent. But how did it happen?

I believe an abscess in a lung provides a useful analogy. The natural way for a patient to get rid of the contents of such an abscess would be, eventually, to cough them up. However, there is another possibility. A surgeon might introduce a needle into the cavity and aspirate the contents with a syringe. Joan, in effect, had put a psychic needle into that psychic abscess and drawn out all its contents, that is the memory of the experience, which included the noise and the terror associated with it. Unfortunately, she had also herself constituted the 'psychic syringe'. Consequently, instead of Hugo, it was she who experienced the emotion in the ghost, and exceedingly distressing for her it was.

I could not doubt that Joan had performed a valid psychic operation, and probably one that was vitally necessary for the patient because I think the chances are that Hugo would never have been able to contact that ghost himself. However, as I said to Joan, I feel sure there must be a better psychic technique—one that uses the energy of the psychic more economically. Joan's reply was robust: 'Not everyone can do it at all!' I had to agree—and to agree too that for her, her faculties were by no means an unqualified blessing! It was impossible not to sympathise with the cry which occasionally escaped her: 'People don't understand how hard it is to be me!'

The other case was more bizarre.

A Fear of The Dark

In the middle of the coldest winter anyone in our region of France could remember, we received a letter from a lady who lived in the Caribbean, asking if she could come to visit us. Her problem was a fear of the dark that was so intense and such a nuisance to her that she was prepared to travel to France in the hope that we might be able to relieve her of it. Since we were due, within a few weeks, to return to New York, we wrote back that we had a better idea—we would come and visit her. Which is what we did.

Our patient and hostess, whom I will call Denise, was a very competent, down-to-earth sort of person in her middle forties. We had not yet had a formal session with her but on the third day of our visit Joan suggested that I ask

Denise to take me on a tour of the island because she wanted to do some work. When we returned, Joan told us what she had been doing. She had shifted her own level, which she was well accustomed to doing, and had tuned in to Denise's long history. Joan had found that Denise had been a man training to be a priest in Egypt in a fairly late dynasty, by which time the priesthood had lost most of its former knowledge and integrity, and had become corrupt. However, it perpetuated certain rites, including the Initiation Rite. This involved the candidate for priesthood being shut up, for three days and three nights in a chamber constructed like a tomb. At the end of this time, the 'tomb' was opened and a senior priest came to hear the candidate's account of his psychic adventures during his period of entombment.

When this candidate had finished his recital, the priest was terrified because he recognised that here was someone who really knew what he was talking about. The priest left the 'tomb', but instead of releasing the candidate he caused the drop-stone to fall once more, condemning him to darkness—and death.

Joan had learned the technique of 'reading' the 'long history' of others when, during her life as Sekeeta in the First Dynasty of Egypt, she had entered the Temple and become a Priest of Anubis, an order which specialised in this skill. Joan's work that afternoon had clearly been a tremendous strain on her, but Denise's fear of the dark had vanished and has not returned. I suspect it would have vanished even if Joan had not told Denise about her 'hove', which was the family's term for such operations.

We never had a formal session with Denise, but interestingly, shortly after our arrival, she told us that she also had another problem. There was a downstairs room in her house that she was quite unable to enter at night. Joan 'saw' that the present wall between the dining room and the sitting room was in a different position from a former wall between the two rooms. Just where the present wall now stood, Joan 'saw' a coffin. It was occupied by the body of a former owner of the house who, during his life, had been much unloved by his slaves. After he had been placed in his coffin, the slaves had filed past and profaned the corpse in various utterly revolting ways. Joan freed the ghost and thereafter Denise had no difficulty in entering the room at any time.

All practitioners of deep psychotherapy would, I think, agree that their aim is to help the personality of a patient towards integration and hence towards maturity. By 'integration' I think they would mean what I would call reuniting any ghosts with the main stream of the patient's experiences; and by maturity I think they would mean an ability to love, to work, to play, to make decisions and to cope with life in this world as it is. My belief in reincarnation causes me to want to amend only one word in that formula—the word 'maturity'.

There is obviously no virtue in *not* being able to cope with the world as it is, but I would prefer the word 'evolution', which would include maturity and go beyond it. By the word 'evolution' in this context I mean the progress of a soul which will bring the spirit from which it emerged nearer the state at which no further incarnations are needed.

To believe in reincarnation is to believe there are other levels of reality. This, in turn, makes more credible the reality of states of altered consciousness—of which hypnosis is one—that can put us in touch with information that otherwise might be inaccessible.

In my own work, hypnosis has played a large part and in the next chapter, so far as the mere written word permits, we shall be able to follow the progress of a hypnotic regression, which is the most valuable technique of analytically oriented psychotherapy.

10   *Penny—a Phobia of Flying*

The First Session

Penelope, universally known, somewhat to her dismay as 'Penny', was a talented, highly competent young lady of twenty-five. At this young age she had risen to a senior post in a very large company with international connections. There was just one snag. The job entailed a great deal of air travel, and Penny had a phobia of flying. From the moment she had booked her next flight until she had boarded the aeroplane there was an undercurrent of terror to her life; and once on the plane, the terror was on the surface until she had landed. And, of course, as soon as she had landed, fear about the flight home began. The phobia was so severe that even the sound of an aeroplane passing overhead was sufficient to start her praying, fervently if silently, 'Oh God, please put them safely on the ground.'

She had sought my help just when she did because on her last flight, as her aeroplane was taking off, she had grabbed the hand of the total stranger sitting next to her; and when, in due course, he had asked if he might have his hand back, she found to her horror she had driven her nails deeply into his palm.

The phobia had manifested itself on the very first flight she ever took. This was when she was about seven years old and, with her parents and brother, had flown to the resort where they were spending their summer holiday. Since then she had flown very many times, partly because—though English—she had, for some years, been at a school in Switzerland, and she had usually flown back and forth. All these flights had been undertaken in considerable comfort on established airlines, and she had never met with an incident that justified anxiety.

However, the accumulation of trouble-free flying experience had done nothing to reduce the intensity of the phobia. On the contrary, with every flight it seemed to get worse.

The air is not a medium through which it is natural for the human animal to travel, and Penny agreed that a certain number of units of anxiety—we put it at fifty—had, therefore, to be considered normal for anyone new to the experience, or even fairly accustomed to it. But the five hundred units from which Penny, who was an experienced air traveller, suffered each time she flew were undoubtedly excessive. Thus the question to which we had to find the answer was: 'Where were the extra four hundred and fifty units of anxiety coming from?'

I explained to Penny that if we could shift her level, we would probably find the answer far more quickly than would otherwise be the case, and she readily consented to allow me to help her to do this. Penny quickly reached an advanced degree of level shift, whereupon, before going any further, I installed the safety device. I told her that if I called her firmly by her name she would never fail to hear it, and that the effect of hearing it would be to bring her back immediately to present realities. Then I told her that I would count slowly to ten, and that as I was counting, something would be bubbling up to her consciousness that would take us a step towards finding the origin of the energy in her phobia of flying. I warned her that I had no idea what might come, and that what came might seem totally ridiculous, or irrelevant or trivial; nevertheless, it would in fact be a clue to the origin of this energy, so it was essential that no matter what it was, she told me about it.

It is perhaps worth stressing that it is true I had no idea what might come to her mind. As I have said, being in an aeroplane is a situation which might justify some anxiety in its own right and at its face value; but in addition it could also have a symbolical significance that had nothing to do with flying. For instance, being encased in a box which one could not leave at will, and from which one would eventually be ejected, virtually irresistibly, through a small orifice could very well resonate to feelings one had experienced in the womb, or during the process of being born. In short, as was the case with another patient with a flying phobia, the real origin of the problem might have been a birth trauma. Indeed there were so many theoretical possibilities that an attempt to guide her at this stage might easily have steered her down a time-wasting path. Hence I was deliberately non-directive.

In fact, when I reached ten Penny declared that she could see a black dog, standing on an area of concrete.

At this point I started to record the session, and what follows is transcribed from the tape. However, contrary to what might be expected, a complete, unedited, word-for-word transcription of such a tape makes extremely tedious reading. I have, therefore, edited it where this could be done without losing anything of value. I have also interspersed, here and there, a few thoughts and comments of my own. Some of these occurred to me in the course of the session, others while I was transcribing it. The initial 'P' denotes Penny speaking; 'K' designates me.

P: It's standing on concrete...it's my dog...I'm sort of looking at it from above...it's getting smaller because I'm sort of in the air above it.

K: Become aware of the 'You' whose dog this is...I assume it is not present-day 'you'? Am I right or wrong?

P: Right...I'm going away from them...the rest of them...they are on the ground...I can't see the ground any more.

K: Whom were you seeing on the ground?

P: The others in the hut. (*This was the first mention of a 'hut'.*)

K: Who were the others in the hut?...Were they more dogs?...Or people?

P: People...men...The hut has a green door...it looks like a dormitory inside.

(*Penny is silent for a long minute, and then she appears to be choking back sobs. I ask her what is wrong and tearfully she replies*):

P: It's my dog...and I don't know why but I won't be seeing it any more!

(*Now there is an even longer silence. At last I ask her what is happening.*)

P: I don't know...nothing really. (*Yet another long pause.*) It's confusing ...lots of bits.

K: I will snap my fingers and it will become clearer. (*I do so.*)

P: It's some sort of shop kind of place...there's a counter...and we're given sort of bundles...I don't know what is in them because they are all tied up.

K: What do you do with the bundles?

P: It sounds strange...we say a prayer over them. Then we stand in a row with our bundles and we have to look at them.

K: Right...and what are they?

P: Straps and things...and brown linen stuff...we just look at the straps and then we put them on.

K: How do you put them on?

(*There is a long pause. Eventually I ask:*)

K: Can you feel where the straps go?

P: Over the shoulders...under my arms...through my legs...

K: Yes...and what happens now?

(Every response has to be dragged out of her.)
    P: I want to bend my knees.
    K: OK, you want to bend your knees. What happens now?
    P: Don't know.
(I sense there is very strong resistance here. At length, with long pauses between each sentence, we get:)
    P: We put our hats on.
    K: What sort of hat is it?
    P: A skull cap.
    K: Is it really a skullcap, or is it more like a beret?
(I make this suggestion hoping to push things along a bit.)
    P: Well, it's brown.
    K: OK...and when you've all got your hats on, what happens?
    P: A lorry arrives.
    K: And you all climb into it?
    P: Ummm...
    K: Good...*(encouragingly)*...and where does the lorry take you?
    P: *(After another long pause)* Across the concrete.
    K: Yes, across the concrete...and where to?
    P: The aeroplane.
(With a long pause before every response, Penny tells me that they all enter the aeroplane. She cannot tell me how many other men are in the group and I do not press the point. Once in the aeroplane she moves towards the back. Her seat is just behind the wings. Being in an aeroplane feels very familiar. She has often been in one before.)
    K: Why are you in the aeroplane? What is your job?
    P: Something on the floor...sort of trap door.
    K: How do you feel about being in this aeroplane?
    P: All right.
    K: Do you know where you are going?
    P: No idea.
    K: I see...what do you do about this trap door?
    P: *(After a very long pause)*...Can't remember.
(I sense there is still very strong resistance, and since we have been working for more than two hours I ask Penny if she would like to stop at this point. She would. I take her through a résumé of the ground we have covered, checking that she agrees with each point, and then give a very strong suggestion to the effect that at our next session she will be able to shift her level very easily and return to this point of being

in the aeroplane. I then bring her back to the present day. When I am satisfied she has fully returned in time, I bring her back to normal waking consciousness, repeating frequently as I am doing so that under no circumstances will she slip back spontaneously into a level shift.)

The Second Session

The next session took place just a week later. When her level was shifted, I told Penny that as I was counting to twenty she would find herself back in the aeroplane at the point at which we ended the last session. I stressed again that she had nothing to fear because if I addressed her by her name she would always hear it, and the sound of her name would bring her out of whatever scene she had been absorbed in and back to the present.

K: You are back in the aircraft?

P: Yes.

K: Try to tell me what is happening...and what you are aware of...

P: There is a wall of the plane at my back...and I'm up against a wall on my right hand side...

K: Do you feel you have a job to do on the aeroplane?

P: Not really.

K: What position are you in?

P: Sitting down...

K: What is in front of you?

P: Space.

K: What is at the end of the space?

P: Can't really see because it's dark.

K: Good...let's move on a bit and see what happens...the story will move on.

P: We are going up.

K: Good...and how are you feeling as you are going up?

P: Slightly lop-sided...

K: Have you any fear?

P: No.

(There was a note of mild surprise in her voice, as though surprised at the question. But what an interesting reply, in view of her present-day phobia! There is certainly no evidence of a phobia at this point.)

K: Do you know where you are going?

P: There is a phrase for it...I can't remember what it is...

K: As I snap my fingers, the phrase will come back to you. *(And I snap them.)*

P: Something like 'a mission'...something like that.

K: Is this something you have done before?

P: Yes.

K: All right...the story will move on a bit further...what are you aware of now?

P: We've flattened out...we should be crossing the water soon...

K: Can you see out of the plane?

P: No...I could if I went up front.

K: All right...the story will move on a bit further...what are you aware of now?

P: Still flying...

K: And this is something you are quite used to? No fear?

P: We are not very high, you see.

K: *(I do not understand the significance of that last remark and I ask:)* How high do you think you are?

P: I don't know, but not very high...we can't fly very high.

K: Move on an hour in time...What is happening now?

P: Nothing.

K: Still just flying?

P: No...

K: NO?! *(I am astonished at this answer)* What are you doing?

P: Floating.

K: *('Aha', I think, she has baled out and is parachuting...)* Are you still in the aeroplane?

P: No.

(That is the answer I expected...I feel sure that I'm on the right lines—but how wrong I am soon proved to be!)

K: Well, let's go back a bit...how do you get out of the aeroplane? You will be aware of leaving the aeroplane in a moment .

(She has suddenly started to look very frightened and distressed.)

K: Can you tell me what is happening now?

P: We're bumping...the aeroplane is bumping...

K: Why is it doing that?

P: We're being attacked...from the ground...bits of things are coming into the aeroplane...

(Her voice is very frightened indeed now and she is choking back sobs. Suddenly she claps a hand to her shoulder.)

K: Why are you clasping your shoulder?

P: It hurts...

K: Has something hit your shoulder?

(She is finding it very difficult to hold back tears. I ask:) Has anybody else been hit?

P: Don't know...hurts...

(She is sobbing and whimpering with her hand still clasping her shoulder.)

K: What is happening now? Are you still in the aeroplane?

P: *(Scarcely able to talk)*...Can't swallow...

K: What is stopping you from talking? Have you been wounded...? I'm going to put my hand on your neck and then you will find you can talk. *(I do this and ask:)* What's happening?

P: There's blood in my throat...I've got to get out...

(She is still gagging, so I put my hand to her neck and throat again and her speech becomes clearer.)

I've got to get out!...I wish my shoulder didn't hurt...

K: Try to tell me what is happening to the aeroplane...is it badly damaged?

P: There's a fire...at least I suppose so...It's hot...and I can't see anything...

K: Does the order come to bale out?

P: No...nothing! Nothing!

K: Can you move the rest of your body?

P: I want to get out and be on the ground...*(This is a wail!)*

K: Can you get out? The picture will become very clear...Can you get out?

P: It's dark...I can't see...

K: You can't see anything? Is there much noise going on?

P: Don't know...want to get out! *(This is a truly piteous wail!)*

K: Now here is a curious question: Are you still alive?

P: Don't know...

K: You don't know if you are still alive...Now...if you did get out of the aeroplane still alive, you will find yourself outside it now...Do you ever find yourself on the ground again? Do you reach the ground?

P: No...I was pushed against this wall...

K: You were pushed against the wall and you couldn't get out of the aeroplane...Is that right?

P: Yes...it is the wrong way up and I'm pushed against the wall...

K: The aeroplane is the wrong way up...so the place you ought to get out by is above you now?

P: Yes...

K: Is there anything the pilot can do to get it the right way up again?

P: No...*(and now pleading, agonisingly)* Oh, put me down on the ground again...safely...I want to be on the ground!...PLEASE...put me down...!

K: *(At this instant something in her voice suggests to me the possibility that she might momentarily have slipped out of the aeroplane scene and into a scene from childhood when an adult had picked her up and was swinging her round and round, at which she was becoming frightened. So I ask:)* Whom are you talking to when you say, 'Please put me down?'

P: God. *(Imploringly)* PLEASE...put me DOWN...!

(I think she has had as much as she can stand, which is hardly surprising. Even just guiding her through this experience has been harrowing. So I call her name, firmly: 'PENNY!' And this gets through at once.)

K: You are going to remember very clearly what you have been experiencing, but come back now...come right back to the present.

(I repeat these suggestions until I am satisfied that she is completely back in the present day—though still in a state of level shift. I ask her then to tell me what she remembers of what she has been experiencing. She replies that it is all very confusing, and I ask her if she would like me to help her to sort it out a bit. She would. So I start to recapitulate the story, seeking Penny's agreement over each point: 'Yes', she remembers very well embarking on the plane and sitting with her back to one wall with another wall on her right hand side, and that it was dark. She remembers feeling lopsided as the aeroplane takes off, and she remembers too that there is no trace of fear at this point, though she knows she is on a mission. Penny agrees that the aeroplane levelled off and it occurred to her that soon they would be over the water; that she cannot see out but that she could if she went up front. At this point I will quote again from the tape:)

K: Now, you are flying along quite happily until suddenly the aeroplane starts to bump all over the place?

P: Yes...

K: You are being attacked from the ground and great bits of metal are hitting the aircraft and flying through it. Is that right?

P: Yes....

K: And then one of these pieces of metal hits you on the shoulder?

(Now, for the first time, Penny corrects me—firmly!)

P: It's a piece of the aeroplane.

K: A piece of the aeroplane? It's a piece of the aeroplane that hits you?

P: It sort of curled in...sort of the lining of the plane...

K: Something from outside had broken a piece of the aeroplane up... does that feel right?

P: Somehow the metal lining of the plane sort of curled in...

K: It curled in and speared you in the shoulder? Is that right?

P: Yes...

K: And then you found your throat full of blood?

P: Yes. Then it gets very hot...I'm sure there was a fire...up front.

K: And that is when you start to pray like anything...'Please put me safely on the ground?'

P: Yes...it starts going down but the way out is in the tail and that's the wrong way up...because it's sort of uphill from where I am...

K: I see...and with the pain in your shoulder you have not got the strength to make it...does that seem right?

P: Yes...

K: And the prayer, 'Please put me on the ground.' This grows more fervent every second?

P: Yes...

K: *(At this point I pause to reflect upon the next step. At length I say:)* You will know the answer to this question with complete certainty: Did you ever get down to the ground alive?

P: No.

K: You died before you got to the ground. Does that feel right or wrong?

P: Right.

K: *(Here, I think, is the explanation of her response that so surprised me after I had suggested she move on an hour in time and then asked if she were still in the aeroplane. Before an hour had passed the aeroplane had been hit, was on fire and out of control and she—perhaps I should say 'he'—had died. How very mistaken I was in thinking he/she had baled out and was parachuting down. It never became completely clear whether he died when the aeroplane crashed, whereupon his soul had lost no time in leaving it; or whether—which I'm sure would have been possible, and even more probable—he had lost consciousness as if in a 'faint', as the plane was coming down, and thus had effectively 'got out of his body'. This would account for the response that he 'was floating'. But be that as it may. At this point I say to Penny:)*

K: Well, Penny, now we are going to change that picture. I want you to go back to the moment when the plane is tilted downwards and the tail is up in the air...which is uphill from you...

P: Don't want to go back to that...don't like it...

K: All right...just lie there a moment while I think...The aeroplane is quite level at the moment...right?

P: Yes.

K: You have got a pain in your shoulder, I know, and you are very uncomfortable, but the plane is level...it is no longer so hot...and the plane is flying.

P: *(protesting, urgently)* But you can't change it!! It's real! *(Now she is sobbing, violently)*...It's REAL!!

(I had no doubt whatever that Penny had been reliving an episode that was part of her total experience. However, since it belonged to a former lifetime, it could not be held in any physical form in her present body. Hence, it had occurred to me it could possibly be reshaped if sufficient energy of the appropriate kind could be brought to bear on it. However, Penny was obviously so upset by the idea that I abandoned the attempt. Instead:)

K: Yes, indeed it is real. Now listen. You had a terrible experience on that aeroplane, a truly terrible experience. You were on a mission: you ran into anti-aircraft fire which hit the plane and set it on fire. You longed for God to put you safely on the ground; but before you could get to the ground you died. When you died, that part of you which contained the experience of the horror inside that plane and the desperate longing to be safely on the ground became split off from the rest of the soul of that soldier and—as I call it—'stuck as a ghost'. What happens now is that whenever present-day Penny even contemplates flying in an aeroplane, the mere idea resonates to this ghost and, in effect, wakes it up. Then, all the energy in the fear that is locked up in the ghost, all the energy in that urgent longing to be safely on the ground that was never fulfilled, all this energy surges up to Penny's consciousness and attaches itself to the prospect of flying or the actuality of a flight. To put it another way, any present-day flight or thought of flying attracts to itself all the fear from that horrific experience from the past; all the energy in the wish to be safely on the ground, which that experience evoked. Does that make sense?

(Penny has been listening intently to what I have been saying and bursts out with a most enthusiastic 'YES!' I resume:)

K: And part of that wish, when it was formed, was awareness of all the circumstances associated with it: of being at war, of being in an aeroplane belonging to the RAF to be dropped behind enemy lines. So when the wish to be safely on the ground comes to Penny's consciousness in respect of a present or forthcoming flight, there is, in the background, the fear of being attacked and of the whole experience being repeated. Even if such thoughts do not reach Penny's consciousness, the fear associated with them must surely be a part of Penny's fear of flying. Thus, even if Penny is on a pleasant, peacetime commercial flight, and possibly safer there than when she is at the wheel of her sports car, she experiences all the terror that was felt by that soldier.

(Penny is looking completely relaxed now, and I continue:)

K: But now that we have recovered that earlier experience, it is no longer in an unconscious area of your mind and so can no longer affect you in the same way. If the fear recurs when you are in an aeroplane now, it will only be through habit, and you will be able, instantly, to banish it by reminding yourself that you are on a peacetime flight, that no one is going to attack you, and that all you need to do is to relax and enjoy it. Or be bored by it!

(I repeat this theme several times, with variations. Finally, I guide Penny on a fantasised flight to the South of France to visit friends. Since she is still deeply under hypnosis, this is as real to her as an actual flight would be. She starts with driving to the airport; then she goes through the formalities and boards the plane. I check at each step for any fear. She seems to have no fear at all. Next, in response to my suggestions, she experiences, in fantasy, the plane taking off and of being aware of its tilt as it climbs. When it has levelled off, she accepts a drink and settles down to enjoy the flight. In due course, she lands safely and disembarks. The whole trip has been accomplished without a trace even of uneasiness. Then I bring her back to normal consciousness. She seems completely relaxed and is able to talk unemotionally about the events of the session. Her only complaint is that she has a nasty taste in her mouth. I ask if it is the aftermath of the blood in her mouth when she was on the plane that was shot down. She feels it might well be. I help her to shift level once more, suggest that the unpleasant taste will disappear, and bring her straight back again to normal waking consciousness. The unpleasant taste has gone. Musingly, Penny remarks:)

P: I still don't know what I was doing on that plane. I would rather *like* to find out.

K: I'm sure we have dealt with the worst part of the experience, and it might, therefore, not be very difficult for you to do that.

(Penny is relaxed, happy and smiling. As she is going out of the door she says:)

P: I've just had a thought: my dog was called Penny, and that is why I can never think of Penny as a real name to give a person!

The Third Session

The third, and as it proved to be, the final session, took place two days later. It opened with Penny telling me that since our last session she had had no thoughts about flying and had not even worried about planes flying overhead.

I help her shift her level, stressing yet again that she will always hear the sound of her name and respond to it by coming out of whatever scene she is engaged in and returning to present realities. I suggest that since she has recovered the end of the story she will probably have less difficulty in recovering the beginning—the explanation of her presence on that aeroplane. I tell her then that as I am counting to ten, something will be bubbling up to her consciousness that will be a clue. I have scarcely reached ten when she announces firmly:

P: Heather.

(This proves to be almost the only response in the course of this session that is not preceded by a pause of, at least, many seconds.)

K: Where are you in relation to the heather?

P: Crawling through it.

K: Why? What are you doing?

P: It's some sort of exercise. I'm sheltering behind a stone...not a very big stone...actually not big enough...

K: Are there other people around?

P: A couple on either side of me ...ten or twelve yards away...

K: Are you carrying anything?

P: My gun...there's a great pack on my back which keeps getting up above the stone.

K: Can you see what you are dressed in?

P: Apart from the fact I've got bits of bleeding heather sticking out of me from all corners, I'm in khaki.

K: Army rather than Air Force?

P: Yes.

K: Do you know what is the object of this exercise?

P: We've got to surround and...anyway, we've got to take that rock! Stupid!

K: You are training for something?

P: I feel sick.

K: Is it sick you feel, or frightened?

P: Both.

K: Are you frightened about what you are doing now or about what lies ahead?

P: ...I don't know...it seems all darkness...

K: Darkness!

(Very often a response of 'darkness' or 'blackness' is a sign of resistance, but sometimes the darkness or blackness is itself the clue. I try, therefore, to cover both possibilities. I tell her I'm going to count slowly to twenty, whereupon the channels of memory will become clearer. I count, and ask:)

K: Where are you now?

P: It's a sort of stone room!

K: Yes...what are you doing there?

P: Don't know...it's a sort of cave...

K: Why are you in this cave?

P: Fog...a fog came down. I've got to spend the night here...

K: Is this part of the exercise?

P: Not meant to be...

K: Anybody in the cave with you?

P: They're asleep...

K: What's happening now?

P: I'm cold.

K: I'll cover you with the other rug.

(I do this because people often tend to feel cold when they have shifted level a long way. However, I suspect the cold she feels is the cold of the cave.)

K: Now, I will count to ten and you will move on three hours.

(I count, and ask:)

K: What's happening now?

P: Sunshine.

K: Are you aware of the purpose of this exercise?

P: It was meant to be to surround and take that bleeding rock...

K: What country is this in?

P: Scotland.

K: Is this important stuff to remember, or should we move on a bit.

P: It's a lot of practising...

K: Do you know what you are practising for?

P: We're supposed to be going to do it over there but...don't know when...

K: Over where?

P: Well...against old Jerry.

K: How do you feel about that?

P: Better than down the mines.

(This is a reference to the scheme introduced by Mr Ernest Bevin who was Minister of Labour during the Second World War, whereby conscientious objectors were employed to mine coal. They were known as Bevin Boys.)

K: What's happening now?

P: Feeling giddy again...and sick.

K: Where are you now?

(There is such a long pause after this question that eventually I repeat it.)

P: I feel sick...*(rather plaintively)*...

K: Again, is this due mostly to fear?

P: It's sort of like being seasick ...I'm swaying...

K: Yes...what is causing you to sway?

P: *(Very puzzled)* ...I'm swinging from a rope...horrid!

K: Where is the rope?

P: I'm still rocking backwards and forwards on the rope...

K: What is the rope attached to? Are you climbing it? Is it a bridge?

P: It's on a sort of scaffold thing.

(Interesting that she ignored both of my suggestions. I was pretty sure that this was part of her parachute training and those last and the next few questions were designed to evoke contradiction.)

K: Are you climbing it?

P: No...hanging from it...

K: By your hands?

P: Sort of under my arms.

K: Is this a parachute?

P: No...it's in the gym for it...

K: Are you training for parachuting?

P: Yes...as well as other things...it's all we do...train...

K: The scaffolding thing...Is that the tower you are learning parachuting from?

P: Yes...

K: Do you enjoy that bit of the training?

P: No...feel giddy.

K: Are you a paratrooper?

P: I expect I will be...I'm not yet though...

K: But that is what you are training to become?

P: One day...yes.

K: How do people call you? When they talk to you, how do they address you?

P: ...Mate...

K: Do you know your name?

P: No...

(She sounds rather worried by this and I assure her that it is nothing to worry about. In my experience, in this kind of work one tends to recover only what is of immediate importance, and her real name was probably not in her mind as she was swinging from that rope. On the other hand, it would have been quite possible that friends or an instructor were talking with her, which is why I put the question in the way I did.)

K: There comes a time when you have finished your training...am I right or wrong about that?

P: Right...but it's ages off yet.

K: Are there important things we've got to look at before your training is finished?

P: No, but the fact is that it is better than being down the mines.

K: I see...and that is where you would have been if you had not become a soldier, is that right?

P: Yes...Bevin Boys they're called...Bevin Boys.

(There! We have it! They were indeed known as Bevin Boys. This phrase was commonly heard in those days, but it was certainly a surprise to hear it uttered in such a matter of fact way by Penny, who was not even born until well after the war. Incidentally, once she was hypnotised and had regressed, her voice and speech had been typical of that of a young working-class man.)

K: Much later there is a time when you were in an aeroplane...in an aeroplane, flying towards Europe...nothing dramatic is happening...your back is against the wall and there is a wall on your right hand side...can you remember that?

P: No!

(That was an extremely stupid question! From her present point in time, that flight has not happened yet!)

K: Do you remember your dog, Penny?

P: I've got her!

K: Where are you now?

P: In a sort of sitting room—with chintzy chairs.

K: Are you married?

P: No...

K: What will happen when your training is finished?

P: Don't know exactly.

K: What sort of thing do you expect to happen?

P: Bits and pieces of what we've been doing...

K: Are you looking forward to that?

P: I think some people do and some don't...

K: Are you looking forward to it?

P: I don't mind...*(Insistently:)* It's better than down the mines!

K: Now go ahead a week and tell me where you find yourself.

P: I'm in a terribly squashed train...I'm on my way back from leave.

K: OK...let's go on another week...what's happening now...what are you aware of?

P: Something wrong with my teeth...I've got toothache.

K: OK...go ahead another 24 hours...what's happening now?

P: Nothing really...

K: A time comes when you get your orders for going overseas...is that right, or wrong? Can you get a feeling about that? *(She is looking very worried.)* What's happening now?

P: I'm thinking of that front room...

K: Which front room?

P: The one at home...

K: The one with the chintzy chairs?

P: Yes, I wish I were back there...I want to go back home...

K: Where are you in fact?

P: Yorkshire.

K: What are you doing in Yorkshire?

P: It's just where we are for the moment...

K: Where is your home?

P: In the South of England.

K: Let's move on a week...what's happening now?

P: Don't know...

K: What are you aware of?

P: I've got a pass to a dance at Wetherby.

K: Do you like going to a dance?

P: Have a few drinks and things...I'm standing up again.

K: Let's move on another week...what are you aware of now?

P: Sort of floating again.

K: More parachute practice?

P: Yes, but this time it's proper.

K: Do you enjoy the sensation?

P: I don't feel nearly so seasick...it doesn't sway so much...it's rather nice...if I waggle a leg I go a different way...I just have to remember to relax and roll over.

K: Have you done this before?

P: Not properly, like this.

K: Are you still in the air?

P: No...

K: You've landed.

P: Yes

K: Safely?

P: Yes...now I've got to fold it up.

K: How do you do that? Is there a special way?

P: The wind gets in the way...do it as quickly as possible...you're not allowed to tear them because there's a war on.

K: Let's move on another week...what's happening now?

P: My heart's going thump.

K: Why

P: I'm feeling nervous.

K: Yes...what are you feeling nervous about?

P: We do it for real to-night.

K: Where are you going?

P: Haven't been told...

K: You just know that you're off?

P: Yes...and I feel nervous.

K: OK—what is the first thing you have to do when you start?

P: Check our packs.

K: Yes...and what then? What do you do then?

P: I'm feeling very nervous ...I don't want to go...

K: You are feeling very nervous...and I suppose the next thing you have to do is to collect your parachute. Is that right?

P: No.

K: OK—what is the next thing you have to do?

P: Go for a briefing.

(Again, it is interesting how promptly and firmly she rejects any suggestion of mine that is inaccurate.)

K: Aha! Where do you go for that?

P: Along to the Mess Hall.

K: All right...now you are at the briefing. What are you being told?

P: Can't remember...I can see him standing there...

K: Do you know what country you are going to?

P: There is a map on the blackboard....

K: Which country are you going to?

P: It's France, I think...

K: Are you going alone, or how many are there of you?

P: About half a dozen of us...I don't want to go.

K: I don't blame you! Have you got a special job to do?

P: Blow up something...

(It might have been interesting to pursue the subsequent events in detail, but I feel it is not therapeutically necessary and, therefore, that it is not justifiable to risk inflicting upon her the distress it might cause. Instead:)

K: All right. I think that is enough for the moment. I'm going to bring you right back to the present. You will be able to remember what you have been telling me this morning but you will be able to place it firmly where it belongs, in the past! It is something that is all over now...it does not even belong to Penny's lifetime! Now, come back to the present day.

(I count from twenty down to one. In fact, to make absolutely sure she is back in the present I do this several times before I tell her that I am now going to bring her back to normal consciousness. At length:)

K: Are you back with us again?

P: Yes.

K: Do you remember all that fairly well?

P: I thought I was going to be sick...the swaying and swinging on that rope...The real parachute was much easier...on the rope is rather like the difference between when you look at a film from the driver's point of view...you feel sick because you think you ought to be moving and you're not...sort of same sensation of sickness because you know you ought to be falling but you're not falling...but you're going backwards and forwards and round and round.

(She laughs, apologetically.)

K: A thing that came out, over and over again, was that it was better than going down the mines. Do you remember that? *(She looks very thoughtful.)*

K: What are you thinking about?

P: I'm trying to think...I didn't know how to get the parachute together without tearing it...it has to be folded up and used again, you see...and if you tore it...twigs and things...brambles...

K: That must have been very tricky...and I suppose it had to be folded in a very special sort of way?

P: Somebody else folded it—but we had to make sure it was not torn. *(All through this conversation it felt as though one were talking with someone who was recalling events from some years ago in this present life.)*

K: Are there any other questions you want answered?

P: It was a nice sitting room...had a sort of feel of being a sort of Victorian house...solid...(*very thoughtful again.*)

K: And what are you thinking about now?

P: The sensation of being totally mindless and always being told what to do ...you don't have to think...

K: Did you like that?

P: No...because all it left you to think about was emotional things, if you see what I mean—emotional rather than practical.

K: Good...well...let's leave it at that, unless there is anything else you would like to talk about?

P: It's like reading somebody else's letters, if you see what I mean...like reading a letter that you've written that is lying on someone else's desk. Because you wrote it you know what's in it, but because you sent it it's no longer yours...slightly confusing and embarrassing...strange sensation...Literally like reading a letter you wrote; like letters I wrote to my parents from school...hard to believe now that I wrote them. But I did...because they are in my handwriting...and strange how familiar that room felt.

K: Have you any doubt that these were valid memories?

P: No. None at all.

And so ended the treatment of Penny's fear of flying.

Some Reflections on the Therapy

I also have no doubt that the experiences, which Penny recovered under hypnosis, were valid memories, and this assertion invites several questions. Perhaps the most obvious of these is: 'How do you know that they were not all a fantasy, based—perhaps—on some film she had seen?'

The simple truth is that I do not, indeed cannot, know. There have been several films since the war depicting the interior of an aircraft in a horrific situation.

One of these, *The Dam Busters*, even featured a black dog, the Labrador that belonged to Wing Commander Guy Gibson who led the raid on the Mohne Dam. To complicate the issue, after leaving on that mission, at least according to the film, Wing Commander Gibson never saw his dog again, though not because he was killed but because, before he returned, the dog was run over. However, a detail like that would not negate the possibility of Penny's story being a fantasy, based on that film.

But even if Penny had seen a film of that kind, so have countless other people, and they have not all developed an intense phobia of flying. If Penny's phobia were indeed a reaction to seeing such a film, this would surely indicate that the film had detonated something explosive that was already within her but was not within the others. And what could be more explosive than the personal experience, at some time in one's long history, of such an episode as that which Penny at least appeared to relive? Moreover, the relief of her phobia was immediate, complete and is bidding fair to prove permanent.

Along the line of a spectacle resonating to something already inside one, another case comes to mind. The patient was a young man whom I also saw in the 1970s. The problem he presented was an acute sensitivity to noise. During a 'level shift' he experienced himself as the rear-gunner in an aircraft which had run into anti-aircraft fire and was falling out of the sky. On returning to normal waking consciousness he exclaimed, 'Now I understand why a certain experience in this life was so terrifying.

'It was a firework display. I was taken to watch these fireworks from a point on the top of a ridge that overlooked a valley. The fireworks were being let off on the floor of the valley, but the site was completely hidden from our view by a belt of trees below us, on the side of the ridge. Consequently, we did not see the rockets until they burst at about our eye level. Obviously, nothing could have looked more like flak.' (Anti-aircraft fire.)

The next question might be: how do you know that Penny, since she was in a state of hypnosis, did not produce that story just to please you?

Again, the truth is that I do not and cannot know. But consider the energies involved. There is surely no doubt that there was a tremendous amount of energy in the phobia. Now, if Penny was prepared, at any level of her mind, to subject herself to the distress she suffered in that session just out of a desire to please me, there must have been an equal amount of energy in that desire. Similarly, if she repressed her phobia after the treatment just out of a desire to please me, there must have been at least as much energy in that desire too as there was in the phobia. Hence, in either of these events, one would surely have expected

Penny to find some way of preserving a contact with me, at least for some weeks if not months.

What happened was precisely the reverse. I did not hear from Penny again until some six months later, and then it was only because *I* telephoned *her* for news. She seemed rather surprised at my call. She told me that she had just flown to a Third World country and back and not even a thought of a fear of flying had ever entered her mind.

Next, if Penny's story had been only a fantasy, and if her recovery had been only a flight into health—that is to say tantamount to the ache in a tooth which ceases as one enters the dentist's waiting room—then I would have expected it to have returned long ago. It has not done so. Flying may never be Penny's favourite activity, but the phobia has not returned.

Lastly, it could be argued that the fantasy flight that I induced Penny to take while still under hypnosis—a flight that was completely enjoyable and free from fear—was a major factor in her recovery, and invalidates the case from the point of view of supporting the idea of reincarnation.

This argument pinpoints a conflict with which a therapist often finds himself confronted, namely the interests of his patient versus the interests of science. I felt it would benefit Penny to take her on that fantasy flight, which is why I did it. Having done so, I cannot say what the result would have been had I not done so. But if it were to be seriously argued that the fantasy flight was the crucial factor in the relief of Penny's phobia, I would again point to the units of energy involved in each instance. It is surely impossible to believe that the fantasy flight carried a charge of energy that could be compared with that in the phobia. Moreover, my experience suggests that the patient's problem will not be completely resolved unless the recall is absolutely accurate and—where appropriate—he accepts responsibility for what occurred.

Taking all these factors into account, I am convinced that by far the most reasonable explanation is that the therapy enabled Penny to find the source of the energy responsible for her phobia. The source was the ghost of the young soldier that was left behind as a consequence of the horrific circumstances in which his lifetime ended. Through reliving the experience, Penny reintegrated it with the rest of her totality and it was no longer in a position from which it could affect her.

Part II

In this second part of the book I shall try to show how acceptance of the fact that the soul has a history of many lifetimes on this planet can contribute towards the answer to some of the riddles that still surround the question of how the character is formed. It will become clear that a certain particular character trait frequently plays a significant part in the development of a variety of individual neurotic conditions as well as being responsible for widespread human misery.

We shall encounter some of the ways in which this character trait can manifest and how, in many instances, the aim of therapy is, firstly, to help a person recognise the trait within himself, and then to choose to change it. We shall also see that a person can indeed change a trait in his character if he can muster a sufficiently strong wish to do so.

It is surely not an insignificant additional point that the successful treatment of an individual is the successful treatment of a cell in the body of mankind.

11   *Reincarnation and Character*

Growing awareness that the recall of details of earlier lifetimes is possible is opening the door to new dimensions of our understanding of ourselves.

Sometimes these recalls are the crucial step in relieving a condition that has not, and probably never would, respond so completely to any other form of therapy. Such occasions illustrate the most spectacular kind of contribution that psychiatry can make in support of a belief in reincarnation; they also illustrate the most dramatic contribution that a belief in reincarnation can make to psychiatry.

However, I have come to believe that of at least equal value are the insights which appear, in the light of a belief in reincarnation, into the subject of 'Character', for these extend beyond psychiatry into every aspect of living. Contrary to what many people may believe, reincarnation highlights the importance of the here and now. Quite frequently it is a character trait that was responsible for the traumatic situation in a former lifetime, the repercussions of which are affecting the individual in his present life.

Of course, psychiatrists have long been familiar with what have been called 'Character Disorders'. To quote Reber's *Dictionary Of Psychology*: '*The term serves as a general label for persons who chronically and habitually engage in maladaptive behaviours, who are inflexible, restrict their own opportunities for growth, and usually manage to function in ways that evoke unpleasant reactions from those around them.*'

However, these are not the kind of conditions that we shall be considering here. We are about to concern ourselves with character traits that are usually considered normal, sometimes laudable, and certainly well within what is socially acceptable; yet, they are a fundamental factor in innumerable cases of neurotic conditions.

The Bully in Rick: A Definition of Character

To take a relatively trivial instance. Many years ago I was lucky enough to be the guest, for several weeks, of a couple who owned a hotel on an island in the Caribbean. One day a lady, who was also staying at the hotel, approached me. She told me that she had heard I was a psychiatrist and was wondering if I would agree to see her husband, Rick. She went on to explain that his therapist had recently discharged him as cured of the severe anxiety from which he had been suffering, but she did not think he was really any better at all.

She warned me that Rick would probably attribute his condition to two recent episodes, in each of which he had only very narrowly escaped a bad motor car accident. However, in her opinion it had started long before they had occurred. She knew he had been overextending himself in his business; he had been sleeping badly; and he had been drinking a lot more than usual. Then she added—not by way of a complaint but purely for my information—that he had always tended to take out on her the frustration that had built up during the day, and that this tendency had become very much worse.

On the following day I saw Rick, a man in his fifties. As his wife had predicted, he attributed his state to the two near misses. Then I began to feed back to him some of the points his wife had made to me. He readily agreed he had been overextending himself in his business, but felt that this was of no significance. 'In my business you can't stay still...if you are not going forwards you are going backwards.' He agreed too that he had been sleeping badly for a long time and probably had been drinking a bit more than usual. Finally, I told him that his wife had mentioned he had always tended to take out on her frustration that had accumulated during the day, and that this tendency had recently become much worse. He thought his wife was probably right.

I asked him then why he did not let his feelings go at the people who had evoked them. 'Oh, I couldn't do that!' was his immediate reply. 'These are important people...they could damage my business if I offended them.' I paused for a moment before asking: 'Has it ever occurred to you that your wife might leave you?'

'She couldn't do that', was the equally prompt response. 'She hasn't any money.'

This reply inspired me to ask Rick how he would define a bully.

'A bully? I suppose a bully is someone who would not tackle anyone his own size but does not mind having a go at someone who is smaller than he is.'

'And what do you feel about bullies?'

He could not have been more vehement or, I'm sure, more sincere, in his condemnation of bullies. When his tirade had run down, I just looked at him, perhaps a shade quizzically.

It took Rick a moment or two to see the point but when he did he was appalled, truly devastated as he realised the implications of the way he had been treating his wife.

When he had recovered his composure, he asked what he could do about the situation. From what he had told me, it sounded as though he were in a line of business that was very competitive, and I asked him if there was anything he could think of doing that would be less so. He replied at once that he thought there was. In the course of travelling around the islands, it had occurred to him that there was no finance company for the black people and he had been thinking of starting one.

I enthused about this idea and, on the assumption that there would not be any shareholders, suggested he ran it along the following lines: 'Instead of aiming to get the highest interest on your loans that you can, try charging the lowest interest you can possibly afford. Make your clients your friends and I'm sure you will find that they will not resent the interest they have to pay; and you will have no need to fear competition because you will already be operating at rock-bottom rates.'

He thought for a bit, then commented that it had never occurred to him to run a business like that, but he would give it a try.

The next morning Rick and his wife both came to see me. They were bubbling with happiness. Immediately after the session he had told her all about our talk. Distress on both sides about the way he had been treating her had quickly been healed, and they had determined to start a business along the lines Rick and I had discussed. His anxiety had vanished and he had had the best night's sleep he had enjoyed for many months.

Why do I regard this case as essentially a character problem?

The word 'character' means different things to different people. I use it to mean 'the sum of a person's *fixed predispositions* to act or react in a particular way under a particular kind of circumstance.'

As I understand it, Rick's anxiety had been due to the mounting pressure in his unconscious of the 'unlove for himself' that he had been accumulating on account of the way he was repeatedly behaving towards his wife. To the significance of his behaviour he had succeeded in blinding himself. In fact, until our talk he had had, by his own definition, the character-trait of a bully. The intensity of his distress when he realised the point, together with the enthusiasm with which he greeted the notion I offered him of lines along which he might run the new business he was contemplating, promised well for his future. They suggested that the way he had been running his old business, and indeed much of his life up to that point, reflected principles that he had acquired as he was growing up, but which were really contrary to what I would describe as the most evolved part of himself.

Interestingly, and perhaps significantly, symptoms are very often a sign of protest by the most evolved part of a person that, it seems, has often become buried beneath, but has remained in conflict with, some of the principles he has absorbed from the prevailing ethos. This is a point with which we shall later be deeply concerned. However, of more immediate moment is the question: 'How is the character formed?'

The Building of Character

If one does not believe in reincarnation, one is compelled to account for a person's character in terms of his heredity and his environment, meaning, of course, the environment of his present life. Obviously an explanation along these lines must go a long way, but is it the whole story? Is it enough to explain the exceedingly marked difference that sometimes occurs between two children of the same family?

Professor Ian Stevenson, talking on a BBC Radio 4 programme, made an important contribution to this debate, and I am grateful to the BBC and to Professor Stevenson for permitting me to quote from the broadcast.

The Presenter: 'Professor Stevenson, formerly the Professor of Psychiatry at The University of Virginia, has spent a considerable part of his professional life investigating at first hand cases of apparent reincarnation occurring in different parts of the world. A common story is along the lines of a young child starting to speak in considerable detail about a previous life with another family, one of whom the parents had no knowledge whatever. Eventually steps would be taken to verify the child's statements and they would be found to have an average accuracy, Professor Stevenson found, of ninety per cent.'

Professor Stevenson then related the case of two brothers who were twins.

Professor Stevenson: 'They lived in Sri Lanka. One (of them) remembered the life of a simple, quiet school-boy, and everything he said turned out to be correct about the life of a rather simple schoolboy who died of some illness when he was about twelve or thirteen. In that case the families were quite unknown to each other and lived about 50 kilometres apart.

'The twin had a totally different memory. He started out to say that he was an insurgent; and there was an insurrection in Sri Lanka in 1973 which was put down with a good deal of bloodshed. He wanted to say more about it and did say a little bit, but the family ridiculed him so he shut up...but the differences between the two twins were very striking. What we may call "the Insurgent Twin" had sort of insurgency habits. He talked about bombs and guns, and he was a tough; yet also, in his way, quite fearful, tending to hide from strangers. The other boy was quite different; bookish, quietly sociable, but dignified and comfortable with strangers...he did not feel hunted...'

The special significance of this story lies in the fact that the brothers were not only twins but also *identical twins*. This meant that they had both developed from the same egg, and that their genetic endowments were, therefore, identical. Moreover, since they were brought up together, it is surely inconceivable that their environments could have been sufficiently different to account for the pronounced differences in their characters. Thus, even if one does not believe in reincarnation and, therefore, discounts any influence due to different experiences in former lifetimes, one is still forced to postulate some factor in addition to their genes and their environments during their present lives.

Believing in reincarnation as I do, I can accept that their respective memories of former lifetimes were valid; and it seems to me that by far the most feasible explanation lies in the different characters of their respective souls. In other words, a person's character consists, in large part, of *the character his soul has built up in the course of its long history and has brought into the present life.* This would be something apart from, and in addition to, what was brought in by the genes. In respect of character, the effect upon an individual of his genes and of his environment would largely be limited to reinforcing or modifying features that were already there. But accepting that notion still leaves us with the question: 'Just *how* does a soul build up his character?'

It may be that we shall never know the complete answer to the question: 'How is character formed?' Suffice it to say that I feel certain the process begins during the prehuman phase of our history. Anyone with experience of animals can testify to the difference in character between, for instance, one horse or one dog, and another. But the matter does not stop there. What, for instance, are the factors which result in one animal rather than another being the dominant beast, in the family or the group? I would not presume even to hazard an answer. I am convinced, however, that the soul brings with it something of the qualities and experiences of its prehuman history, just as, I am sure, the genes do.

However, once the human phase of our history is reached, we can recognise a factor that is unquestionably of crucial importance. This is the human being's *freedom to choose* how he will act or react under any particular circumstance. This freedom is arguably the feature that most noticeably distinguishes the human animal from his precursors, since the latter, to a greater or lesser extent, are the prisoners of their instincts. A rabbit that feels threatened does not need to have been taught to bolt for cover underground. It does not need to consider what it will do. It is programmed by its instincts to respond in a particular way and it has no choice. If it is free to choose this hole rather than that one, this is probably the limit of its field of choice. Similarly, a squirrel is programmed to make for the nearest tree.

I do not wish to join the debate about whether the human being has any instincts at all, but it is certain that in his brain, his hands and his speech apparatus he has the potential to break out of any prison in which instincts might tend to confine him. These assets give him a field from which he is free to choose his response and, very probably, the means to implement his choice.

As I have said, I am defining the word 'character' as 'the sum of a person's *fixed predispositions* to react in a particular way to a particular kind of circumstance.' At this point, the reader may be wondering: 'If a predisposition has become fixed, what has happened to the "freedom to choose"?'

Fixed Predispositions and Freedom to Choose

I believe the answer is along the following lines: if our choice of action or reaction has a result which, so far as we see, is satisfactory, then we become predisposed to repeat that choice the next time a similar situation arises. If the result is again satisfactory, the predisposition becomes stronger, and the next time stronger still. In short, the predisposition becomes stronger with each successful repetition, and the stronger it becomes, the more quickly it enables us to make our choice.

So far, this is fine. This is the proper use of experience; and it matters not how quickly we make our choice, *so long as there always is a moment of choice.* The possibility is, however, that the occasion will arrive when the stimulus is followed by the response immediately: that is, *without even a moment of choice.* This is a significant occasion because it indicates that the predisposition, which has been growing steadily stronger, has suddenly become *fixed;* and once a predisposition has become fixed, it seems to acquire certain properties.

First, it becomes very stable; that is, it is extremely unlikely to change spontaneously. If, on some occasion, the habitual response—which is really what it has become—does *not* bring the expected result, the tendency will be to repeat the reaction but harder, rather than to stand back and consider whether there might be some other and more effective way of tackling the problem. The reason—and this is the second property—is that a fixed predisposition seems to blind its possessor to the very possibility of any alternative approach.

Although, strictly speaking, the incident does not concern the character, the point was beautifully illustrated when a friend of mine was trying to loosen the wing nut that secured one of the wheels of his new sports car. He had dealt the nut several increasingly vigorous blows with the hammer supplied for the purpose, but to no avail at all. Happily an AA scout, one of that band of roving experts who are a boon to the stranded motorist, appeared on the scene and he had the nut off in a trice: he had tapped it in the opposite direction! My friend, in order to loosen a nut, was predisposed to apply pressure this-a-way. This predisposition was sufficiently fixed to blind him to the possibility that to undo this particular nut you had to turn it that-a-way!

The effect of the combination of these two properties, the stability and the tendency to obscure alternative approaches to a problem, is to make it very unlikely that the end of a lifetime will be the end of a fixed predisposition. On the contrary, it becomes a part of the character—a character trait in fact—and a feature of the very shape, so to speak, of that which reincarnates.

Allowing a predisposition to become fixed is one way in which we can forfeit part of our field of choice and hence our freedom to choose until, with outside help, possibly in the form of therapy, the predisposition becomes unfixed. But there is also another way in which one can forfeit part of one's freedom to choose.

In the course of a session, a lady happened to mention that she hated the colour green. She made the statement with such vehemence that I felt it would be worthwhile to try to find out just why she felt so very strongly about this colour. She was already under hypnosis, and in a few minutes she was reliving the occasion when, as a very small child, she had gone into the bathroom *alone*! This, as she well knew, was strictly forbidden. We can assume, therefore, that she was feeling a good deal of apprehension simply on account of being there. And, no sooner had she entered the bathroom than she found that the cat had been sick on the floor.

The smell was revolting and, next to the smell, the most striking feature about the deposit was that it was *green*! The smell of the vomit, combined with her feelings about being in that place at all, had generated such a charge of negative emotion that, in effect, she had said to herself, 'I wish never to be reminded of this incident.' And since the colour green might have brought it back to her, we can be sure that this wish included the wish to avoid that colour. In due course the memory of the episode, including the whole wish, became unconscious.

I am sure this lady would have asserted that she was perfectly free to choose any colour she liked, be it for a dress, for curtains, for a carpet in her living room or for anything else. In fact, however, she would have been mistaken. The presence of that unconscious wish made it *impossible* for her to choose the colour green for any purpose, even if every artist, dress designer and interior decorator in the world had been in unanimous agreement that green was precisely the colour that was needed.

While gaining insight into the reason for her aversion did not suddenly render green her favourite colour, it certainly reduced the intensity of her aversion to the extent that she could accept the colour when it really was appropriate to do so. In other words, she regained her freedom to choose in this respect.

This case solved a problem for me.

It is frequently asserted that a human being has 'free will', an expression that I feel is better rendered as 'freedom to will' or 'to choose'. On the one hand I had always felt, intuitively, that this was true, whilst on the other there seemed to be much evidence from patients to the contrary in the form of unconscious wishes which effectively limited that freedom.

I'm sure now the fact is that we always retain freedom to will or to choose, *within our totality.* But when, for whatever reason, we permit or cause something to fall into our unconscious, we forfeit part of that freedom until we have raised the repressed material to our consciousness again. My attachment to the grey car—which features in Chapter 2—would certainly come under this heading. Until I had brought back to my consciousness the experience I had repressed, which made me see the car as a symbol of my mother—as I saw her when I was aged five or six—I was powerless to choose to get rid of it.

Frequent repetition of a particular pattern of reaction can also lead to the development of a different kind of mechanism. Repeat a pattern of, for instance, blind obedience often enough and you can wear yourself into a groove. Eventually you decide that the groove leads nowhere so you turn round. But if the groove is deep enough, all you can see is the other end the groove, which is, of course, blind disobedience. And herein can lie an illusion. The subject of blind obedience cannot deny he is virtually a puppet, moving in accord with the hand of whoever is the puppet-master. But let the string run over a pulley, and now it is when the hand of the puppet-master goes *down* that the puppet jumps *up.* And though this may lead the puppet to think that he is no longer subject to the whims of the puppet-master, in fact of course, he is just as much a puppet as he was before. Only by sticking his head out of the groove can he regain his freedom to choose—and it may be difficult, unaided, fully to realise that he is in such a groove.

In the next chapters we shall be considering the character trait that, understandably, is almost universal, is accepted and even encouraged, but which is the seldom-recognised root of a large proportion of psychological problems.

12   *Claude and Albert Introduce the Power Merchant*

I find there is one particular character trait that underlies a considerable proportion of psychological problems, and many years ago I concocted a little
story to illustrate to a patient some of the points connected with this trait.
The story proved so effective that it became almost a standard item of my diag-
nostic and therapeutic equipment. The original patient happened to be French,
which is why the two characters have French names—the first two names to
come into my head.

The Claude and Albert Story

'Claude and Albert are two young men who have just started their respective careers in business. Albert is a large muscular fellow and very bright, while
Claude is just a little guy and rather dim. At the time with which this story is
concerned they each have a room in the same boarding house. It happens that
both these young men wish to take a tub each morning at precisely half-past
seven, but this is impossible as the establishment has only one bath tub.'

At this point I usually invite the patient to tell me how he—or she—thinks
the situation then developed. Almost invariably the reply is along these lines:
'Well...Albert was the stronger so I expect he got the tub when he wanted it.'
Then there is often a pause, followed by: 'Well no...actually I expect they com-
promised...took it in turns...each had the tub at seven-thirty on alternate days...
something of that sort.' And then we would discuss these replies.

It is easy to imagine that, on their first morning in residence, Albert arrives at
the bathroom promptly at seven-thirty to find Claude actually in the tub. Flexing his muscles ominously, he threatens Claude that if this should happen again
he will lift Claude out of the tub and throw him down the stairs. Claude assures
Albert that he has got the message and will take care in future to be nowhere
near the tub at half past seven...So, by his strong-arm technique, Albert has
indeed got the tub at the time he wanted it. But at what cost?

If Albert had ever carried out his threat he might have broken Claude's neck, which would have brought the whole weight of the law down upon Albert. But a long way short of that, threatening Claude would not have turned Claude into a friend. Consequently, henceforth, Albert would have needed to divide his energy. He could look where he was going with one eye, but with the other he would need to keep looking over his shoulder in case Claude, possibly with the help of friends, were plotting revenge. Clearly, this policy of Albert's would prove to have disadvantages, even in the short term.

In the long term, if Albert were to make a habit of using his muscles to get what he wanted, he would gain a reputation for so doing. In due course he would find that if arms were extended at his approach, it would not be in welcome but to fend him off. In time, Albert would become very lonely and loneliness, the realisation that no one is other than indifferent to one's very existence, is something that the human animal cannot tolerate for long. Thus the power ploy would not prove beneficial in the long term either.

The compromise is obviously an improvement on the power ploy, but it too has its shortcomings. For one thing, a compromise is never entirely satisfactory to either party. Consequently the conflict is not resolved but merely buried, and anything that has been buried has a way of coming to the surface again, sooner or later. Moreover, if a time comes when one of the parties feels he is in a position to get things all his own way, history suggests that he is liable to tear up the agreement.

Now the story continues: 'Predictably, after a week or two, Albert has become discontented with having the tub at the time he wants it only on alternate days—or whatever the arrangement was—and reopens negotiations. However, this time he starts off with a question.' And I invite my patient to tell me what he—or she—thinks the question was. Very rarely have I received the answer that I have in mind. However, when I reveal it, the reaction is nearly always: 'Of course! Why didn't I think of that!'

The answer I have so seldom received is: 'Claude, just *why* do you want the tub at precisely half-past seven?'

This question, so simple, and, one might have thought, so obvious, is supremely important because it is the first step in the process of Claude and Albert *empathising* with one another. I have chosen this word in preference to 'identifying' in an attempt to convey a sense of going beyond just *understanding* what the other fellow is feeling so that one can put oneself in his place, to actually feeling the other fellow's feelings. In effect, each is trying, for the moment, to *become* the other. The point is that to the extent that each of the parties in conflict can, in effect, temporarily *become* the other, any course of action that would hurt the one would hurt the other no less, and would, therefore, scarcely seem to merit discussion.

Clearly, so long as we are on this 'down-here' level of density, each of us encased in our own physical body like the drivers of so many saloon cars, we cannot empathise with one another to that degree. However, if only people who start in opposition will try *hard enough* to empathise with one another, they will often find that a possible course of action emerges which resolves the conflict because it is obviously to the advantage of them both.

The Third Direction

I call this possible solution, hitherto unrecognised: *The Third Direction.* I do not find it surprising that it should appear. A compromise may be the best arrangement two people in conflict can achieve so long as they are both rigidly determined to stick to their original positions. But genuine effort to become, for the moment, the other person implies a willingness at least to consider changing that position; and any change of position, physical or psychological, brings new things into view.

This, essentially, is what happened with Claude and Albert. To Albert's question Claude replied, 'It's very simple, Albert. I like to spend as long as possible in my bed, but I have just acquired a new and ravishingly attractive secretary. I wish, therefore, to get to my office at ten minutes *before* nine looking as spruce as possible. A tub at 7.30 enables me to fulfil all these requirements. But,' Claude finished courteously, 'what about you, Albert?'

'Well, Claude,' Albert said, 'it's a funny thing but I too like my bed and I too have just acquired a glamorous new secretary and I too...' It was immediately apparent to them both that they were in precisely similar situations.

Having reached that point, they quickly realised that in concentrating upon getting the tub at precisely seven-thirty they had been focussing on the wrong target. The object of the exercise, for each of them, was to spend as long as possible in his bed consistent with getting to his secretary at ten minutes before nine, looking and smelling like a metaphorical rose. To this end, *the tub* at seven-thirty was merely a means and, as they were also quick to see, not the only possible means. A shower would do just as well and there was plenty of room to rig a shower over the bathtub. Two showers if necessary. Thus the conflict was resolved to the entire satisfaction of them both. And also, incidentally, to that of their landlady, who gained a shower and lost nothing.

This simplistic little story extols the virtues of seeking what I have called the

'Third Direction' but, I must admit, it says nothing of the difficulties that may lie in the path of adopting that approach. One of these is that the approach may require a great deal of time and patience and at least a modicum of skill, because one may have to start by helping one's opponent to clarify in his mind precisely what it is that he wants and why he wants it before he can make it clear to you. And that may be only half of what is involved, since you may have to accept his help to get the similar points absolutely clear, for the same reasons, in your mind.

This latter part of the process may cause one to ask oneself, rather ruefully, 'How could I have been so stupid as to think I really wanted that?' And since, at the start of any negotiations, there may not be a bottomless well of mutual trust and good will, the thought might occur to one or other or both parties, 'But if I put all my cards on the table I shall be leaving myself vulnerable and defenceless. I am certainly not going to do that!' Furthermore, if the parties come from different cultures and have different mother tongues, the stage is set for misunderstandings which can cause a host of other problems.

Seeking the Third Direction could justifiably be called the 'Positive Approach' to a situation of conflict. However, in view of all the possible obstacles that may lie in the way of adopting that policy, it is understandable that the negative approach may offer a temptation that, in the course of our long history, we have surely all, more than once, found irresistible. This approach is nothing more complex than using whatever form of strength we may have which might enable us to exploit a weakness in our opponent and compel him to do what we wish. I call the character trait from which this policy arises the 'Power Merchant' trait, and a person who displays this trait to a very marked degree I think of as a 'Power Merchant'.

Since this trait plays such a large part in human affairs, it is worth conjecturing where it originated.

Introducing the Power Merchant

In the first part of this book I explained my belief that every living organism is alive only because and so long as it is incorporating a non-physical component. I explained too my belief that this non-physical component starts its history as the animating force of the smallest particle we would describe as living. From that point it evolves by becoming the animating force of a succession of forms, first of plants and then of animals, of increasing complexity until it has become sufficiently evolved to be the animating force of the most complex organism we know of, a human being. At this point I cease to use the term 'non-physical component' and speak, instead, of a 'soul'. In other words, I believe the soul has, in its history, a long prehuman phase.

During this prehuman phase, the ethos was the Law of the Jungle, that is, 'Survival of the Fittest'. And one can see the part it played in the evolution of physical forms. When living by that law, catching one's next meal—or avoiding becoming someone else's—might call upon the extremes of one's speed, strength and stamina, and the individual who, on account of some feature, had an edge over his fellows had the best chance of survival and therefore of handing his special feature down to his progeny.

Under that regime the last thing one wanted was even a trivial injury. To that end, when one belonged to a species which led a social existence in a family, a herd or a tribe, one was endowed with instincts which enabled one to establish a modus vivendi that kept physical confrontations with other members of the group to a minimum. Once the pecking order had been established one would have accepted it, as animals still do. Of course, physical confrontations would still occur between animals of the same group, mostly over territory or mates, but it was seldom an impulsive rush into battle. The contestants would start by making the equivalent of fearsome faces at each other, and even at that early stage one of them might decide it was stepping out of its class and withdraw. If it came to blows and one of them only then realised that his opponent was too strong, it was similarly free to retreat. In such conflicts between just two animals, neither of them armed with anything but its own teeth and claws, at the very worst, both might die, one immediately and the other later of its wounds or because it was rejected by its group and could survive only briefly on its own. Moreover, the victor would be the better beast, which would be to the benefit of the species.

During this prehuman period it was surely natural and right to use any form of superior strength we had as we were programmed to do by our instincts. There was every advantage in being the beast with the mostest. Could this not have been the seed from which sprang what I have called the Power Merchant trait of human beings? During the prehuman period when, one can suppose, the emphasis of evolution was upon physical form, it is difficult to imagine how the ethos of survival of the fittest could have been bettered. However, with the emergence of *Homo sapiens* the situation began to change.

Quite simply, *H.* self-styled *sapiens* developed three features that made the ethos of jungle law too dangerous. These features were his intellectual capacity, the power of speech, which extended his powers of communication, and his manual dexterity. Taken together they ensured, in the first place, that a conflict was not necessarily confined to just two animals. It might spread to whole families or tribes, involving any number of individuals. Secondly, they enabled complex strategies to be planned and executed. Thirdly, they made possible the construction of ever more sophisticated tools and weapons.

It is noteworthy that when anything is used as a weapon it loses any absolute value. Money illustrates the point perfectly. Used benignly, any sum of money has an absolute value, whether in terms of the amount of candy it can buy, the comfort in which it permits one to travel, the house it will enable one to build—and so on upwards. But at an auction, where money is undisguisedly used as a weapon, any sum of money is rendered valueless by a rival who can spend just a bit more.

More to the point, perhaps, consider a club. Used benignly for knocking in posts or cracking nuts, a club has and always will have an absolute value. Used as a weapon, however, while it might be of some use against someone who is unarmed, against someone who has a bow and arrow that he knows how to use, the club becomes valueless. To early *H. sapiens*, wedded to a large extent as he was—and as present day *H. sapiens* still is—to the jungle ethos, the only answer to appear then, as too often it is even now, was a more powerful form of bow and arrow. *Homo sapiens* was all too able to design and construct such things, thereby making escalation inevitable with the results—on every scale from the individual to the global—we now know all too well. A stupid weakling can now destroy in an instant the most magnificent specimen of humanity, mental or physical, that ever lived; or mow down any number in seconds. And we have the means to make our planet uninhabitable by pressing a few buttons.

When a non-physical component embarks upon the human phase of its evolution as a soul, it retains its instinct for survival and its adherence to the jungle ethos. But, and this is a point I cannot make too often or emphatically, the soul of a human being acquires what is frequently referred to as 'free will', a quality that—I feel—is better expressed by 'freedom to will', or 'freedom to choose'. And no matter whence we obtained the direction to use our assets as we did during our prehuman phase, as time went on, *H. sapiens* came to use them in a similar way but as a matter of choice. I suspect the short-term results of the choice seemed so rewarding that the choice was repeated, again and again, until it became a fixed predisposition and a character trait. As such, it became a feature that reincarnates and which, since it blinds the individual to any alternative approach to a conflict will, if left to itself, continue to do so. This has occurred in such an overwhelmingly large proportion of human beings that the use of Power Merchant strategies and tactics is widely accepted as a matter of course and even encouraged!

Now the fact is that this policy, which once played a vital part in the evolution of physical bodies, those vehicles essential for the evolution first of non-physical components and then of souls, has now become the single most common cause of all the miseries that exist, between Peoples, amongst people and within individuals. So much so that I have come to regard possession of the Power Merchant trait as *The Human Sickness*.

The outlook for human beings and indeed for the planet would be one of unrelieved gloom were it not for one bright feature: *within his totality every human being always retains the freedom to choose* how he will react in any present situation. He can retain his instinct for self-preservation, but it does not have to remain wedded or welded to the Power Merchant trait. He has the freedom to choose other ways of resolving conflicts, and the repeated exercise of that freedom will displace the Power Merchant policy as his *automatic* approach to such situations.

An Echo of Alfred Adler

In this context I would agree wholeheartedly with Alfred Adler who was one of the first to join the psychoanalytic movement of Sigmund Freud in the early years of this century. They parted because while Freud insisted that the basic cause of neurotic problems lay in the sexual drive, Adler, while not denying the importance of the sexual drive, had come to see the fundamental cause of neurotic conditions as the conflict between the individual's urge for power and dominance on the one hand, and the various obstacles it encountered both within and outside himself on the other. Part of Adler's therapy centred, therefore, on efforts to help his patients to adjust more satisfactorily to the realities of life and of themselves. After 1916, however, the core of his teaching was to the effect that Man, for his own sake and for the sake of society as a whole, must cease to be egocentric and direct his interest towards his neighbours.

I think there would have been no gulf between Adler and myself. I'm sure he would have agreed with me that whatever a man's role in life may be, the most important task to which he needs to apply himself is to recognise what I call the Power Merchant within himself, and work towards changing it. And if, in truth, the trait in a human being is no longer due to instinct but to a fixed predisposition that has resulted from the repetition of a certain choice of action or reaction, then, in addition to clinical experience, there is a rational basis for my certainty that an individual can change the trait *by repeating a different choice.*

I believe that recognising one's own Power Merchant trait and changing it into something more benign is the essence of the evolution of character.

The Hole in the Bucket

The effects of the Power Merchant trait upon individuals who possess it to a marked degree range in severity from simply limiting, in a trivial way, what the person puts into life—and hence what he gets out of it—at one end of the scale, to neurotic conditions causing profound distress at the other. Why are its effects so far-reaching? I find the logic of the following answer irrefutable.

It starts from another question: 'If someone were to use his superior strength to twist your arm to compel you to do his bidding, would this cause you to like that person more or to like him less?' Under any normal circumstances the answer must surely be 'less'.

Now the next point: 'If you would like somebody less because they had behaved in a certain way to you, then, if you behave in a similar way to someone else, you can confidently expect that person to like you less.' I'm sure this truth has been recognised since before the dawn of recorded human history. But there is an additional twist that seems often to be overlooked or forgotten. Rick-in-the-Caribbean vividly illustrated it, and it is this: 'that you cannot avoid *also liking yourself less.*'

The feeling of 'liking oneself less' or—to use a word for which I am indebted to a former patient—to have a feeling of 'unlove' for oneself—is the essence of a feeling of guilt, and I cannot doubt that most of us, at some point in the human part of our history, have experienced that feeling after twisting someone's arm. We would have been wise to have heeded the feeling as a warning that we had done something which, as we saw in the story of Claude and Albert, was, to say the least, unwise. And it would have been so easy, in theory anyway, to set the feeling at rest. All we would have needed to do would have been, first, to admit to our victim that we had done him a wrong and ask him to take back what we had extorted from him, or tell us how else we could make amends. Secondly, we would have needed genuinely to regret what we had done; and thirdly, we would have needed to resolve to try never to do anything similar again.

But I doubt whether, at any period of our history, we have relished admitting we have been at fault. I'm sure, too, we often felt that what we had just gained was too important to hand back; and finally, far from genuinely regretting what we had done and resolving to try never to do such a thing again, we often decided, 'this is a most efficient technique for getting what I want and I propose to repeat it.' And repeat it we did. But each time we did so we were assailed by these feelings of guilt which were—as indeed such feelings always are—uncomfortable. This posed a problem: 'How could we continue to twist arms without suffering these feelings of guilt?'

I believe that each of us, many lifetimes ago, solved this problem by constructing the system of defences that keeps thoughts and feelings, which—for whatever reason—would be unwelcome, from reaching our consciousness. This is the barrier that Sigmund Freud so brilliantly elucidated. We found it so effective that we brought the tendency to build the barrier anew back with us into each new lifetime.

With this barrier in place it seemed that we could now twist arms in perpetual peace, free from any feelings of guilt; but this was an illusion. When the late President Lincoln observed that you cannot fool all of the people all of the time, he might well have added: 'and you cannot fool *all* of yourself *any* of the time.'

The fact seems to be that the part of our mind behind the barrier always knows precisely what we are doing. If we are twisting an arm, this part of our mind sends out feelings of self-unlove that are just as powerful as before, but on their way to our consciousness they become blocked by the barrier, so we are not aware of them. But *behind the barrier they accumulate.*

It happens—and from an 'Upstairs' point of view, possibly not by chance, that the human is a very interdependent kind of animal. No human being can exist without some cooperation from others of his species. Life might be restful if we knew that in the last resort we could rely upon anyone to do what was necessary to keep us alive and happy, simply out of general goodwill if not personal affection for us. However, it is clearly impossible to believe that one can be loved by anyone to a greater extent than—within one's totality—one can love oneself: than one can deem oneself to be loveable. Hence it may be a misguided policy to encourage someone simply to love himself. It might be more helpful to explore with him, first, just how loveable or otherwise he really is and, if necessary, show him how he could become more loveable.

For the fact is, as I have already remarked, that one cannot possibly fool the whole of oneself. After one has twisted a certain number of arms, one will have acquired so much unlove for oneself—it may be behind the barrier but it is still part of one's totality—that it is impossible to believe, to the depths of one's being, that anyone can love one really very much. To introduce an analogy I use very often, *the unlove for oneself that one has accumulated in one's unconscious will act like a hole in a bucket, through which any assurance that one is loved will rapidly leak away.*

This leads to another question: 'If it is essential that a person renders one a particular service, but one cannot rely upon him doing it willingly, out of affection or for a just reward, how can one be sure of getting him to do it?' The answer, in the last resort, seems to be, 'only by being able to twist his arm'. But, in order to be able to twist a person's arm, merely to be strong is not enough. It is essential to be, in some way, *stronger than* the possessor of the arm one feels one may have to twist. Gradually, one's whole peace of mind can come to rest upon the fact, *or the illusion,* that one is the strongest tiger in whatever corner of the jungle one happens from moment to moment to find oneself. By this time, the appetite for this reassurance may have become insatiable, but each time one seeks more of it, the probability is that one is going to increase one's unlove for oneself, which is going to make it still more impossible truly to believe that one is loved. In effect, it will enlarge the hole in one's bucket, whereupon any reassurance one gets will even more rapidly leak away and the need for reassurance that one is the strongest tiger will come to seem still more urgent. One has trapped oneself, in short, in a very vicious circle.

A picture of the eventual outcome that I find realistic starts with the notion that the walls of the unconscious are elastic. They expand to accommodate more and more of this unlove for oneself before it reaches one's consciousness. Eventually, however, this accumulation develops pressure, so much pressure that it begins to smoke, and the smoke comes through the barrier in the form of symptoms. An accumulation of unlove for oneself is obviously not the only cause of psychological symptoms, but it does account for a considerable proportion of them.

It may be more than one lifetime before one realises that one pays for everything one gets, including unmerited peace of mind bought at the expense of accumulating justifiable unlove for oneself behind the barrier. But the bill will come in eventually. Inevitably. And it may arrive at a most inconvenient time and be uncomfortably heavy. It may take any of a variety of forms. It may take the form of a neurotic illness or of a psychosomatic condition, or the misery of just plain loneliness, to name but three. But there is no escape from it—except by recognising the trait in time and choosing to change it. This fact gives the clue to what I frequently see as the aim of therapy: to help the patient to recognise his Power Merchant trait and show him an alternative way of reacting to the inevitable conflicts of life.

Before ending this chapter I should perhaps emphasise that of course there is nothing wrong with power per se. Power is the ability to produce an effect; energy is what actually produces it. The more powerful one is, the more energy one has at one's command. Money is a symbol of energy, and the more money a person has, the more power he has. Everyone can envisage benign projects that can be brought to fruition—or disasters that can be averted—only by using all the power one has, all the energy one can muster to bear upon the situation. A person whose power in a certain kind of situation is such that other people will, of their own volition, yield a portion of their own autonomy in order to be guided by him, is a natural leader.

But I must stress that the possession of power carries responsibility. In every situation in which one is involved, one must accept one's share of responsibility for the outcome. For instance, if a patient seeks my advice as a doctor and I undertake to give it, it is important that I recognise the power I probably have to influence his subsequent behaviour, and therefore my responsibility for its outcome. In this particular kind of situation my power and therefore my responsibility are probably very much greater than my patient's, nevertheless it is his responsibility to decide whether or not to act on my advice.

In the next chapter we shall see Power Merchants operating in a variety of ways.

13 An Assortment of Power Merchants

I consider I have been fortunate in that during my life I have been at least brushed by so many different kinds of emotional experience that it is unusual for a patient to tell me about something that he has done or that has befallen him without causing me to feel: 'that reminds me of the time when...'; and many a patient has told me that he has found it helpful when I have shared such recollections with him. If I have picked an appropriate one, he feels assured that I really do understand what he is talking about, and also that he is not alone!

In addition I have had the privilege of being married to Joan Grant for upwards of twenty-five years. One of Joan's faculties was an uncanny ability to gain instant insight into motives for behaviour, even when these lay deep in the unconscious of its perpetrator; so much so that one sometimes felt one was living under a sort of psychic spotlight. This was not always comfortable but it was instructive. Very instructive!

As a therapist, Joan was direct. I think that is *le mot juste*. With extended arm she was inclined to point a finger and declare, 'The trouble with you is...' A variant of this was, 'You can't be as silly as that!' It was a technique—if one can call it that—which did not suit everybody, but it was probably the only one that would have pierced my defences so quickly. However, I think I can fairly claim that, at least at a conscious level, I was eager to learn truths about myself, even if, as was often the case, they proved to be unpleasant. Some of these I have also shared with patients, many of whom have told me that this often made it easier for them to recognise and accept aspects of themselves. For this reason, I will also mention, amongst other personal experiences, some of the insights into myself, which I gained through Joan.

The Power Merchant trait, as I have already said, is the name I have given to the character trait of readiness to use whatever form of strength one has that may enable one *to exploit a weakness in somebody else*; figuratively to twist his arm in order to compel him to do one's bidding. In addition, when speaking of a person in whom this trait is very marked, I find it convenient to refer to him (or her!) as a Power Merchant.

Why a 'Power Merchant'? In my early schooldays, which was when my enthusiasm for reading about cricket and cricketers began, some writers used to refer to a bowler who relied upon the speed with which he delivered the ball to get his results as a 'speed merchant'. I think, therefore, it came very naturally to me to refer to someone who uses his power in the way I have described above to gain his ends as a Power Merchant.

Weapons of Power Merchants

Of the assets and attributes commonly used as weapons by Power Merchants, amongst the most obvious are such features as muscle, money, status—social or professional—intelligence, charm, and sexual attractiveness.

Needless to say, all of these can be used benignly. Muscle does not have to be used to threaten or to dominate the less robust: there is no end to the situations in which it can be used to help them. Equally obvious are the innumerable ways in which money can be used to increase the sum of human happiness. Intelligence, rather than being used to take advantage of the less bright, can be employed to help them with their problems. Status can sometimes be used, perfectly ethically, to cut through red tape to get results more quickly than would otherwise be the case. Charm, an invaluable item in the armamentarium of a confidence trickster, can also be used to help people to feel relaxed so that they can the more quickly indicate where the pain is, thus making it possible the more quickly to set about relieving it. And I am thinking of pain in every sense. Sexual attractiveness may be a great asset in initiating friendships and can obviously give immense pleasure to a beloved. It does not have to be used to boost one's ego or to inveigle people into bed, to the bank or to the altar. Nor does it have to be used consciously, or, as in the following case, unconsciously, as a means of control.

Sex as a Weapon

Tessa was an attractive married lady in her late twenties, with two children. Her problem was that since the birth of her second child she had been almost completely incapable of any sexual activity with her husband. I say 'almost' because once or twice a year, for a period of about a week, her sexual capacity would return, and by the end of that week her husband would be one tired citizen.

Her incapacity for the rest of the year was a source of distress to them both, and they had received much psychotherapy, separately and together, from a succession of therapists, but to no avail. Recently they had even tried looking at pornographic pictures, but this had proved equally unhelpful. Their last therapist, knowing of my interest in former lifetimes, had referred the lady to me in the faint hope that an approach along these lines might provide the answer.

Taking her history brought one or two factors to light, which caused me to suspect that the cause of her problem might be some traumatic episode involving her mouth. It was soon to transpire that I was partly right, but had missed the most important point.

At an appropriate moment I helped Tessa to shift her level and told her that if there had been an unhappy experience that concerned her mouth, she would quickly find herself reliving it.

Almost at once she was experiencing herself as a girl of about ten-years old, lined up in the kitchen with her brothers and sisters while her mother went down the row, popping into each mouth a spoonful of a glutinous tonic, which Tessa happened to find most disagreeable. However, this episode did not seem to have enough steam in it to have produced her symptom. Moreover, it had occurred very much later than anything of the sort that I had in mind. Accordingly I told her that if there were something earlier, she would now find herself back in that situation.

I had scarcely finished speaking before she was turning her head violently from side to side. I asked her what was happening. Through tightly clenched teeth she uttered, furiously, 'My mother keeps trying to put her nipple in my mouth and I DON'T WANT IT!'

'What do you do,' I asked, in a deliberately gentle voice, 'when your mother tries to do this and you don't want it?'

'I bite and I scream and I kick!' came the reply.

'But does that not make your mother very angry?'

'Yes, it does!' Emotional steam was issuing from the patient as if from a vigorously boiling kettle.

'And aren't you very frightened when she becomes angry with you?'

'NO, I'M NOT! IT JUST MAKES ME MAD!!'

This was no pathetic infant who wanted only to be burped or who feared being smothered by a large breast. This was an infant battling for dominance. By now we had been working for more than two hours and, feeling she had done enough for one session, I brought her slowly back to the present day and then back to normal waking consciousness. As I was doing so, I frequently repeated the suggestion that at the next session we would resume from this point.

The suggestion proved effective. On her return, two days later, Tessa's level shifted easily and she was immediately back in the scene with which the previous session had ended. When it was as clear to her as it was to me that the battle over being fed was indeed a struggle for dominance over her mother, I said to her: 'I suspect you have always been fighting someone, right through your life. Come forward in time now to the age of...let us say five, and let us see whom you are fighting then. As I reach the count of ten you will be five years old.'

I counted to ten and asked her how old she was.

'I'm five,' came the reply, casually yet confidently.

'And where are you?'

'At home,' she replied, in a tone that suggested studied unconcern.

'Is there anybody else there?'

'No...' Again that elaborately casual tone. Then she continued: 'Mummy has gone to fetch my sister from school. She usually takes me with her but it's raining today so she has left me at home.'

I sensed drama was on the way—and I was right.

'Do you mind being left at home alone?'

'No.' Yet again that tone of elaborately casual unconcern. 'But'—and now a note of relish was discernible—'I did something when she was out of the house. I spat on the gold cushions in the drawing room; and then I rubbed in toothpaste! Then I turned them over and'—now glee was undisguised—'my sister got blamed!'

As a teenager she found herself in a furious dispute with her mother over something as trivial as ironing a frock. It was abundantly clear that she was determined to be in control of every situation. At length I asked her: 'And how do you control a man?' The reply came in a very small voice, full of shame: 'In the bedroom.'

From that point the explanation of her problem soon emerged. She resented the fact that her husband had a much closer relationship with their second child—indeed with both the children—than she had, and she had become determined that in all other respects it would be she who ruled the marital roost. This determination had to be kept at an unconscious level because she was genuinely extremely fond of her husband and, as her voice testified when she realised what she had been doing, she would have been too ashamed of her policy to carry it out consciously.

In fact, she would probably have been unable to do so. If the intention had been only at a conscious level, she probably would not always have been able to restrain herself from responding to her husband's overtures; and as her unconscious saw it, to have responded would have cost her all her control of the situation. As it was, her unconscious had ensured she would not respond by forming a very strong wish *not* to do so. The effect of this wish, so long as it remained unconscious, was to make a response genuinely impossible for her. Once she had raised this wish from her unconscious to her consciousness and had understood the mechanism, she realised that the periodic brief returns of sexual function were motivated by anxiety to keep hope alive, in both her husband's heart and points further south.

She was then quick to see that each time she rebuffed her husband she loved herself a bit less, making it the more impossible to believe that he really loved her and, therefore, seemingly, the more essential to keep turning the screw. She did not need me to suggest that her life might be happier if she were to aim at being a more loveable person rather than one determined to be always in control.

Events moved more swiftly than I had anticipated. The next and, as it proved to be, the final session, occurred two days later. Tessa arrived beaming with happiness and the news that her problem had vanished overnight. No further work was really necessary but she was eager to have a glimpse, if possible, of a former lifetime, so I shifted her level once more.

She quickly became aware of herself as an unlovely lady sitting on the doorstep of her house. She was wearing a black dress, though it was a hot sunny day. There was a general impression that the scene was in Spain. She was the butt of much teasing by the local children, and the only way she felt she could control matters was by frightening them, with curses. We did not seek to learn anything of her history before that life, but I would guess that difficulties over the benign use of control had long been a prominent feature. This would explain why it was so important for her always to be in control in her current life. This had led to her basic problem: she always sought to improve matters—as countless others have done before her and still others will do in the future—by turning the screw in the wrong direction.

For years thereafter a card from Tessa at Christmas would confirm that her new approach to life was continuing to bring great happiness to her husband, to herself and, indeed, to the whole family. Thinking of Tessa's case always reminds me of an elderly lady in a village in which I used to live. In respect of looks it would be difficult to imagine someone less favoured than she. Yet such was the sweetness of her expression and her nature that she was the most loved person in the village.

The Power of Weakness

So far we have concentrated on the ways a Power Merchant may use obvious strengths, but let us never forget the power of weakness. Many a chronic invalid has ruled a household with threats of 'another attack' if hints were not taken or expressed wishes not promptly gratified. Such an invalid may come to be regarded as an infernal nuisance rather than an object of great affection. However, even the weakness of a chronic invalid may be second in power to that of a baby. A baby in a household will be the person who determines its routine; and if a mother can neither take the baby with her nor find a baby-sitter, the baby will imprison her in her house more securely than could any bolts or bars. And whilst adults are programmed to respond sympathetically to a baby's cry, thus making its cry an essential part of its survival kit, material emerging from hypnotic regressions suggests that some babies seem to be aware that with their cry they can drive strong men up walls. In the baby's weakness lies its strength.

But even a healthy, averagely good-natured adult—which I would claim to be—can unconsciously be using a weakness ploy. The use—or misuse—of superior strength as a weapon is usually obvious. But, I as I was to learn, the use of weakness in a similar way can be far more insidious. Two episodes, which illustrate the point, are engraved in my memory.

The Washing-Up Story

The first episode involved myself and illustrates what I meant by 'living under a psychic spotlight'. Joan and I had been together only a few weeks and had just moved into a new flat. Joan had been busy all day working on curtains and other jobs aimed at making it habitable. As we were finishing supper that evening, Joan said, 'I'm awfully tired—do you mind if I go and have a bath and leave you to wash up?' 'Of course not,' I replied, and so far as I was aware I meant it, right down to my boots. After a cup of coffee I shifted everything to the sink and embarked upon the operation.

After her bath Joan returned to the kitchen. For some moments she stood watching me as, happily, at my own speed, I was getting on with the job. That was and remains my story. Joan saw the situation differently. Her view was that I was just pushing the mop round and round the same plate, and after a minute or two she spoke. 'You think,' she said, 'that if you take long enough over this and do it badly enough, I will do it for you. Well, let me tell you, I won't!' Her words caused my mind to snap back to a certain summer evening when I was about four-years old. I had been getting on everybody's nerves and was just about to receive a well-deserved smack when, with a stroke of what, to my shame, I still regard as a stroke of genius, I said, pitifully, 'But I is a *tired* little boy.' This brought the entire situation under control in a flash. The hand about to chastise was checked in mid-air; my Nanny was sent to put my fairy-cycle away; and I was plunged into a nice warm bath. With a duck. And after that it was cocoa and biscuits in bed.

I am not convinced that on this particular occasion Joan was not projecting a bit of herself upon me, but no matter; she had caused the recall of this incident, which resulted in a piece of insight that has proved most valuable. It concerned the feelings of intense, almost overwhelming fatigue which could assail me from time to time. With this insight I realised that these spells occurred only when I was confronted by some particularly irksome chore, such as a large pile of correspondence. I could now see clearly that on these occasions I was virtually regressing to childhood, when a convincing exhibition of tiredness might result in someone doing an uncongenial task for me. In the present day, of course, there was no one else who could possibly do it, so such fatigue was entirely non-productive. Indeed it was counter-productive because if I allowed myself to become, in effect, smaller than I really was, the job would appear correspondingly larger than it really was, but it still had to be done. However, with the insight that the feelings of fatigue were a sign that I was regressing, came also the realisation that I had *freedom* to *choose* either to let the regression continue or to snap out of it. I found I had only to ask myself, 'Are you being a *tired* little boy?' to return promptly to my true size, whereupon the appearance of the job would shrink accordingly. Since discovering this technique, the frequency of these regressions has dwindled almost to nothing.

The crucial point of this experience was the discovery of my *wish to remain small* because of the power to evoke pity that I had discovered lay in the weakness of childhood. This wish was unconscious, but as we have seen in other cases, an unconscious wish can, if it is strong enough, have the effect of a real fact. Not only can an unconscious wish to be unable to walk have the effect of paralysing one's legs, but this episode shows that an unconscious wish to remain small can have the effect of making one feel one really is small. And when one realises that for many a baby it must seem that simply to exist is enough to win universal approval, it is not surprising if, as it begins to discover that in addition to existing it is expected to *do* something to justify its existence, it longs for the perpetuation of its babyhood. One hopes it will find that the rewards of growing up make the process worthwhile; but the individual who has brought a lot of Power Merchant in with him may feel that they do not compensate for the loss of the power innate in infancy and also in childhood. It can in fact happen that the energy in the wish to remain small, if that wish persists in the unconscious, is a perpetual brake upon the maturation of the personality.

The second incident occurred a couple of years after the washing up episode. It shows the potential for far-reaching unhappiness that may lie in the use of weakness as a weapon.

The Helpless-Little-Girl Ploy

Betty, who came to stay with us for psychotherapy, was another attractive young woman with a sexual problem. It was somewhat similar to Tessa's, but in her case the incapacity really was total. She was referred to us by a colleague from whom she had already received a great deal of analytically oriented psychotherapy, but to no avail.

It was during dinner on the first evening of her visit that, quite unknowingly, I took what proved to be the essential step in resolving her difficulty. The moment came when someone was handing round the cheese board, and one of the cheeses was still in its wrapper. Betty was sitting next to me, so it was to me she turned with appealing eyes and, imploringly, said, 'Could you please undo it for me...it is so difficult!' I do not know what possessed me at that moment, but my reply was: 'You are a big girl now, you can undo it yourself'! The poor woman blushed scarlet.

When supper was over, I took Betty to my consulting-room. Referring to the cheese incident, I explained sympathetically that I had recognised that she was using the well known 'helpless-little-girl' ploy, which disguises the aggressive intention of turning someone into one's slave. To her great credit she responded, 'You must tell this story, in front of me, to my husband when he visits me here next week.'

Her husband duly arrived, and as I was relating the incident a most comical expression spread slowly over his face in which indignation and amusement were nicely blended. When I reached the end of the story, he took his cigarette lighter from his pocket and, holding it towards Betty, said, 'Could you please change the flint for me: it is so difficult!' She had used—but successfully—precisely the same technique on him! Understandably he had thought: 'Here is a most attractive girl who thinks I'm next to God because I can change the flint in her lighter. This must be Heaven!'

As a child, this patient had found that the power she had as an appealing little girl brought such rich harvests that she had formed the wish to remain one. If it had ever been conscious, this wish had slipped into her unconscious, but certain kinds of situation would resonate to it and activate it, whereupon it would cause her to behave accordingly. Alas, the fact is that sooner or later, in one way or another, we always have to pay for everything we get; and she could only continue to play the helpless-little-girl by day at the cost of being a thoroughly inadequate woman by night, and this was threatening her marriage. However, until the unconscious wish to remain a small girl was brought to her consciousness again, there was little she could do about it. Raising this particular wish to consciousness was not the whole story, but it proved to be the crucial factor in her recovery.

Four Cases Reviewed

We have had a brief look at four people with fairly well marked Power Merchant traits, and it is interesting to note some of the features they share and some of the differences between them. The people were Rick of the Caribbean, whom I mentioned in Chapter 11. Then there was Tessa who, amongst other things, rubbed toothpaste into the drawing-room's gold cushions; Betty of the cheese unwrapping and the flint-in-lighter changing; and myself, the—according to Joan—dilatory washer-upper. The first similarity is that we were all using our weapons in order to get something.

Rick was perhaps the most obvious. His nature had incorporated a streak of the bully. He had been gaining a measure of relief from tension by taking advantage of his wife's relative physical frailty and her financial vulnerability to displace upon her the anger he had not dared to express against the figures who had evoked it.

Tessa, to a considerable extent, was controlling her husband by withholding sex from him in order to rule the household. At an unconscious level she knew very well that she was deliberately using her sexuality as a weapon.

Although Betty's problem was similar to Tessa's, its origin was quite different. Her inability to perform sexually was a side effect of her unconscious choice of technique for getting people to serve her. She was continuing—with considerable success—to exploit people's vulnerability to the pleadings of an appealing small girl.

As for myself, if Joan's diagnosis was correct and, I admit that it probably was, I was employing a small boy's version of the same technique. In the particular episode that had come to mind, I was using it to avoid a well-deserved smack, but I have no doubt I used it also on other occasions to gain different ends. However, I was more fortunate than the others in two respects. Firstly, my attacks of fatigue were not so frequent or so severe as to constitute a problem.

I never even thought of mentioning them to anyone, let alone seeking advice for them. And if I had thought of seeking advice, it would never have occurred to me that it was the advice of a psychiatrist that I needed. My second piece of good fortune, therefore, was that Joan's faculties brought her near enough to the diagnosis to spark off that memory which, in turn, led to the helpful insight before the attacks had become a problem.

This is something that rarely happens. Far more often, as in the other cases I mentioned and as a general rule, neither the Power Merchant nor the victim is aware of the significance of the former's behaviour. As a result, the Power Merchant's ploys are successful for long enough to cause their use to become a habit—in effect a character trait—and for distressing problems to develop. Rick had developed severe anxiety and had caused his wife much distress. Tessa had been cutting off her own nose as well as spiting her husband's face and, in addition, had been causing some distress to the whole family. Eventually, no doubt, she would have seriously endangered her marriage, while Betty's marriage was already in jeopardy. In short, to put it at its mildest, the Power Merchant trait carries the seeds of eventual misery, in one form or another, both for the individual and for those around him.

In the next chapter we shall be looking at certain attitudes, certain states of mind that, very often indeed, are associated with the Power Merchant trait.

14 More About Power-Merchantship

Anyone, from time to time may find himself in a situation in which it is essential for him to be and to remain in control. However, in order to feel secure, the Power Merchant has a constant need to feel he is in control; that he is the 'Strongest Tiger' in whatever situation he happens to be. Some of this need may be fully conscious, but the force of his reaction if he feels his supremacy is threatened may indicate clearly that a large proportion of the need is unconscious.

It is the presence of this unconscious element of the need to be in control that causes the basic attitude to life of the Power Merchant to have an element of hostility. It makes him like someone—if you can possibly imagine such a person—who is frequently throwing tennis balls at the walls that surround him, while remaining completely unaware that he has ever had a ball in his hand. Of course the balls will bounce back at him but he, unaware that he threw them in the first place, can only conclude that the walls are throwing balls at him! The walls, of course, consist of the circumstances and the people around him with whom he has any link.

Consequently, he is ever ready to feel he is under attack, and is prepared to react—as it seems to him—appropriately. His mental energy is largely bound up with his own safety, and he has little to spare for benign concern about any-body else. Hence, if he waves a greeting at a friend on the other side of the street and it is not returned, he is less likely to consider the possibility that his friend is preoccupied with a problem of his own than to feel that his friend is deliberately ignoring him. In short, the Power Merchant is likely to become a somewhat paranoid person.

Moreover, it seems that even 'down-here', at an unconscious level, we assume that we communicate by thought transference. Thus, the more unconscious hos-tility we are harbouring, the more probable it is that we will take it for granted that the person in front of us is aware of it and is assuming that it is directed against him. This leads our own unconscious to assume that he is preparing retaliation, which will put us in danger.

The barrier we have constructed, which divides the conscious part of our mind from the unconscious, protects our consciousness from feelings that might cause us distress, mainly those feelings of unlove for ourselves that we call guilt. However, if, at an unconscious level, we feel we are in danger, then within our totality we shall feel that we cannot afford to let our consciousness remain unaware of the fact. Consequently, we may have feelings of apprehension or of suspicion, though *we will probably be unaware of the real reason for them.*

Such feelings of suspicion may have consequences of their own. On the basis that the best means of defence may be attack, our unconscious hostility may cause us to have an aggressive attitude to life. Though its function is in fact defensive, it can nonetheless lead to any potentially friendly encounter becoming a hostile confrontation—which may escalate to any height.

I sometimes remind patients of the story of the man who was driving very late one night along a country road when his car sustained a puncture. Preparing to change the wheel, he discovers he has no jack. 'Only thing to do,' he thinks to himself, 'is to walk until I come to a house where I might be able to borrow one.' At length he sees a light in the distance and starts towards it. On the way he is ruminating upon how he would react if some stranger woke him up in the middle of the night and asked if he could borrow a jack. He reaches the house and knocks on the door. A head soon appears at the lighted window and a kindly voice enquires, 'What can I do for you?' Unfortunately, the jackless one's soliloquy has reached a point that causes him to respond angrily, 'All right then, *keep your blasted jack.*'

Yet another consequence of the unlove for himself that, as a result of the trait, the Power Merchant has accumulated in his unconscious, is that, at some level in his mind, the Power Merchant is likely to be saying to himself, in effect, 'Because I am so unlovable I cannot rely upon anyone to look after me but me!' As a result, so much of his energy becomes bound up with himself that there is little to spare, which can flow out spontaneously in a benign way to other people. Thus he gains a reputation for being selfish: a person who loves no one but himself. Selfish and self-centred he undeniably is, but for a reason that is precisely the reverse of loving himself. Unfortunately, his self-centred behaviour is perpetually turning the screw in the wrong direction.

As I explained in Chapter 12, some degree of the Power Merchant trait is almost universal amongst human beings. Nonetheless, on the whole, at least on the surface, we seem to manage our lives fairly well. But even a slight degree of the Power Merchant trait, if it is not recognised and efforts are not made to change it, can grow into a trait that menaces both the happiness of its possessor and of those around him.

Pride

This is an appropriate moment to introduce a subject that is a virtually inevitable concomitant of the Power Merchant, namely, pride. I took advantage of an occasion when Joan had shifted level to ask her how she understood pride. Without a moment's hesitation she replied: *'True pride is the honourable acceptance of the responsibility, implicit in one's assets and attributes, to help those who are weaker as and when they need protection.'* I had never heard that definition before, nor have I since, but I doubt if it could be bettered. It has some far-reaching implications.

For instance, it underlines the importance of that age-old injunction: 'Know thyself'. Only to the extent that one knows oneself can one know what one's assets and attributes are. Or one's weaknesses. It implies too that *true pride,* in one of its aspects, is the acceptance of how far one has travelled, and that *true humility* is the recognition of how far one still has to go. On any road.

It is noteworthy that Joan specified she was talking about *'true pride'.* True pride is in contrast to 'false pride', which is the kind of which the Power Merchant usually has an abundance. False pride consists, in large part, of *the illusions we create* to enable ourselves—and to cause other people—to feel we are larger than we really are or that the ice we are standing on is thicker than it really is. It also contains, often, the feeling that we have the right to look down upon those less favoured than ourselves and to make use of them.

The point about the illusions is particularly important because, once we have accepted a truth about ourselves, we no longer have a fear of being faced with it. By contrast, we may go to any lengths to protect our illusions from being exposed for what they are, to ourselves as much as to anyone else. Hence the false pride of the Power Merchant is the principal factor which prevents some Power Merchants from coming anywhere near a psychotherapist and which, in general, makes it difficult for anyone to help them. The need to maintain his illusions and to appear whiter than white may cause the Power Merchant to become an inveterate liar, to himself no less than to others.

There are three kinds of emotion that the Power Merchant is particularly likely to harbour, and these we will consider next. They all have the potential for effects that range from the trivial to the tragic. I refer to envy, to jealousy and to possessiveness. Let us start with envy.

Envy

Envy is the wish to destroy the pleasure a person is taking in some aspect of his good fortune. It may extend to wishing to destroy the fortunate person as well. An advertisement in a glossy magazine that caught my eye indicated how widespread this sentiment is. Inadvertently, I suspect, it also revealed how lethal it can be, for beneath a picture of a luxurious motorcar was the legend: 'Arrange a trial run down your street and *watch your neighbour break his heart.*' (The italics are mine.)

I happened to be staying in a hotel at the time so it was easy to show the page to a number of people and ask them what they felt about it. The almost unanimous response was: 'Jolly good advertising.'

Since the object of an advertisement is to sell the product, it is pertinent to ask what the factors in the advertisement were that its designers anticipated would contribute to its intended effect. The picture of the automobile was obviously one, but the legend would surely not have been added unless it was deemed to provide extra punch.

How was it expected to do this? How else but by playing upon the capacity so widespread amongst us for the feeling we call envy; or upon the wish to evoke that feeling, which is merely the other side of the same coin. To what else could the prospect of watching one's neighbour breaking his heart at the sight of something one possessed be expected to appeal? And if experience had not shown that this kind of legend appeals widely and strongly, the advertisers would not have included it.

A capacity for envy and for the wish to evoke it are both hallmarks of the Power Merchant trait, and we have only to look just below the surface to see why the sentiment is potentially so dangerous, so unhealthy and so widespread. *'And watch your neighbour break his heart.'* That expression was presumably intended to convey the idea that at the sight of you in the car, your neighbour would be gripped by an intense and extremely unpleasant emotion. Now, suppose for a moment that all of the neighbour's controls against putting his feelings into action were to break down, what form would the action take? Surely nothing less than an attack upon the car and quite possibly upon its prospective owner as well. It is this desire *to destroy* the pleasure a person is taking in some aspect of his good fortune, which is the essence of envy and which makes it so dangerous. This is in contrast to a wistful, 'I wish I had one too.' Such a wish, if it is powerful and reason tells one that it will never be fulfilled, might be exquisitely painful, but it would be ethical, and psychologically healthy.

Why should the prospective owner of the car be expected to derive pleasure from seeing his neighbour suffering such distress? The most probable explanation is that the sight would enable him to infer that his neighbour was admitting that he, the prospective owner, was in a position to acquire something that the neighbour was not, and that he, the prospective owner, was, therefore, in some way that was important to the neighbour, superior to him.

But if the prospective owner is going to derive pleasure from such an admission, this must surely indicate that he desired it. But why should he desire it? The most probable answer is that his desire has sprung from his need—conscious or unconscious—for reassurance that he is the strongest tiger. And since it is inconceivable that one could enjoy the spectacle of someone whom one loved suffering from envy over one of one's possessions, the capacity for envy supports the notion that the basic attitude of the Power Merchant is one of constant if unconscious hostility towards the world in general.

However, as I explained in the previous chapter, each time the Power Merchant seeks reassurance that he is the strongest tiger, he increases his unconscious load of unlove for himself and so enlarges the hole in his bucket. Thus any reassurance of superiority, indeed any sense of satisfaction he may get from the sight of his neighbour's distress will be short-lived; and by increasing the pressure of the accumulation of unlove for himself in his unconscious, he is moving a step nearer to having undeniable 'down-here' problems of his own.

A person who is in the grip of a chronic, smouldering feeling of envy is probably keeping his body permanently in the state which was designed only for emergencies, thereby opening the door to the whole range of psychosomatic problems. A common one of these is a blood pressure that is constantly too high, a condition that carries with it an increased liability to heart attacks and strokes. Moreover, a strong feeling of envy that is not resolved before this lifetime ends may lead to a ghost being left, which may be a source of trouble in a subsequent life. This is equally true of all kinds of negative feelings.

Anxiety is a frequent consequence of a capacity for envy, or of the desire to evoke it. The case of a lady whose husband was very rich indeed illustrates the fact perfectly. Since he grudged her nothing, one might have supposed that she would be enjoying a life that was singularly free from worry on her own account. In fact a persistent feeling of anxiety, which she could not explain, tormented her.

She usually arrived for her session festooned with jewellery, but one day she arrived displaying only a ring with a vast solitaire diamond. I duly commented upon it, whereupon she told me she had asked her husband to buy it for her that very morning as she was lunching with a friend (her word), who also had a solitaire diamond and she was determined to make her friend's ring look small.

Satisfaction from evoking envy was only one manifestation of the Power Merchant in this lady's character, but to her credit she quickly grasped how it was causing her daily to add to her store of unconscious unlove for herself, which was already under such pressure that it was threatening to burst through to her consciousness: hence her anxiety.

Equally quickly, she saw ways in which she could use her many assets to contribute to the sum of human happiness rather than to its misery. And she realised too that one benign function of jewellery is to enhance the appearance of its wearer and so add to the pleasure of anyone who happens to see her. Her changed approach to life very soon caused her to become a much happier person.

Incidentally, Joan, on another occasion when she had shifted level, recalled that when she was the Pharaoh during her life as Sekeeta in the First Dynasty of Egypt, no one grudged Pharaoh the contents of her treasure chest because the people knew that these contents stood between them and any disaster which might threaten the nation.

Closely allied to envy is what Stephen Potter brilliantly termed 'One Upmanship'. It can take a variety of forms of which one is name-dropping, which requires no explanation. Another is a need, which may amount to a compulsion, to try to convey that one's own experience, one's own choice of whatever is superior to that of the other person's. It is perhaps pertinent to mention that One Upmanship of this kind is sometimes a rather unfortunate means of attempting to compensate for unconscious feelings of inferiority. Such unconscious feelings constitute a genuine inferiority complex, the term often mistakenly applied to feelings of inferiority that are fully conscious.

There are two thoughts in particular that have seemed to help some people who were suffering from envy. The first is that while destroying the pleasure someone is taking in some aspect of his good fortune may reduce the difference between the 'he who has' and the 'he who has not', thereby perhaps giving the latter the feeling of having enriched himself, the feeling is only an illusion. On the other hand, if the 'he who has not' can find it in himself to congratulate the other on his good fortune, he will, in a sense that is very real if not material, have enriched himself. Sooner or later he will become aware of this.

The second thought is relevant when it can be seen that the envied object is in fact envied mainly because it is a symbol of a *status* that is envied. The point here is that since the envied object is only a symbol, its destruction will not affect the reality of the status of its owner. You can surreptitiously inflict an ugly scratch upon the smart car which it is your boss's privilege to drive and in which he takes such delight, but he will still be your boss! It is undeniably exciting to be at the wheel of a beautiful piece of machinery, but one should be able to survive without that luxury, especially if one has adequate transport of a sort. In any case, your own transport facilities will not be improved by disfiguring the boss's car.

Such thoughts may help to dispel specific feelings of envy, but they are not, of course, dealing with the underlying Power Merchant trait. However, before coming to that topic we will consider the second of the reactions of the Power Merchant trait that I mentioned earlier: jealousy. This emotion can be no less agonising and dangerous than envy.

Jealousy

If we consult Reber's *Dictionary of Psychology* once more, under this heading we find (all the italics are mine): 'Generally, any emotional state classified as a special form of anxiety and *assumed* to derive from a lack of security in the affection of one *who is loved*. Distinguish from envy, where there need be no loved one, merely a desire for things possessed by the rival.'

I am not entirely happy with this definition because it does not mention a point that, to my mind, is an essential component of jealousy. This is *the wish to destroy* the rival, and possibly also the so-called loved one. 'So-called' because jealousy and love do not have any link with each other. The reason is clear. I will state it from the point of view of a heterosexual male, simply because this is the view that comes most naturally to me, but the principle holds good no matter what the genders of the people involved may be.

To the extent that one truly loves a lady, one will wish above all for her happiness. Of course one will be thankful if one is the main source of that happiness; but if it becomes clear that it is someone else who has come to occupy that role in her life, though one may be agonisingly *sad,* one will not suddenly cease to love her. One will not, therefore, wish ill upon the person upon whom her happiness depends—or appears to depend. Only time will tell whether, for her, her new love is the real thing or will prove to be just a passing fancy.

Moreover, the sadness of unrequited love is the pain of a clean wound; and though, initially, such a thing may seem impossible, the wound will in fact heal. And as the healing progresses, one may find it possible to tell the rival that so long as he is doing all he can to ensure the lady's happiness, he can count upon one as a friend. After all, if the lady is indeed the kind of person one believes her to be, it is unlikely that her new love is not a kind of person whom one too would like. And such is the strangely benign way that such matters sometimes work out, not only may one become a valued friend of them both, but one may come to feel that, after all, such a relationship with this particular lady is preferable to marriage to her. What could have been a distressing triangle becomes, in fact, a happy trinity.

This is the antithesis of jealousy because—and this brings us back to the element I feel is missing from the definition—jealousy, as I have said, incorporates a wish to destroy. There will certainly be a wish to destroy the rival and quite possibly the lady too. It is admittedly a different matter if the rival is a proven rascal of some kind or a man who is a notorious Don Juan. In such a case, since it is seldom profitable to appeal to the reason of someone who is in love, probably the best one can do is to warn the leopard he would do well to change his spots. One can also pray that, if the person one loves comes to realise that what she was living in was just a dream world, she will awaken from it in a way that causes her the minimum of distress; and that one will be there to pick up any pieces there may eventually be! What then are the feelings from which jealousy may arise?

Certainly not unrequited love. Jealousy is a form of hate and while love may dwindle to indifference, it can no more turn to hate than a violin, upon falling silent, can turn into a saxophone. A violin may be *replaced* by a saxophone, but that is a different matter. Moreover, if love for someone has genuinely diminished to indifference, there is virtually no link left, so it is highly unlikely that hate would arise. However, with *desire* the case is different. If desire is frustrated or unrequited, it may certainly turn to hate.

The other very common source of jealousy is a threat, if not an actual blow, to one's false pride. This is where the link with envy may be very close. Many a man in love is gratified if the sight of his beloved evokes envy, and this suggests that an element of boost to his pride is involved. 'If a man envies me my girl, I have got something he wishes he had, and this must mean that I'm a better man than he is!'

However, circumstances may arise which cause the lover to fear that his belief that he is the only and the permanent object of his lady's attentions may be proved an illusion, and as we have noted more than once, a Power Merchant may go to any lengths to preserve an illusion. One is reminded of the fable of the princess who was so enamoured of her beauty that she had the corridors of her palace lined with mirrors so that she could constantly enjoy her reflection. However, the time came when, rather than face the fact she was getting a bit plump and needed to watch her diet, she smashed the mirrors because they no longer reflected an image of herself that pleased her. In the case of the jealous in-lover, the mirror may be the mere thought of *his* lady with another gentleman; hence the desire to smash them both.

But is it not natural for a person in love to want exclusive rights in his beloved and to wish to dispose of any rivals? The reply I would offer to that question is, admittedly, sheer speculation.

Believing as I do that our soul has been through a long phase when it was the non-physical component of a series of different kinds of so-called wild animals, I find it conceivable that the state of being in love has a forerunner during that phase. A propensity for jealousy might have tended to ensure that the best physical specimens of females were acquired and retained by the best physical specimens of males. Such an arrangement would surely have been to the benefit of the species and, moreover, might have contributed to the evolution of physical forms. I am not qualified to explore the notion further. I will add only that I am aware that not all species display sexual jealousy; neither, I understand, do all human individuals or societies.

I shall not discuss the complex factors involved in the state of being in love. Suffice it to say that it is a state comparable to an obsessional neurosis. Indeed, if the word 'neurosis' did not imply an abnormal condition that may require treatment, I would say that a person in love is in a highly neurotic state, ineffably paradisiacal though it is. Perhaps one should look upon it as the 'Heavenly Neurosis'!

What are the symptoms of this 'Heavenly Neurosis'? The most prominent one is the tendency—in the eyes of the rest of the world—to overvalue the love-object. Anyone who offers any criticism of her just 'does not understand...' The proof that the condition is, in a certain special sense, outside the normal, lies in the fact that 'cure' may happen quite suddenly, and when it occurs the erstwhile in-lover is often left wondering what he ever saw in her. (Let me remind the reader I am writing only from the point of view of a heterosexual male!)

Economic considerations aside, is it perhaps partly because parents have lived long enough to know from experience that the state of being in love is liable to be transitory that in some cultures it is they who choose the marriage partners for their children?

Lastly, I would make the point that, except to in-lovers, the state of being in love is only a very narrow band indeed in the whole spectrum of loving.

Possessiveness

Since a person in love is likely to place his beloved on a high pedestal, it is probably normal for him to have a degree of fear that he is really not worthy of the blessing of having his feelings reciprocated by such a goddess in human form; and that, therefore, for one reason or another, the blessing might be withdrawn. However, it may happen that no matter how much absolutely sincere reassurance a lover receives, on account of the hole in his bucket his anxiety is so intense and so persistent that he is constantly seeking—even demanding—still more. At a certain point this anxiety may lead to the state we shall consider now: possessiveness.

It is not, of course, only people in love who may become possessive. Parents can become possessive of their children—and vice versa I might add; friends can become possessive of friends; people who are in need of constant care, of their carers. In short, one or other, or indeed both of the parties in any emotional relationship may become possessive.

The possessive person is usually one who, at an unconscious level, has so much unlove for himself that he cannot believe anyone would stay with him because being with him is the place where, most in the world, any particular person would want to be.

I shall refer to a person who is possessive as a 'possessor' and—for simplicity's sake—as male, though female possessors are just as common. And I shall refer to anyone in the clutches of a possessor as the victim and—also for the sake of simplicity—as female, though male victims are not uncommon. The aim of the possessor is to keep his victim with him. Thus he will try to minimise the chance of her encountering circumstances that might awaken in her the desire to escape, or reinforce any desire to do so—which the possessor is likely to assume is already there.

He may have a variety of techniques for keeping his victim at his side. Financial restrictions, applied through threats of disinheritance, or through wages or even just pocket money, are one group. A liability to develop at any moment a symptom that demands instant attention is another. Always finding an excuse that prevents the victim from attending a function where she might meet and become interested in someone is a third; and a fourth is a threat of suicide. A previous more or less convincing attempt at suicide will add weight to such a threat. And let us not forget the simple sulk or other offensive behaviour if the victim is not where he wants her to be at any particular moment.

At a conscious level, the possessor may possibly be able to hide what he is doing from the world under the cover, for instance, of the 'such wonderful care he takes' of the person who is in fact his 'bullyee' or victim. To some extent he may even deceive himself, but within his totality he knows perfectly well what he is doing, and for this reason each time he uses one of his ploys he increases his unlove for himself and enlarges the hole in his bucket. This, of course, increases his fear that he may lose his victim; however, his character trait of possessiveness blinds him to the possibility of any other reaction than that of strengthening the bars of the prison. To mix the metaphor, this is, in effect, yet another example of repeatedly turning the screw in the wrong direction. The situation is heading for misery, even tragedy, but it may be very difficult to help.

The first person to seek help will almost certainly be the victim. She may be suffering from any of a variety of psychological or psychosomatic conditions, or even from just perfectly rational feelings of frustration and despair at being in a prison from which she sees no escape. It is true that there may be factors in her character which led her to put herself in the position of being a victim in the first place, and to stay in it when it is really in no way essential for her to do so. And it may be possible to give her helpful insight into these factors. However, there may still be obstacles of a worldly nature, which prevent her from setting herself free.

Not infrequently these are entirely financial, and it may or may not be possible to help her to overcome them. There may also be—and this can be far more difficult to deal with—a fear of the reactions of the bully if the bullyee were to present him with any sort of hint or threat of leaving. These could range from violence against the bullyee to threats of suicide, as I have mentioned before. The victim may also have a fear that is more or less realistic of the reactions of other members of the family, and even of public opinion.

By the time the possessor has driven his victim to seek help, the possessor's fear—conscious or unconscious—of being faced with unlovable aspects of himself may prove an insurmountable barrier in the way of persuading him to accept any therapy. In short, possessiveness can lead to difficult and even dangerous situations.

In Chapter 11, after stating what I mean by the word 'character', I offered some contributions, revealed in the light of a belief in reincarnation, towards understanding how the character is formed. In Chapter 12 we had a preliminary look at the character trait that I call the 'Power Merchant' trait; and I explained why I consider it to be *The Human Sickness*.

In Chapter 13 we looked at some of the ploys that a person with marked

Power Merchant traits might use in his efforts to retain control of any situation. In this chapter we looked at false pride as well as at three distressing emotions to which a person with a strong Power Merchant trait is particularly prone.

In the next chapter we shall explore some of the reactions of the Power Merchant—and their consequences—when he has failed to get his own way.

15   *Anger and the Power Merchant*

Part I: Anger

At a certain point in *Winged Pharaoh*, which—the reader will remember—is the story of her life as Sekeeta during the First Dynasty of Egypt, Joan relates the following incident. One day Sekeeta, quite unjustly, lost her temper with a servant and struck him repeatedly across the face with a heavy whip that happened to be to hand. Later in the day her father, the Pharaoh, summoned her. 'Sekeeta,' he said, 'Remember! Anger beneath your will is a flail in your hand, but uncontrolled anger is lash upon your shoulders.'

He could not have spoken a truer word. In one way or another, anger lies at the heart of much of the misery in this world—not least, anger that is locked within the individual.

Anyone with a large measure of the Power Merchant trait in his character is particularly liable to feel anger and, moreover, to harbour resentment. The latter is particularly dangerous. If feelings of anger, and the desire for revenge with which they are often associated, are not resolved before the individual dies, those feelings are likely to be a feature which the soul brings with it into a subsequent life, or to cause a ghost to be left. In a later life, such a ghost can be a source of problems.

What exactly is anger?

As befits its name, the Concise Oxford Dictionary gives us a definition that is both brief and comprehensive. It tells us, quite simply, that anger is *extreme displeasure*. It is an emotion. I stress this obvious point because, as we know, an emotion always embodies a wish, implicit if not manifest; and a wish contains energy.

Anger is most likely to occur when some block prevents the energy in a wish from achieving its object. It is thus a natural response to frustration and disappointment. It is also a natural response when one's territory is being invaded.

The word 'territory' in this context includes one's psychological territory no less than one's physical territory. Under some circumstances, as in an underground train during the rush hour, one may be tightly squeezed on all sides without feeling that either one's psychological or one's physical territory is being invaded. Under other circumstances, however, any restriction of one's freedom of movement may be perceived as an invasion of one's physical territory, while, for instance, a prolonged stare may be sensed as an invasion of one's psychological territory.

One's physical territory will include one's personal possessions, while one's psychological territory will include what one takes to be one's rights. Thus a theft on the one hand or anything one perceives as an insult on the other can evoke anger. Briefly, anything that one feels diminishes one is likely to evoke anger.

An immediate gesture of apology may well resolve the situation before the anger is more than a spark. Failing such a resolution, the spark may become a blaze. One will wish to take such measures as may be necessary to remove the offending factor and, quite possibly, to punish it—by causing it pain, physical or psychological. (If the block happens to be inanimate, one may cause more pain to one's toe than to the block.)

But what if the offending factor cannot be removed? The person with no more than a small amount of Power Merchant trait will be able, albeit regretfully, to accept the situation. 'Accept' is the operative word here because it implies that the person is no longer, at any level of his mind, fighting the situation, trying to change it. Not so, however, with the Power Merchant.

To the Power Merchant, inability to arrange matters to his liking is tantamount to a defeat, and a Power Merchant may do anything to avoid having to admit to a defeat. He may, for instance, adopt the sour grapes technique, and in doing so may succeed in deceiving the world at large, and himself too—at a conscious level. But he cannot deceive the whole of himself. The memory of the defeat will persist in his unconscious, as will resentment that was associated with it. It will be added to any store of anger, which he has already accumulated and is carrying around in his unconscious. This store of anger in his unconscious can, as we shall see shortly, be the source of a variety of problems.

The tendency to anger brought in by the Power Merchant trait may manifest very early in infancy with consequences that can affect the person for the rest of his life. I personally was more than forty years of age before I learned this truth—through yet another incident that involved Joan.

The Po Under the Bed Fantasy

From time to time Joan would put her arm round my neck. It was just a light-hearted gesture of affection but for some reason it used to irk me. I tried not to show it, but one day I unthinkingly shrugged her arm off and her expression of dismay prompted me to admit my feeling. It was so clearly out of proportion to the circumstance that we decided to try to discover the reason for it.

Adopting a technique I had used before to shift my own level with Joan standing by, I relaxed in an armchair and fixed my gaze on the flame of a candle on a table in front of me. Then I asked 'Upstairs' to cause such thoughts or ideas or memories to come into my mind as would take me towards the understanding I was seeking.

The first thought to arrive was that I had never been able to recognise my true size. I knew that at six feet one inch (1.85 metres) my height was above the average and that I was likely to be one of the taller members of most groups. Nevertheless, if I saw myself reflected among a crowd of people—in a shop window for instance—I would often find myself wondering, 'Who is that big guy?' With surprise, I would realise it was myself.

In a different direction, my interest in hypnosis caused me to be invited to talk to groups of various kinds, but I could never really believe that anyone could be sincerely interested in anything *I* could have to say, so I tried to turn my talks into something of a comic turn. Rather on the principle that if you can make them laugh they are less likely to shoot you!

Next came the realisation that this difficulty had been with me throughout my schooldays. Notions of ever being top of the form or getting into the school team at football or cricket, for instance, never even entered my mind. That was for the 'big boys', and it never occurred to me that I would, or indeed had become one of them. It was only after many years, when I met some of these erstwhile 'big boys' in various situations, that I realised that neither intellectually nor athletically were they significantly superior to me.

Then, abruptly, the scene changed. I found myself in what I had come to call 'My Po Under the Bed Fantasy'. I started to have this fantasy quite frequently about a year before I met Joan, whenever I allowed myself to daydream. I would experience myself in a small room of which the ceiling, on one side, was sloping. There was a black iron bedstead with a white cover on it, and a chamber pot beneath the bed. And there was a window. I would look out of that window and see the world passing by. No one knew I was in that room, or cared; and there was nothing I could do about it. I would just have to stay in that room until I died.

The fantasy was accompanied by a feeling of desolation.

Suddenly, the scene changed again. I was experiencing myself now as an infant in my mother's arms and she was trying to feed me. I was resisting her efforts as strenuously as I could, vigorously turning my head away. But each time I did this she was able to yank it back again because *she had her arm underneath my neck!* The emotions accompanying this scene were vivid. It was infuriating to be powerless to resist this monster, but far worse, it was intolerably *humiliating* that she could do what she liked with me *because I was* so *small...*

Humiliation, of course, as I have remarked elsewhere, is what we feel when some circumstance has forced us to accept that we are not as big as we have chosen to believe that we are. It is a blow to our false pride.

Then something happened which, while it was occurring in my level-shifted state, and regressed as I was to this infant of only a few weeks old, seemed perfectly natural. It was only in retrospect that I realised how extraordinary it was that I should have experienced it. I became aware of thinking to myself: 'It is only when I try to fight her that I am forced to realise how small I am. I wish I could stop *wanting* to fight her...' As the wish formed in my mind I actually felt myself splitting off any wish to fight my mother from the rest of my experience. To use the technical term, I felt myself 'repressing it'!

At that point I came forward in time spontaneously and found myself back in the room with the po under the bed. Then, for the first time, I heard myself saying: 'But there is no need for me to *stay* in this room! There is nothing to stop me from walking down the stairs and joining the world outside!'

In almost the same moment I realised where the different elements in the fantasy had come from. The attic room with the bed and the po beneath it was based on the cubicle I had had during my first term at my public school, aged thirteen. The window was a composite of the window of that cubicle and the window of a lavatory in which I had been forgotten, before I was old enough to manage self-service. But the real steam in the fantasy—and it had a great deal of steam—came from the period *before I had any mobility of my own: the period when—as it seemed to me—I would have* to *stay wherever my mother dumped me until she chose to rescue me.* It is surely not just coincidence that I started to have the fantasy at a time when I began to contemplate making a big change in my life which I knew would incur the wrath of my mother.

I realise that in being aware of splitting off from the rest of my experience any wish to fight my mother I was unwittingly implying that as much of my experience as I was conscious of, or which I could easily bring to my consciousness, remained in one part of my mind, while any wish to fight my mother was pushed into another. It is difficult to see how this 'other' could be anywhere but the area of the mind we call the unconscious. This, in turn, implies that the unconscious is part of our mental equipment at birth, and indeed I believe this to be the case. I was in fact using the same mechanism which, a few years later, I employed to protect myself from experiencing again the emotions I felt when I saw my mother disappearing—as I believed, for ever—through the door en route for South America. I described this occurrence in the chapter that relates the episode of the Grey Motor Car.

In the same chapter I explained how, when we repress a memory, we create what I call a ghost. I explained too of what a ghost consists, and how it can affect the way we feel and the way we behave.

The experience of the regression to my mother's arm around my neck explained my reaction to Joan's gesture to my complete satisfaction, but, of course, it did not cure my Power Merchant trait. However, I learned a bit more about it.

Because the attitude to life produced by the Power Merchant trait is basically hostile, the infant whose personality contains a generous measure of this trait—and mine unquestionably did—arrives expecting from the start that life will be a battle. Things that are going his way he takes for granted, as a matter of course and of right, but the moment whoever is looking after him does something that is not to his liking, he is liable to feel that his anticipations have been confirmed. 'There you are!' he tells himself. 'I knew it! Life is going to be a battle and that'—pointing a mental finger at whoever is taking care of him, quite probably his mother—'is my first opponent.'

Of course, situations will inevitably arise in the life of every infant, which bring him into conflict with whomever is looking after him. Even if that person can understand what it is the infant wants, it may be impossible for her to grant him his wish. For instance, no matter how clearly an infant indicates that he wishes to taste one of the tablets from that intriguingly shaped bottle beside his mother's bed, one cannot permit him to grab a handful of her sleeping pills.

The attention of most infants can quickly be turned upon something else and the incident is genuinely integrated and forgotten, like an unremarkable and easily digested meal. The thoroughgoing Power Merchant, however, is likely to see any restraint as an example of nothing but malicious opposition, and it may precipitate a battle that, of course, the infant cannot win. Nevertheless, his Power Merchant trait is not going to allow him to accept defeat. In effect, he says to himself, gritting his gums: 'I may not have won this battle but I have not lost it. I'm still in there fighting!'

Well, in due course other things come along to push the skirmish out of the forefront of his mind and most of his soul gets on with the job of growing up. However, the chances are that a part of it remains stuck in this battle, to become another bit of the 'child-that-once-he was' that he may already be carrying with him in his unconscious. Later in life, certain circumstances will resonate to various of these stuck bits of child, releasing some of the energy bound up in it. This energy will then be a factor in determining how the individual responds to the later circumstance.

My mother's determination to feed me against my wishes caused me to see her as an adversary. And her ability to do so despite my most strenuous resistance made her an adversary against whom I could not hope to compete successfully and, of course, to compete unsuccessfully made me feel small—the feeling which, above all, I wanted to avoid. One effect of repressing any wish to fight her was that for several years I never did see her as an adversary whom I ought or wanted to challenge. Thus I avoided one kind of situation that would have made me feel small.

But, there was a price. The ghost came to see any challenge that I could not be sure of overcoming as a symbolical repetition of the original challenge presented by my mother, and hence prevented any idea of accepting it from entering my mind. I never actually felt too small or too weak to gain a place in the school football team, or too stupid to reach the top of the form; the idea of even trying to do so was blocked from ever occurring to me. Without realising it, I was living by the principle, 'if you don't try you cannot fail, and if you don't compete you cannot lose.' The fact that you also cannot win never bothered me because the possibility of competing successfully was not on my mental map. I was a chronic underachiever. If I had gained this insight as a schoolboy, I think the comment 'could do better' might have featured less frequently in my school reports.

What I had repressed had other effects too. It was many years, for instance, before I allowed myself to realise that because someone was older than I, he or she was not necessarily 'better' or 'wiser'; and that I was entitled to look critically at a book that was an expression of an author's ideas, even if that author was a widely acclaimed authority.

However, a Power Merchant is typically quick to see how he can use what assets he has as a weapon. I suspect I had learned the power that lay in being small long before the episode, which Joan's comments upon my washing-up technique brought to mind! But there is one point that I must make with all possible emphasis. It is that my mother was in no way whatever responsible for my reaction to her attempts to feed me. My reaction was no one's responsibility but my own. It was an expression of a facet of my character, for which I alone was responsible. I am not yet free of the trait, but I can usually recognise when it is about to determine my reaction to a situation, in time to choose a different one.

But how can a small baby be held responsible for its character? Let me reiterate: a baby is a *person*, whose soul has a long history during which it has developed its own character traits which it has brought with it into its current life. This is a point that was well illustrated by Tessa, whose use of withholding sex as a weapon was related in Chapter 13.

Life would obviously be impossible if we instantly gave expression to all the anger we felt, and learning not to do so is part of the process through which we all have to go to become so-called civilised members of society. Unfortunately though, this training process is directed principally to teaching us to control our anger. Control is essential, but for two reasons it should not be thought of as more than a halfway house. One reason is that controls are liable to break down; the other is that control may progress to repression. It would be beneficial if more emphasis were placed upon helping people to recognise the Power Merchant trait in their character, and the need to change it.

At the stage of spiritual evolution that the human race as a whole has reached so far, existence would be impossible without the mechanism of repression. Indeed, Freud once remarked that repression is the price of civilisation. But, undeniably, repression can lead to much distress.

In contrast to the person with a minimum of the Power Merchant trait in his character, who can often transform the energy in a disappointment into interest in something else, the person with a marked Power Merchant trait, if he does not express it, is likely to repress a considerable proportion of any anger he feels. But no matter how great the proportion that he represses, what remains in his consciousness is likely to be slow to evaporate and to be expressed in a sulk. It was largely through Joan that I learned how dangerous sulking could be—for the sulker—and the subject merits a section to itself.

Part II: Sulking

Sulking and Depression

What exactly is a sulk?

Interestingly, Reber's *Dictionary of Psychology* does not include the word, so I will offer my own view. I see sulking as the somewhat covert expression of anger that, for one reason or another, the individual chooses not to express overtly.

Throughout one particular day at the beginning of our life together, Joan had been writing steadily in the study while I had been seeing a succession of patients in my consulting-room, on the top floor. I had just shown my last patient out when it occurred to me that it would be fun, after supper, to look at photographs of our recent holiday, which had just been developed.

However, as I came into the kitchen, Joan was putting supper on the table and was bursting to tell me about her writing. Her enthusiasm was infectious and I forgot about the photographs until supper was almost finished. I was on the point of suggesting that we look at them when Joan announced that she was very tired and intended to have a bath and go to bed. I was disappointed and responded, rather coldly, 'Of course if you're tired you must have a bath and go to bed.' And off she went.

And off I went too! Through the other door, the one that opened into the study. I sat down at my desk and within minutes a mood of dejection had enveloped me like a black cloud. 'What a life!' I said to myself. 'No one cares what I might want to do'—and a great deal more in a similar vein of self-pity.

Some twenty minutes later, having had her bath, Joan came back into the kitchen. 'I'm going to make myself a cup of tea,' she called to me brightly, through the doorway. 'Would you like one?'

'No, thank you,' I replied, in a voice as flat as I could make it. 'If I wish for a cup of tea I am quite capable of making it for myself.' Joan disappeared with her tea, back into the bedroom...and the cloud of my 'depression' grew thicker and blacker. Somewhere about half past ten I was thinking: 'And why should I share her bed anyway...I'll make myself a bed upstairs'. However, by about eleven, this had changed to: 'Oh what the hell! I can't be bothered to make a bed upstairs...I suppose I'll have to sleep in our bed...' And I made my way to our bedroom.

What did I find there? I found Joan asleep. Asleep! Sleeping peacefully and happily!

Well! I knew there was something wrong about THAT! Nevertheless, I started to undress as quietly as I could. It was, of course, entirely by accident, that I dropped a shoe—and the noise woke Joan up.

Instantly she bounced up in bed, exclaiming, 'Darling! I've just had a rivet tingly interesting dream!' And without so much as enquiring solicitously whether I was tired and would prefer to hear about it in the morning, she proceeded forthwith to relate it! And it really was an interesting dream; so interesting that I could not help myself from being drawn into a discussion of it. By the time I was ready to get into bed, the 'depression' had almost completely disappeared.

I was about to get into bed on my side when I checked. I thought to myself: 'You have been a real so-and-so this evening, the least you can do is to apologise.' So I walked round to her side of the bed and said: 'I'm sorry...I was not very nice to you this evening.'

'Oh, weren't you?' Joan responded. 'I never noticed!' And then she did a double take. 'My God!' she exclaimed, 'when I said that your jaw dropped! You were doing it ON PURPOSE!'

Once more she had hit a nail on the head. I had not realised it fully at the time, but now that Joan had charged me with it, it was impossible to deny. Indeed I had done it—that is, brought on my mood—on purpose. I had in fact been sulking. Withdrawing—which is what I had been doing—is a frequent feature of sulking, and I had intended it to hurt. *That* was why Joan had had no business to be sleeping so peacefully!

The insight I gained from that small episode extended rapidly—and usefully. I had frequently suffered from periods of what I used to think of as a 'depression'. I put the word in inverted commas for two reasons. One reason is because, compared to a state of true clinical depression, my states were trivial. They had never been severe enough to prevent me from working. But I have experienced, albeit mildly, many of the feelings common to people who are in a genuine depression. These include, for instance—in addition to feelings of gloom, worthlessness and a generalised 'what's the use?'—the feeling that people are looking at one strangely or talking about one, and that a headline one glimpses in a newspaper is really directed at oneself. The other reason for the inverted commas will appear later.

I was able to recall some of these episodes in sufficient detail for us to examine them, and it became clear that in each case the 'depression' had been a reaction to being thwarted, to not getting my own way about something. I had been angered but too ashamed to admit it to anyone else and even, fully, to myself. And a day or two later a 'depression' had started. Looking back upon them, these 'depressions' indeed seem to have been nothing but delayed and protracted sulks. Had Joan's dream not been so interesting as virtually to drag me out it, that particular sulk could very well have progressed to another of my 'depressions'.

This experience led to the discovery of a tactic some patients have found useful if they have been 'depressed' for a couple of days, or even longer. One simply reviews the forty-eight hours before the 'depression' started—it seems one seldom needs to go further back than that—looking for an episode in which, being as honest with oneself as one can, one is less than proud of the way in which one has behaved. When one finds it, it usually appears that either the anger was justifiable, but for some reason—no matter what—one did not protest as one should have done, and one is ashamed on that score; or it was unjustifiable and one was too ashamed to admit fully, even to oneself, that one had felt it. In either case, one's self-respect is liable to be bruised, sometimes rather painfully, but one's 'depression' will quite probably cease. I was soon to experience for myself how effective this measure can be.

On a certain occasion, I realised I had been increasingly moody for several days and was wondering why. Suddenly there came to mind the memory of an incident that had occurred a few days previously. Joan had casually presented Johnny, her four-year-old grandson—an enchanting child by the way—with a particularly luscious looking pear whose ripening I had been monitoring very carefully. I had felt anger but had quickly suppressed it because I had been too ashamed to admit, even to myself, that I could be so mean as to grudge the kid a pear. With that recollection and insight my moodiness disappeared. It had, in fact, been nothing but a sulk. Experience of other occasions suggests it might otherwise have progressed to one of my 'depressions'.

It can happen that the relief, which follows the discovery of the particular incident that precipitated the sulk, is short-lived. The moodiness returns. When this happens, it is probable that the incident that came to mind was, in effect, only a trigger. It may then be necessary to find what it was that the trigger caused to explode, and if the symptoms are sufficiently severe, this may require professional help. In fact, there is a rider to this episode of the pear.

My moodiness had not returned, but Joan was astute enough to suggest I try to discover why an established psychiatrist in his mid-forties should have been so upset by such a triviality as the loss of a pear, no matter how luscious its appearance. It did not take me long to discover that the loss of the pear was the origin of only part of the anger in the sulk.

If Joan had asked me if I would mind her giving the pear to Johnny, I think I would have been disappointed for a minute at losing it but I know I would have answered: 'Of course not'. In fact, she had given the pear to Johnny *without any reference to me whatever,* and I resented this on two counts. In the first place, it was, to say the least, somewhat discourteous. I think I should have voiced the indignation I had felt, and I had in fact been reproaching myself for my weakness in not so doing. Secondly, that particular instance of discourtesy—in which I had been ignored—had stepped on one of the toes of my Power Merchant trait. It was anger coming from the Power Merchant trait that was the fundamental origin of much of the energy in the sulk.

This insight led to the other reason that I have put my states of 'depression' in inverted commas. If there is a basic difference between a sulk and even a mild clinical depression, it lies in the origin of the two conditions. The energy in a sulk is the energy in anger directed at some person or thing outside oneself, but not expressed as such. A true depression, by contrast, is essentially due to anger that is imprisoned in the unconscious and therefore cannot be directed against anyone but the self.

Depression is a form of illness that is very widespread and can cause endless misery. The distress of a person in the grip of a severe depression may cause him to take his own life. Even now, the condition is by no means fully understood. What I think is clear is that in certain cases of depression chemical changes have occurred in the way that cells in the brain conduct their business. I'm sure it can happen that sometimes, if the true origin of the unconscious anger can be brought to the patient's consciousness, these changes in the chemistry of the function of the brain cells can right themselves. Often enough though, the help of antidepressants may be required, and in these cases no psychotherapy is likely to be effective until the medication has started to take effect.

I feel certain that the psychological element in a depression is anger. That is a widely held concept that was brought home vividly to me by what I think of as The-Breast-But-No-Milk case, which I described in the first chapter. In that case, the reader will recall, an infant was less than three weeks old when it experienced the anger that, it believed, had caused her mother to vanish.

Belief in reincarnation makes it possible to postulate that the true origin of the anger causing a depression may sometimes be found in the events of a former lifetime. When the anger originally arose it had an effect that so frightened the individual experiencing the anger that thereafter a large proportion of any anger evoked was blocked from reaching the individual's consciousness. The major portion remained imprisoned in his unconscious and, turning upon himself, caused the depression. When reincarnation gains credence by the medical profession as a whole, I'm sure that improved means of access to former lifetimes will be discovered, and the answer to a number of cases of depression, amongst other medical problems, will come to light.

The next section will be concerned with accounts of three patients whose symptoms, though originating from a sulk arising out of the Power Merchant trait, differ from anything we have encountered thus far.

Sulking and Cutting Off One's Own Nose

Cream Cakes and Zoos

Alec, a man in his forties, was suffering from a depression that was manifesting itself in an unusual way. He started every session by telling me that I was being of no help to him, implying that he was regretting he had taken the trouble involved in coming from Los Angeles to see me. One day I realised he was getting a perverse kind of satisfaction out of feeling justified in saying this, and I felt prompted to concoct a little story. It rang the bell for him immediately and, as other patients have also identified with it, I feel it is worth recording. I have an uneasy feeling that the episode is essentially autobiographical, but I have not been able to put my finger right on it. The nearest I can get to it is an occasion when, as a very small boy, my mother was giving me my tea in the nursery and she either did or refused to do something which caused me to exclaim, 'Mummy! I don't think you are a BIT pretty.' This arrow was to prove to have been not only shrewdly directed but also barbed because my poor mother was never able to forget the incident.

The story I concocted also concerns a small boy, aged about four years, having tea in the nursery with his mother. The moment comes when he announces: 'Want another cream cake.' 'No, darling,' his mother replies, 'you have already had three and if you have another you will be sick.' The child has learned that it does not pay to make a rude noise at his mother or even to put his tongue out at her, so his jaw just sets with the corners of his mouth turned firmly downwards. His mother does not want him to be hungry so she offers, in succession, another piece of bread and butter? With jam on it? A chocolate biscuit? Each offer is declined with a curt, 'No.'

His mother is wondering how she is ever going to get a smile back on the little beast's face when she has what strikes her as a brilliant idea. 'Darling!' she says, 'you love going to the Zoo! Let's all go to the Zoo tomorrow afternoon!' 'No,' comes the response. 'Don't like the Zoo.' On this note teatime ends and in due course bedtime arrives, but not before the child has sensed that if he persists in saying no for long enough, he can evoke a gratifying degree of anxiety in those around him.

Next day, as lunch is coming to an end, Mother says brightly, 'Now Darling, off we all go to the Zoo!' 'No. Don't like the Zoo' comes the response yet again, and this time it precipitates a potentially difficult situation. His mother now has the choice of either dragging the sulking child with her and risking at some stage a public tantrum, or of cancelling the expedition altogether, to the dismay of the other members of the family. In the latter event the child may well realise that in his sulk he has indeed a very powerful weapon. But suppose Mum can call upon a baby-sitter! In that case she may decide to say: 'Very well darling, we will all go to the Zoo and you can stay at home with Nanny.' Whereupon they all prepare to leave.

Unless, at the very last moment, the child says he really would like to go with them after all, he has dug himself into a corner. Either he has to admit to himself that he has behaved very stupidly and done himself out of a treat that he really would have enjoyed very much; or...he has to convince himself that he *genuinely* does not like the Zoo.

If he has come into life as a thoroughgoing Power Merchant, his false pride will probably make it impossible for him to admit the defeat implicit in the first course so, perforce, he adopts the second. In effect, at an unconscious level in his mind he *forms the wish not to enjoy the Zoo*. The result of this wish will be that he grows up, genuinely—so far as he knows—not liking the Zoo. In due course, he will produce a variety of plausible explanations for his aversion to the Zoo, and indeed to zoos in general. He does not like to see wild animals in cages, for instance. However, they will all be rationalisations, covering the real truth that has long since been unconscious. This is that his dislike of zoos started as a means of enabling him to continue to avoid admitting defeat over the matter of cream cakes when he was four years old.

But his real problem was still more fundamental. It was the Power Merchant trait in his character. This character trait had caused him to see his mother's refusal to allow him another cream cake as a hostile act on her part, thus casting her—or more probably by that age, confirming her—in the role, sometimes, of an adversary. From that point, largely at an unconscious level, it became essential that he refuse to admit defeat because he had to maintain his superior position. This is what the battle was *really about*; the cream cakes had been merely a casus belli. It was only his Power Merchant trait that had prevented him from seeing the denial of another cream cake as no more than a disappointment. To repeat an analogy, it would have been like an unremarkable, but easily digested, meal that would have been swallowed and soon forgotten.

According to the story, the pleasure of zoos—such as it may be—was all that his Power Merchant trait had cost that person. However, Alec recognised immediately how closely the story applied to him. All his life, he realised, he had taken a malicious delight in denying other people the pleasure of knowing they had pleased him. But the only way of ensuring that he gained his pleasure was by making certain that he genuinely did not enjoy something that had been provided by someone else. Hence he had formed the wish, which until this particular session had been largely unconscious: 'I wish *not* to enjoy anything provided by someone else.'

The effect of the wish was, of course, to produce a conscious 'I cannot...' or 'I do not...' And the inability to enjoy anything provided by someone else had been a feature of his life long before he became obviously depressed. By the next day he had begun to realise of just how much pleasure in life he had cheated himself; and the realisation was saddening to him. To his credit, he was able to free himself of his false pride, accept the sadness—and choose to enjoy life henceforth.

Alec's sulk reaction had cost him dear. Nonetheless, it had brought him into less real danger than did Mark's, whose case we will look at next.

Mark: An Acute Mental Illness

Mark was a young man of 22 when we first met. Halfway though his final term at University he had developed an acute mental illness. Convinced he could fly, it was with difficulty that his family had restrained him from launching himself off the balcony of his home. He had then eluded them, got into the family car that happened to be standing outside the house and driven off. He was convinced that he had divine protection, permitting him to drive through red traffic lights. However, any feeling of protection he may have had of that nature was not shared by the police and, fortunately, before he had damaged anyone else or himself he was safely in a mental hospital. Within a couple of weeks Mark's acute symptoms had subsided and shortly thereafter he was discharged into our care for psychotherapy.

It was several weeks before it emerged that his problems arose from his almost lifelong determination, at an unconscious level, to cause woe to everyone in authority, particularly his parents and schoolteachers. Again and again he would lead them to expect great things from him and then, at the last moment, in one way or another, on one pretext or another, he would let everybody down. He was sufficiently astute to do just enough in the way of passing exams to avoid being thrown out, and he used his considerable power to charm so successfully that he avoided all retribution. However, as his last term at University was coming to an end, he realised that he was inescapably going to have to face *Life*, and that he had neglected to equip himself to do so. This was the situation that had precipitated his illness. He could not go backwards, he feared to go forwards and only one direction was left—upwards. This, metaphorically, was the direction he took.

So expert was Mark at giving every appearance of sincerity of intention and of regret at failure that it was several months before I tumbled to the fact that—not entirely at an unconscious level—he was now using all his ploys against Joan and me. An unconscious that was able to hoodwink Joan for so long would merit a place in a psychological museum—if such an immaterial establishment existed on our level of density.

However, a day came when his explanation of his failure to keep a certain promise strained our credulity beyond breaking point, whereupon the whole pattern became clear. I have since wondered whether, in cricketing parlance, his unconscious did not give his wicket away! I suppose a footballer might have called it a deliberate own goal; but be that as it may, in a long talk I was able to show Mark how he had repeatedly led us to believe we could rely upon him for some service, and he had then let us down. Mark soon appreciated the truth of what I was telling him and was able to relate it to the whole of his life up to that moment. I think it is no exaggeration to say that our talk that afternoon brought an end to his illness.

At times during his therapy Mark had recovered fragments of former life-times and they had repeatedly revealed a large element of Power Merchant in his character. This trait was unquestionably the real origin of his troubles. A significant occasion which had mobilised the trait early in his present lifetime came to light when—as an afterthought, his real therapy having finished—he mentioned that he had a fear of water. Although he was a powerful swimmer, he had to overcome this fear before he could enter even a small swimming pool. He hoped I might be able to free him of it.

I helped him to shift his level as I had often done before, and told him that in a few moments he would be aware of something that would take us a step towards the origin of his fear of water. Almost immediately he found himself back as a small boy at the seaside. He was happily building a sandcastle when his father swooped down upon him, scooped him up and marched into the sea with him. In water that was no more than ankle-deep he set Mark down.

Mark felt furious with his father for inflicting upon him what he saw as such indignities, but of course his father was much too big to attack. Providentially, from Mark's point of view, a wavelet came along at that moment broke against Mark's legs and splashed him. It would have been too humiliating to have to admit that he feared the retribution of a mere father if he were to express anger against him, but there was nothing humiliating about being afraid of THE SEA! Mark immediately displaced the anger with his father, and his fear of what the consequences might be if he were to express it, upon the sea. From there, the fear had spread to water in general. After all the work we had done, ten minutes sufficed to free Mark of his phobia of water.

Mark made the best possible use of his therapy. He first became a schoolmaster, for an excellent reason. As he explained: 'There is no ploy for taking the mickey out of parents and schoolteachers that I cannot spot a mile away, and I can convince any kid who tries one of them that in order to spite other peoples' faces he is really cutting off his own nose; and that in the long run the policy does not pay.' Mark went on to gain a Ph.D., and is now a successful therapist.

Mark's lifelong sulk had run him into danger on two counts. Firstly, for a short time during the initial phase of his illness he was a menace to himself and to everyone else. Secondly, while the outlook for recovery from an acute illness such as he developed is good, one can never be sure of recovery until it has occurred.

Homosexuality

I have included the next case in this chapter because the origin of the condition, homosexuality, seemed to be anger that had been evoked—albeit it in a former lifetime—and not fully expressed. It had remained in the soul until the current lifetime when it had found expression, but in such a heavily disguised form, that the condition could be described as a form of sulk, though a very unusual one.

Nigel was homosexual. He was a good looking, athletically built and very competent man in his mid-forties. He was consulting me because of his depression. On the face of it, he was depressed because his feelings, which were predominantly of sexual desire, for a man whom we may call Douglas were not being reciprocated. However, this did not seem to me an adequate explanation of the severity of his state. I suggested, therefore, that he allow me to hypnotise him with a view to trying to discover if there were more to his state than appeared on the surface. Over several sessions an interesting story unfolded. It started with a lifetime when Nigel had been a young woman who fancied her charm and had set her cap at a young man of considerably higher social status, who eventually jilted her. In rage, she took her own life. In a later life—possibly the next one—she was in domestic service. Once more she was a very good-looking girl and she fancied her chances of seducing the master of the house and improving her status. Again she was totally unsuccessful. It is not clear how that life ended but what is clear is that she became violently resentful of and vengeful towards both men and women.

In the present life, this soul was born into a thoroughly adequate male body. However, the soul was carrying the bitterness and desire for revenge it had developed whilst in female bodies. Feelings of sexual attraction towards a person can be a cover for intense aggression, and this, it seemed, was at least a powerful factor in this man's attraction to members of his own sex. Once this point was on the surface, it soon became clear that the cause of his depression was less unrequited love than unconscious anger against the man who was the present object of his feelings because he was not reciprocating them. Therapy did not change Nigel's sexual orientation, but he now has a non-sexual friendship with Douglas, which—I believe—enriches the life of both of them. I am of course aware that the story of this case cannot be more than—but I think this much is just possible—a minute contribution to the understanding of an exceedingly complex condition. With the possible exception of the subject of the last case, who ended one lifetime in rage, we have not been concerned with the consequences of physical violence on account of loss of temper. We will look at this subject in the next part.

Part III: Uncontrolled Anger

The quotation from *Winged Pharaoh* which features in the opening paragraph of this chapter will bear repetition: 'Sekeeta, remember anger beneath your will is a flail in your hand, but uncontrolled anger is a lash upon your shoulders.'

The consequences of an outburst of uncontrolled anger may be tragic. The victim may be seriously injured, even killed, while his assailant may spend the rest of his life in prison. And there is reason to believe that its effects may not be confined to the same lifetime. The reader will recall the case I described in Chapter 7 of the man who reacted so strongly when I asked him if 'dying with his boots on' meant anything to him. He suffered from periods when he could not move more than a mile from his bed. This patient was convinced that in a former lifetime he had committed a crime of violence and for safety had taken refuge in a monastery. There the area of sanctuary extended for a mile from the altar. He was convinced that in this life he had unconsciously identified his bed with that altar, and I feel no reason to doubt his hunch.

That case, admittedly, was unusual. A more common sequence of events, which may involve more than one subsequent life, is less dramatic but no less distressing. The starting point, as in the case of the patient I have just mentioned, is an incident of violence committed in temper in which the perpetrator seriously injures or even kills someone. He is overcome with remorse and, in effect, he says to himself: 'This anger of mine is extremely dangerous. I must control it.' And it may be that, for a time, his determination to control it is successful. But, eventually, a situation arises in which, if he does not explode in a tantrum again, it is only by the narrowest of margins that he restrains himself from doing so. As a result, he becomes so frightened of his anger that he embarks upon the next step in the sequence.

Now it is as if he says to himself: 'If I *feel* all the anger that something has stirred up in me, I fear that *I may not always be able to control it. I wish, therefore, that out of every ten units of anger that are ever stirred up in me, only one unit will reach my consciousness.*' This mechanism may bring the person a measure of peace of mind, but there will be a price, in the form of side effects. One of them may be that the controls, which are the effect of this wish, may themselves get out of control! They become like brakes that are binding and cannot be released. A vivid illustration of such brakes was provided by a particular young woman whose ability to do anything approaching her potential was severely limited. At one point I asked her to let her mouth fall wide open and emit a resounding 'AAAAHHHHH'. The best she could manage was an 'eee', squeaked through clenched teeth.

As we have seen, common causes of anger are frustration and disappointment. Since wishes of so many kinds are liable to encounter obstacles to their fulfilment and hence possibly to lead to anger, at an unconscious level the individual gradually comes to fear allowing himself to wish for almost anything at all. In effect, he becomes afraid of himself! This fear of himself will determine the way he reacts in so many situations that it becomes a character trait. The reality of reincarnation becomes relevant here because, as a character trait, unless his fear of himself is resolved before he dies, it can become a feature of his character in subsequent lifetimes. The effects it then produces will differ from one person to another.

For instance, a person may project this fear upon the world outside himself. As a result, he becomes a somewhat timid person and may suffer from shyness. If he does not give the outward impression of being shy, inwardly he may nonetheless find it difficult to express himself positively and firmly upon any subject, for fear of offending someone. He may even find it difficult to have a firm opinion about or a marked preference for anything. 'Would you prefer to go to the theatre or to a film?' probably elicits the response: 'I don't mind'. And probably this person, so far as he is aware, genuinely does not mind, for by not minding, by not having strong feelings about anything, he is not vulnerable to disappointment or frustration and, therefore, is in little danger of becoming angry. Moreover he can come down equally convincingly on either side of the fence.

The severity of the effects of any ploy to avoid having to cope with one's anger can range from the barely perceptible, through the mildly embarrassing to the socially agonising. The higher end of the scale is especially likely to be reached when sex comes into the picture. A man with an acute fear of his psychological energy may have virtually insuperable difficulties in making a sexual advance without the help of a wise and perceptive woman. A woman with the corresponding difficulty may suffer from what has been called the 'Stop it—I like it,' syndrome. She finds that at a certain point her sexual arousal or even mere interest always encounters a block that she is unable to overcome.

Another possible side effect of fear of one's psychological energy is illustrated by the following analogy: 'A young man has inherited a large fortune. However, he lacks confidence in his ability to handle his money wisely. Therefore he puts the capital in the hands of trustees whom he instructs to allow him only a somewhat meagre income. In real terms he is keeping the major part of his psychological energy imprisoned under guard in his unconscious.

'This young man is talented in many directions, so no matter what ladder he decides to attempt to climb—by which I mean whatever occupation or form of recreation he chooses to adopt—he makes rapid progress to a certain point almost effortlessly and becomes very enthusiastic. However, the time will inevitably come when, if he is to climb any higher up the ladder, effort will be required. For this he will require more psychological energy.

'One might think that in order to get more energy he has only to instruct his trustees to allow him a larger income; but to be responsible for a larger amount of his psychological energy is just what he fears most. Hence, instead of climbing higher he withdraws his interest from that activity and abandons it. He decides that, after all, it is not what he really wants to do. Alas, this pattern of events is likely to recur with each new ladder, with the result that he eventually settles into a niche which makes far fewer demands upon him than, if only he were able to accept control of his potentials, he would be able to meet. Hence he contributes to the world and gets out of life less than he might do.'

Along an entirely different line: a person who fears his psychological energy may have difficulty when finding himself in a confined space from which the way of exit may involve negotiating even simple obstacles. He may experience feelings on a scale from mild uneasiness to panic. The spectrum of situations that can act as a trigger is broad. It can range from a seat at some function, which is in the middle of a row, to the cabin of a lift. This is one cause of the condition of claustrophobia.

Obviously there are other possible causes. In the course of his long history he may have died when trapped beneath a building which had collapsed on top of him. I have had one patient whose fear of being in any situation from which exit might be obstructed symbolised a repetition of the difficulty she had experienced in getting born. She could barely tolerate being in an underground train, on an escalator or in an aeroplane. Reliving her birth and her survival after the ordeal rid her of her phobias.

If claustrophobia is one side of the coin, the other side is agoraphobia. This condition is usually thought of as a fear of open spaces. A sufferer from this condition may be looking upon his house as a symbol of his unconscious, in which he is keeping a large part of his psychological energy safely imprisoned.

However, the word derives from the Greek 'agora', meaning a market place, and I think there may be an additional twist to the underlying cause of the condition. In a market place there is a possibility of being jostled, of one's territory being invaded, which is another common cause of anger, and hence another reason why the sufferer from agoraphobia may feel safer in his house.

Of course, this condition too might be due to an altogether different kind of cause. The patient might have had a life that ended by being assassinated in a crowd, or by perishing, lost, in a desert.

Rarely, a patient may suffer from both claustrophobia and agoraphobia at the same time. A colleague of mine told me of a patient whose presenting problem was difficulty in satisfying himself that he had securely locked his house up and could safely go to bed. On the one hand he unconsciously wanted assurance that his psychological energy was safely locked up in his unconscious which, for him, was symbolised by his house. On the other, he unconsciously wanted it to be free. Thus he was torn by two conflicting unconscious wishes.

Having securely locked the front door, the unconscious wish to be securely guarded was partially satisfied and, one might have thought, would have been completely satisfied when he had also locked the back door. But by the time he had dealt with the back door, his unconscious wish to be free would have come into play. He would find himself feeling uncertain that he really had locked the front door. By the time he had satisfied himself on that score, doubt about the back door would have arisen. Hence he had to go back and forth checking each door several times before he could tear himself away and go to bed.

It seems that ultimately there is no escape from the need to cope with our Power Merchant trait. Only then shall we gain our ability to choose whether or not we shall react to a situation by feeling angry. We shall explore this topic next.

16   On Forestalling Anger and Changing the Power Merchant

On Forestalling Anger

Studying the Nature of the Material: the Draughty Door

Between the free edge of the door to the room in New York I was using as my consulting room and its frame there was a gap of nearly a centimetre, which permitted an annoying draught. One day when the maintenance engineer of the building was in the apartment, I pointed this out to him and asked him if he could do something about it.

'What would you suggest, Sir?' he enquired.

I replied that I thought a strip of wood fixed to the edge of the door would do the trick. He agreed warmly and then asked how I would fix it. 'Oh—just a few screws,' I replied airily.

'You are aware, Sir,' he asked politely, 'that this door is made of hardened steel?'

Well, of course, I hadn't been aware of any such thing. I had assumed it was made of wood, and in fact I had been on the point of going to the hardware store that was only a block away, purchasing a strip of wood and such tools as I presumed I would need, and setting about the job myself.

Imagination supplied the rest of the story. Having decided exactly where to put the screws, I pictured myself trying to make holes to start the screws off, with the bradawl I had bought for the purpose. Finding it made no impression, I could see myself looking for something to use as a hammer and, with frustration mounting with each futile blow, knocking paint off the door and skin off my thumb but getting no nearer to making a hole in the door. The fantasy stopped short of hurling the tools in rage through the window, to the possible detriment of citizens on the sidewalk below, and the lesson of the whole incident began to clarify itself.

It would have been absurd to lose my temper with the tools. They had never claimed to be effective upon any substance but wood. It would have been equally absurd to become enraged with the door. The door had told me no lies about what it was made of. I had simply omitted to ask it. In truth, the only factor in the drama with whom there would have been any justification for becoming angry was myself, for *having neglected to study the nature of the material!* But having made that mistake, the sensible thing would have been to use the energy that became the substance of my rage to return to the shop and try to persuade its owner to take back such tools and materials as I had not used.

Incidentally, I might then have done what I should have done in the first place: bought a roll of adhesive-backed rubber draft-excluder. Why I had not thought of that before I have no idea, but I am glad the thought did not occur to me because the 'Draughty Door' became the basis of a most useful thera-peutic ploy. Since that occasion, when the subject of frustration and anger has arisen in the course of therapy, I have often asked my patient to imagine that he has kindly consented to fix a bolt on my consulting-room door. I explain that I have neither bolt nor tools of any kind but that down the road is a hardware store where he would be able to get anything he wanted. Finally, I ask him to tell me how, step by step, he would undertake the job.

Gratifyingly often the patient has started off: 'Well, I would go down to the shop and...' Those words would be enough to set me metaphorically rubbing my hands in gleeful if unprofessional anticipation of the moment when I would be able to say to him: 'And that is where you find yourself in trouble. You have brought back tools for working in wood, but that door is made of hardened steel, as it would have told you if you had asked it!'

STUDY THE NATURE OF THE MATERIAL! This is possibly the most useful single piece of advice I can offer anyone. If a do-it-yourself enthusiast who is planning to hang a picture starts by examining the wall, he will learn first whether the wall is strong enough to hold a picture as heavy as the one he wants to hang on it. He will learn too what tools he will need and roughly how much time. For a wooden wall and a light picture, a hammer, a small nail and thirty seconds may well be enough. A concrete wall, though, may require a drill, a rawlplug and screw and—to allow for the possibility of encountering snags—at least half an hour. Armed with this knowledge and equipment he will approach the job in the appropriate frame of mind, and the likelihood of frustration and anger will be minimal.

And it is not only the handyman who can profit from this advice. In another direction, study the nature of that small animal curled up in a corner of its cage before you extend a hand to stroke its invitingly silky fur and you may be avoiding the loss of half a finger to a ferret.

The pupil whom the teacher finds exasperatingly slow to learn might be so short-sighted that he has never been able to see the blackboard clearly, or so hard of hearing that he hears but a fraction of what his teacher is saying. Likewise, the employee who repeatedly makes the same stupid mistake may be concealing, behind an adequate social front, a significant difficulty in learning. The applications are endless, but they can all save you the woe that follows an attempt, in one form or another, *to wring a drink out of an empty bottle.*

'But,' I seem to hear a reader exclaiming, 'what in the world has this to do with reincarnation?' Simply this: if studying the nature of the material has become a character trait, it is likely to be part of the soul when it next takes on a physical body. That individual, therefore, is likely to avoid pitfalls into which anger may lead him, and will start off with some of the basic equipment he will need to become a thoroughly competent person.

On Changing the Power Merchant

The problem of anyone who seeks help from psychotherapy may, of course, be a consequence of some trauma that befell him, either earlier in his present life or during a former lifetime. My experience suggests, however, that far more often than not, his presenting symptom should be understood as a bleep from what I think of as his in-built evolutionary compass, indicating that he has departed from what I would term his true evolutionary course; and the factor most frequently responsible for causing him to lose his way is the Power Merchant trait in his character. The symptom is only a manifestation of the problem, *not the problem itself.* Having recognised that this is the case with his present patient, the goal of the therapist is clear: it is *to inspire the patient to choose* to work towards changing his Power Merchant trait.

I do not think it is possible for one person to change another, so to reach this goal the therapist needs to enable the patient *to see for himself* that his Power Merchant trait is indeed closely related to his symptom. Once the patient has really seen and grasped this fact, he is usually anxious to know if the trait can be changed. He will be thankful to learn that he can indeed start changing the trait himself, once he has formed the single-minded, wholehearted wish to do so.

The difficulties the therapist may encounter in inspiring this wish in his patient will vary from one patient to another. Any suggestion that a person would do well to change an aspect of himself, no matter how gently it is presented, cannot avoid at least implying criticism of his present state. For this reason it is advisable for the therapist first to remind the patient of his good points and to emphasise them, for no one relishes being criticised. While this is true of all of us, it is particularly true of someone who is heavily laden with false pride. Such a person is liable to interpret criticism as having tomatoes thrown at him, and he may be too concerned with dodging them or catching them in order to throw them back to make good use of any of them.

I'm sure this is one reason that the Claude and Albert story, adjusted as necessary to suit the therapeutic situation, has proved so useful. Since no finger has been pointed which might evoke a defensive reaction, the patient has almost always been able to relate to the story, of which the explanation of the hole in the bucket and the process of becoming trapped in the vicious circle are essential parts.

I think another reason why the Claude and Albert story is helpful is because the patient is often seeking psychotherapy in the expectation that the therapist himself will do what is necessary to relieve the patient's distress. He is thus not expecting to hear that relief will depend upon his doing something about himself that no one can do for him. Fairly painlessly, the Claude and Albert story, when it is appropriate, tends to set him thinking in the right direction.

Once the patient has genuinely grasped the link between his symptom and the character trait, he can start to change the latter as quickly as, by turning his car around, a man driving south can become a man driving north. The cases of Rick-of-the-Caribbean in Chapter 11 and of Tessa, the-battler-for-dominance in Chapter 13 illustrate the point.

But a driver on a motorway may have to continue for a considerable distance before it is possible for him to change his direction. I think it is more useful, therefore, for each of us to think of himself as the pilot of his own aircraft. Such a pilot is free to change his direction at any moment, no matter how long he has been following a mistaken compass point. He will only be held up if something is jamming his steering mechanism. Such a 'something' is likely to be false pride, an old sense of guilt, a grudge or desire for revenge, all of which may stem from a former lifetime. Finding the 'something' may require professional help. Having found it, the matter of forgiveness may well arise.

Forgiveness

Just what does it mean, to forgive? As always, the Concise Oxford Dictionary is both concise and helpful. Under the word 'forgive' we find, amongst other things: remit, let off, *cease to resent,* pardon…(Italics mine.)

However, without amending the definition or encroaching far upon the territory of philosophers and theologians, I would like to offer some thoughts about the significance of forgiveness, based upon my experience as a therapist.

If someone has cheated one or done one an injury, it is all too easy to resent both the person and the act, and to want at least to get one's own back. If that is not possible, one would like some form of revenge. The Power Merchant trait will cause a person to have such feelings particularly strongly. The problem here is that in harbouring such feelings towards someone, one is *binding oneself to that person.* As a result, the part of one's totality thus linked to the person is anchored, and cannot evolve. If the grudge or resentment arose during the present life, it can happen that it becomes the centre around which a large proportion of one's thoughts, one's feelings as well as one's decisions and activities revolve. If one dies still harbouring such feelings, then that part of one may become 'stuck as a ghost', and—as we have seen—a ghost can be responsible for a variety of problems. Hence, at this level, to forgive is *to free oneself.*

Still on this level, it matters not whether the one who has injured you knows or cares what he has done, or whether or not he expresses any regret or apologises. *It is not for his benefit that you are forgiving him but for your own*—to set yourself free. At this level, I think forgiveness entails no more—and heaven knows, this can be difficult enough—than to cease to harbour resentment or any desire for revenge.

But suppose what the offending one has just done to one is evil and, furthermore, there is every indication that, given the chance, he will repeat his act? What should one's attitude be in this case?

To do nothing would be to condone what he has done, thus encouraging him—in effect, giving him more energy—to go still further off his evolutionary beam, and that can surely not be right from any point of view. It must surely be permissible to do what may be necessary to protect oneself, even if that involves taking the steps that will lead to the offender being imprisoned. But I think one needs to aim at taking them *without feelings of malice or of getting revenge.* No easy task, but I don't believe it has ever been suggested anywhere by anyone that spiritual evolution is easy!

However, I think there is another level of forgiveness.

To the extent that one loves a person, that person is, in a very real sense, a part of oneself. If that person behaves in some way of which one would never have thought him capable and which one finds totally unacceptable, one may then feel, 'You are no longer a friend of mine, no longer a part of me.' If, in due course, that person convinces you that he fully understands what he has done and everything it implies, that he genuinely regrets it profoundly and is sincerely resolved to try never to repeat that act, then, I feel one would be justified in forgiving him, in the sense of taking him back as a part of oneself.

However, it is not only one's fellow creatures one may sometimes have to forgive. It may sometimes be oneself. A case founded on guilt was that of Robert-of-the-painful-legs, which I described in Chapter 8. On the face of it, the origin of the pain was the injury to his neck he sustained when, as a teenager, simply to show off, he had dived into a swimming pool at the shallow end and hit his head on the bottom.

But we soon found that this act of showing off symbolically repeated an occasion, many lifetimes ago when, again through showing off, he sustained crippling injuries which had rendered him a burden upon his wife until he died. His guilt about this long-ago act of showing off, *for which he had never forgiven himself,* had caused a ghost to be left, and it was energy coming from the ghost that was the real origin of the pain in his legs. When I was able to convince him that it was in the nature of young men sometimes to do things that were frankly stupid, he was able to forgive the ghost, to take it back into himself. Thereupon the pain in his legs ceased abruptly and had not returned in ten years.

Your Business—My Business

In connection with the theme of forgiveness, I acquired one day a fragment of insight, the value of which was proved by an incident that occurred shortly afterwards. Since then, it has been valuable so often that I will pass it on. It also illustrates the point that there is no single answer to changing the Power Merchant.

The fragment of insight, which will not be novel to most people, was simply that *what I do is my business and what you do is your business.* For instance, if you choose to be rude to me, that is your business. Your rudeness may diminish you but it will in no way affect my essential stature. Similarly, my response is my business, and while it may diminish—or even, possibly enhance—mine, it cannot affect your real stature.

Within a week of gaining this particular grain of understanding, an occasion arose which confirmed its value. Joan and I happened to be shopping near Piccadilly Circus when, with a certain movement, she wricked her back, and we needed to take a taxi back to where we lived, in Highgate. In the course of the journey it became necessary to ask the driver to be kind enough to drive more slowly, as the jolting was hurting Joan's back. His response was an extremely angry: 'Don't you *ever* say please?' Nevertheless he slowed down considerably.

Some ten minutes later I had to point out to him, which I did as courteously as I possibly could, that he had not taken us to Highgate, which one can think of as lying some six miles to the due north of Piccadilly, but to Hampstead, which is roughly the same distance but to the north west. His response, when he saw that I was right, was unprintable, but admittedly he slammed down his flag, which cancelled the fare for the whole trip, performed a U-turn and drove us to our apartment.

In contrast to most taxi-drivers, whom I have found polite and most helpful, this driver had been outrageously rude to me, in front of my wife, on two occasions. Strangely, however, I did not feel any indignation whatever. Instead, I found myself tuning-in to him, and I realised he was very distressed about something. Hence, when at length he dropped us at our house, I first handed him what I had reckoned was the right fare, with a bit on top. Then I said to him, 'I'm sure you do not usually speak to your passengers in that way: I sense you are very upset about something. I happen to be a doctor, can I do anything to help?' His reply was, 'I'm sorry, Guv. The fact is that my wife was taken to hospital this morning as an emergency. I was about to go to visit her when you flagged me. By law, I couldn't turn you down, and this journey to Highgate has taken me more than an hour out of my way.'

The manner in which this driver had spoken to me was his business. The story he told me was—I believe—the truth, but even if were not, it was still his business. And I hope that my response, which was entirely my business, was one that contributed a mite to the sum of goodwill in the world, rather than one that would have added to the hostility, of which there is more than enough already. If, on the other hand, he went away feeling I was just a gullible mug, that too would have been his business...

I was particularly pleased with my reaction because it had contained no element that *needed to be controlled.* I felt, 'I really have got this Power Merchant problem licked!' However, there was only a brief interlude before such pride as I was taking in the encounter with the taxi-driver had its first fall.

Just a few weeks later, by which time we had started to live in France, a young woman happened to descend upon us, and she remained with us for some months. She irritated me as few people have ever done. I was familiar with the maxim: *'If you find yourself pointing a finger at someone and thinking, "I do not like you because...", it is always worth looking at where the other three fingers are pointing.'* But I still could not understand why she had this effect upon me. Eventually I asked Joan if she could explain it.

'Oh Darling,' Joan began—an opening that should have warned me to be ready to duck—'don't you know? She parades around openly the bossy little beast that *you try to pretend that you are not!*'

In any case, the warning would have come too late, so swiftly and accurately did Joan's reply find its mark. The fact is that this young lady gave the impression of being completely confident that she knew everything about everything, including subjects upon which I felt I was the person in the house who was supposed to know the answers. In short, she made me feel she was taking over my position. Invading my territory, in fact!

Why had I not been able to see the explanation of her effect upon me for myself? The reason is that the barrier we create to protect our consciousness from being invaded by feelings that might cause us more than 'x' units of distress—notably feelings of shame and guilt—prevent even a relatively experienced psychiatrist from seeing behind his own psychological ears. This barrier thus prevents us from seeing those very aspects of ourselves we would do well to look at. In effect, it cuts us off, to a certain extent, from our evolutionary compass.

Since it has this effect on everyone, it may be partly responsible for the fact that awareness of the menace that the Power Merchant trait can be has not become part of our culture. Indeed, behaviour that stems from it may often be not only accepted but also encouraged by Society. It is rather rarely that, with the dangers of the Power Merchant in mind, a person is invited seriously to explore to the limit the implications of something he is feeling, intending or doing. And, so far as I know, the subject has not entered textbooks on psychiatry.

The effect of the insight Joan had given me was striking. I doubt if this lady would ever have become my favourite companion, but no longer did she irritate me. What she did was her business... Had I not experienced the irritation she aroused in me, I might well have suffered from a depression during her stay. This would probably have been an indication that I had fallen into the trap, which—again with acknowledgements to Joan—I call *'Trying to be like Christ too soon'*. This simply means trying to give oneself the impression that one's character is nobler than it really is by preventing feelings which one would deem unworthy from coming to one's consciousness.

To react to someone's behaviour with anger may well indicate a shortcoming within oneself, but one gains no marks for trying to conceal from oneself the fact that one has been angered. If one makes a habit of repressing such feelings, one is storing up for oneself future trouble of some kind. On the other hand, by admitting to oneself that one has feelings which one deplores, one has taken the first step towards understanding the factor within oneself which gave rise to them, and hence towards being able to do something about it.

But to forestall a ghost based on anger being formed, it is necessary, especially before one dies, to ensure that one is not harbouring a grudge or a desire for revenge against anyone. Such a grudge or such a desire acts like a rope that is binding one to that person, and may continue to bind one after death... Hence, before one dies, it is essential to drop one's end of the rope. During one's life, one must not be drawn into, or permit to continue what, in effect, is a game of psychological Ping-Pong, seeking to have the last word or to force from the other person an apology or an admission that he was in the wrong. Recognition that what is really involved is one's false pride, based on one's Power Merchant trait, may make this step easier.

The success of any course of therapy depends upon several factors. For instance, it is important that the form of therapy chosen is the most effective for the patient's condition. It is, of course, also essential that the patient and therapist are compatible and able to form an effective working relationship. Not every patient is suited to every therapist any more than every therapist is suited to every patient.

Patients vary in the extent to which they are able to be honest, even with their therapist, and in their ability to accept insights that are disagreeable, no matter how gently they are presented or reached. They all want help, but some do not want the insights that would help them.

It is perhaps worth mentioning here that there can be what one can think of as two levels of insight. There is insight at the level of the head, and also insight at the level of the heart. More than once, months—even a year—after therapy had ended, I have received a letter saying, in effect: 'When I left you I thought I had understood all that I had learned from you. Now, I *really* understand. Thank you'.

Another very important factor is the attitude of the relatives. It may not always be easy for them if one member of the family is involved in deep psychotherapy. In the course of the therapy, the patient's behaviour at home may come to differ from what the family has been used to. At times, the therapy may release and make available to the patient energy that, hitherto, has been imprisoned in his unconscious. I recall a husband who became so outraged when his wife ceased to be the submissive person that suited him, and began to stand up for herself, that he refused to allow her to continue with her therapy.

Not infrequently, a young patient has been far unhappier with his life at home than the parents had realised. This might have been because they had never really bothered to listen to him, or had been too authoritarian to allow him to express himself. When he finds in his therapist someone who not only listens but is even interested in what he has to say, he is—not surprisingly—overjoyed. At home it does not occur to him to conceal his happiness. From my own experience I know that some parents do not take kindly to seeing their offspring blossom under somebody else's care.

Before closing this chapter I must repair an important omission. I feel I may have given the impression that I believe all the energy to initiate and persist with the process of changing the Power Merchant trait must come from the patient himself. In fact, that is neither what I believe nor had intended to convey. Each lifetime is an opportunity for the soul to evolve towards the state when it will not need to incarnate again. The core of this process of evolution is to increase one's capacity for loving, and no request to the 'Upstairs' people for help to this end ever goes unanswered. I am so certain that this is true that I frequently advise a patient to pray.

Occasionally this advice meets with resistance. The patient 'does not believe in it'. My response is to indicate the telephone. I point out that if he never dialled a number because he did not believe he would ever really hear a voice answering him, he most certainly never would hear such a voice. I suggest that prayer, anyway in one of its aspects, works on a somewhat similar principle—and urge him to try it.

17   *About Life in the Womb*

A word is called for to explain why this and the next chapter did not appear earlier in the book. The reason is that some of the material therein is concerned with the Power Merchant trait, and therefore to say something about that subject and its widespread influence was an essential preliminary.

I have sometimes wondered whether it was something within me that was responsible for my unshakeable certainty that the apparent regressions, first of Clare (of the Breast-But-No-Milk case), to the age of three weeks, and then of subsequent patients to birth, the prenatal period and ultimately to conception were indeed what they appeared to be. Perhaps it was. On the other hand, I feel sure that anyone who had been looking over my shoulder throughout the therapy of these cases would have found himself forced to the same conclusions.

Nevertheless, it is a matter of considerable personal satisfaction that experiences which corroborate, and indeed go far beyond those I encountered and described in the paper I have already mentioned, published in 1953 by the *Journal of Mental Science*, have now been reported by many people, by no means all of them engaged in some branch of medicine. (To anyone who is interested in pursuing this topic, I would recommend *The Secret Life Of The Unborn Child* by Dr Thomas Vernon and John Kelly, containing, as it does, references to other relevant works.)

After 1950 when, for the first time, a patient of mine regressed to the event of her birth, regression to birth and to the period in the womb became commonplace in the course of my treatment of patients by hypnoanalysis. When for instance, a young woman who suffered from asthma reported a dream in which she was a fish that had been pulled out of the river, foul-hooked in its tail, I was not even surprised when she regressed spontaneously to her birth, whereupon it became clear that she was a breech delivery, which means that she arrived bottom first.

Another case comes readily to mind, that of a young man who was terrified of the lightning when a thunderstorm occurred during the night. He regressed spontaneously to his birth and experienced anew the total darkness into which the whole place was suddenly plunged by the power cut that had occurred, just as his head was emerging. The poor kid hadn't known if he was coming or going! Reliving the episode enabled him to review it from an adult standpoint, which banished the horror. However, until Joan Grant came into my life, it had never occurred to me that there could be anything prior to conception.

Of the inferences I drew from my own work on the prenatal period, there are four which I take to be the most important. These are:

1. There is a level or order of consciousness from the very start of and throughout the period in the womb.

2 There is communication between the foetus and some level of the mind of the mother, both telepathically and chemically. This is based on the experience of Marilyn's case which I discussed in Chapter 6.

3. Experiences in the womb and during birth can have a profound effect upon the psychology of the individual for the rest of his life.

4. When experiences before or during birth have later effects that are undesirable, it may be possible—in my experience through the use of hypnotic regression—to relieve these by enabling the patient to bring the relevant memories to his normal waking consciousness and integrate them.

These inferences I still regard as valid. However, I also believed at the time that the character was formed largely by experiences occurring during the period in the womb. This notion was based on the fact that patients who displayed a somewhat paranoid attitude to life as adults, readily suspecting that people were hostile to them, had been equally ready to feel that they were under attack if, for instance, whilst in the womb, they were jolted by the mother sustaining a fall, or suffering a severe attack of vomiting.

Since the idea of any kind of existence before conception had not yet entered my mind, my assumption that experiences in the womb played a major part in forming the character was understandable. That, of course, was one of the notions that were soon dispelled when, with the arrival of Joan in my life, I came to believe in reincarnation. Intrauterine experiences may contribute to the formation of the character but they are by no means the whole story.

How did Joan affect my views?

Early in one's days as a medical student one was taught that conception consisted of the fertilisation of an ovum by a sperm, and it had never occurred to me that this might be only one part of the process. However, when Joan told me that there were in fact two stages to conception, the second being the attachment to the fertilised ovum of an incoming soul, I felt intuitively that her understanding was unquestionably correct. Incidentally, this view supported my belief that Marilyn had indeed relived her conception. Joan would have said she had relived the second stage of conception, the arrival at the ovum of the incoming soul.

Next, belief in reincarnation immediately enabled me to see the incoming soul as, in effect, a *person* who was temporarily without a physical body.

This 'person' does not arrive empty-handed. He will, for instance, be bringing a selection from the experiences he had accumulated during previous incarnations and, quite literally, only the Lord knows when they began. I am not qualified to delve deeply into this topic, but I have often wondered just how and when the first mammal acquired the whatever-it-is that sent it off, the moment it was born, in search of its personal milk bar. More immediately, I have wondered too if someone could possibly become a concert pianist or violinist unless his soul had brought in musical experience gained in some former lifetime.

The soul will also be bringing the character it has built up for itself in the course of its long history and, possibly most important of all, it will be bringing the order of consciousness on which it operated between incarnations. This order of consciousness which functions, of course, without any physical apparatus, I refer to as 'discarnate consciousness'. I am also sure that the consciousness of the soul includes a sense of individuality: of 'I-ness'.

With the case of Marilyn in mind, I feel certain that, on making contact with the fertilised ovum, the incoming soul shares its consciousness with that ovum. Thus it is that the individual has consciousness from the very start of his life in the womb. To my mind, this concept renders entirely credible the notion that with the acquisition of consciousness from the incoming soul, the fertilised ovum embarks upon what will become his career as a 'down-here' person.

By means of its discarnate consciousness the soul is aware of the emotional circumstances surrounding its attachment to the fertilised ovum as well as the event of that attachment itself. Since, on becoming so attached, the soul shares its consciousness with the fertilised ovum, the details of his conception become a part of the total experience of the individual. This part can, therefore, be a factor in the occurrence of emotional problems later on. Indeed, I believe it not infrequently is. I think it is most likely so to be when the nature of the event is such as to cause the soul to wish, literally, that it had never left 'Upstairs'. This wish, which is likely to be reached and be understood in normal waking consciousness only with the aid of intensive therapy, can act like a brake upon any future desire to grow up, to go ahead and to make progress in life. In short, to move further and further away from 'Upstairs'.

Can I prove this? No. I cannot. It is an inference I have felt compelled to draw in more than one case of an apparently healthy young adult who was finding it impossible to decide what he wanted to do in life. When work within the orthodox framework had proved unhelpful, this explanation, after having reviewed his life-situation and encouraged him to have confidence in his potentials, has sometimes had a gratifying effect.

The Tasks Facing the Foetus

Obviously the foetus has to bring its body to a state at which it is capable of an independent existence, but this is by no means all it has to do. Since discarnate consciousness requires no physical apparatus, another task the foetus has to accomplish during its period in the womb is to transform *at least some* of its discarnate consciousness, which—initially—is the only form of consciousness it has, to a certain stage of brain-functioning consciousness. I stress 'at least some' because I suspect that it is with the remains of their discarnate consciousness that people with extrasensory faculties are operating. And, as if these tasks were not enough, the foetus also needs to reach a certain degree of psychological maturity. The ideal degree, I believe, would feature readiness, even eagerness to be released to a wider sphere of activity; in short, eagerness to be born.

It happens that the period we are allowed in the womb is fixed—give or take a week or two—at nine months, which is normally more than enough for the physical body to reach an adequate state of development. It is also usually long enough for a foetus to reach an *adequate* state of psychological maturity. However, for it to reach the ideal state, I suspect the psychological conditions in the womb need to be more perfect than they often are. These conditions will depend upon—at least—two groups of factors. The first of these concerns the psychology of the mother. It will include her deepest feelings about becoming a mother and, more superficially, her feelings about her husband and the general pattern of her life. The second group will concern the character of the foetus itself. I shall not attempt to add to the great deal that has already been written about the relationship of a woman to pregnancy; however, less has been written about the psychology of the foetus.

Unless one believes in the reality of the soul it is easy, even tempting, to think of the mind of the foetus as a blank sheet of paper waiting to be written on, or as an amorphous lump of putty waiting to be shaped by experience. But if one has come to believe in the reality of the soul, then it is easy to believe that it is in the womb that experience begins. This, as I have already said, was in fact the mistaken view that I held for several years.

However, when I came to recognise the reality of reincarnation, it became clear just how mistaken this notion was. I can no longer doubt that the foetus is a *person* whose soul, temporarily, has once again the body of a foetus. This soul has its own long history in the course of which it may have suffered traumatic episodes that have left their mark and caused ghosts to be left behind. Even more important though, as I also remarked earlier, it will have developed a well-defined character. This may include a marked Power Merchant trait, with its concomitants: a basically hostile attitude to life, a somewhat paranoid outlook, and a measure of unlove for itself. A foetus with such a character may well have difficulty in believing in the love of even the most devoted mother! Many a patient has told me that he was an unwanted child and that his mother never loved him, but I have never known a person who had regressed to the prenatal state suggest that he came under attack because he was somewhat unlovable! However, an explanation that does sometimes emerge is that of being the 'wrong' sex.

This particular notion may have a basis in fact, in which case the foetus may easily pick it up, by telepathy. I'm sure a constant, 'Oh, I do so hope it is a boy' in the mind of the mother can be picked up by the foetus, and can cause a female foetus to wish it were male. Later, such a wish in the unconscious of a small girl may be one explanation of her becoming a tomboy. Later still, it may be the origin of—apparently—inexplicable feelings of inadequacy about herself as a female. The unconscious wish to be male acts like a hole in the bucket through which any assurance that she is an adequate female leaks away.

A certain lady who presented with this very problem had a dream that illustrates beautifully the kind of confusion such an unconscious wish can cause. She dreamed that she was at a table in a restaurant and in front of her were two rolls (of bread). She could not decide which roll *(role)* to take! Such terrible puns are not uncommon in dreams.

Incidentally, it occurs to me that a constant wish for a daughter in the mind of a prospective mother might sometimes, possibly, be a factor in causing a male child to be homosexual or to have a penchant for cross-dressing, that is, for wearing the clothes of the opposite sex.

The Placenta Mechanism

I want now to discuss a mechanism which, I believe, has not been reported before. I am indebted to a patient for recognising it. This patient was a young woman who had developed feelings for me that, as she fully realised, were unrealistic. She recognised, in fact, that she was in the throes of a 'transference'. A transference is another jargon expression. It is the technical term given to the situation in therapy when a patient is transferring upon the therapist feelings he once had—usually in his childhood—for some person or object and then had repressed. Many people would argue, and I would agree with them, that relationships in everyday life also very frequently contain at least an element of transference. For instance, I find it impossible to deny that this was the case concerning my attachment to the grey car, which I related in Chapter 2.

When such a transference has developed in therapy, the transferred feelings may be positive or negative. The aim of the therapy, at some point, will be—to use the jargon again—to resolve the transference. This amounts to enabling the patient to realise that he is experiencing once more, but in a symbolical form, the situation or circumstances that were the origin of the feelings he is transferring. When this has been achieved, the therapy will have reached its goal of enabling the patient to recover from his unconscious the part of the child-that-once-he-was that had become split off from the main body of his experiences and that was causing his problems. It will also have the effect of causing the patient's feelings for the therapist once more to become realistic. The development of the transference and finally its resolution might be considered the cardinal feature of orthodox psychoanalysis.

Contrary to what might be expected, transference is unusual and seldom plays a significant part in hypnoanalysis. The altered state of consciousness that makes hypnotic regression possible enables the patient's mind to give reality to memory pictures held in his unconscious. In his regressed state, the scene in which the event to which he has regressed happened, the event itself and the people concerned will be as real as they were when the situation actually occurred. Thus the patient is able to complete any aspect of the situation that was then left unfinished, and there is no time for a transference situation to develop. The figures concerned are often parents, siblings or someone in a regular child-minding capacity.

It happened, though, that hypnoanalysis was impossible with this patient because I was unable to hypnotise her and therapy was therefore conducted by talks in normal consciousness. Over a considerable period, this proved conducive to the development of a succession of transference situations. She had already been through periods when she had been transferring upon me feelings she had had for each of her parents, and these transferences had been satisfactorily resolved. The feelings she now had seemed to have nothing whatever to do with her mother or her father, and this particular transference was proving extremely difficult to resolve. It was characterised by a mixture of exaggerated feelings of concern for me and of dependence upon me. Then, one day, in the course of a session, she suddenly exclaimed, 'I know what it is! I *am a foetus— and you are the placenta!*' This insight quickly led to a reduction of her feelings of dependence upon me. However, she still had the feeling—which she still recognised was totally irrational—that she was completely responsible for my well-being. Again, it was she who, a few days later, recognised the explanation of this feeling. In the course of a session she burst out, '*I know what's happening! I am still a foetus and I am worrying about you, my placenta!*'

The discussion which resulted from that flash of insight resolved her exaggerated concern for me and taught me the basis of much of what I think I have come to know about this mechanism. I believe it is an important one to recognise for three reasons. Firstly, its development is an indication that the patient's intrauterine period was less than ideal and that exploration of it might prove fruitful. Secondly, it may occasionally be the origin of a transference that a therapist is having difficulty in resolving. Thirdly, I think it can be the origin of certain instances of anxiety. I will explain how, I think, the placenta mechanism comes about.

When, for whatever reason, the foetus does not feel loved and secure, it may also feel *lonely*. It longs for a companion, and *it may fantasise a companion out of the placenta.* Not infrequently, a person who has regressed to the intrauterine period may speak of having a twin with him. Sometimes he may indeed have—or, for a period, have had—a twin, but on other occasions I suspect that the notion of a twin is, in fact, a consequence of the 'placenta mechanism'.

The placenta has not, of course, any life of its own, but the foetus endows it with life and personality in just the same way that a child bestows an identity and a personality upon his teddy bear. And just as a child may become most deeply attached to his teddy bear, refusing to be parted from it and dragging it around everywhere with him, so, for the foetus, the placenta may become a real person for whom it develops an intense attachment.

My experience convinces me that a foetus knows that one day it will be born, just as surely as we know that one day we shall die. If, in addition, it has developed the placenta mechanism and has not resolved it, it also knows that birth is going to separate it from its beloved companion. I suspect it also knows that the separation will be permanent. Until that happens, the foetus is as dependent upon the placenta as the placenta is upon the foetus. In short, *precisely the feelings which had characterised my patient's transference.* The knowledge may not only cause the foetus to develop feelings of deep concern for the placenta but may also bring to the event of birth an element of great sadness. I strongly suspect that in his teddy bear the child is trying to replace his former companion, his placenta. This is particularly likely to be the case when the attachment to the teddy bear persists long after toddlerhood has been left behind. In fact, the attachment is a transference situation which has not been resolved. As my patient showed, the distress over the parting from the placenta is an entirely different thing from distress over parting at birth from any aspect of the mother herself. I feel sure it can be a factor responsible for the clinging child and, indeed, for the clinging adult as well.

The anxiety which such people endure—children as well as adults—can be agony for them and a distressing burden for the persons upon whom the anxiety is focussed. Reassurance to such a child that his mother will be back from her shopping very soon is at best of only limited and temporary comfort because the present absence of the mother is not the fundamental cause of that child's anxiety. Though of course unaware of the fact, the child is also feeling again some of the distress it once felt about the placenta from which, it knew, parting was not only inevitable but would be permanent. In later life such a child may become a parent who has exaggerated anxiety about his own offspring, even when they are grown up. If one of them is going on a journey, for instance, the parent may implore him—or her—to telephone at every possible stage to assure the parent that all is well. As with the clinging child, the reassurance is likely to have only a limited and short-lived effect, and for the same reason.

Obviously there can be other reasons for this type of anxiety such, for instance, as unconscious aggression. In this event, though totally unaware of what is happening, the patient is in fact afraid of the effect his unconscious feelings of aggression may have upon the person who is the object of his anxiety, especially if the person is away for any length of time. However, if the anxiety persists after all the recognised causes have been explored, just an explanation along the lines of the placenta mechanism may, at least to an adult, prove helpful.

This happened in the case of a patient who had developed a loving relationship with a married man. However, as there was no possibility of a future together on account of the man's commitments, she had decided, of her own accord, that she would terminate the relationship. Her problem was that whenever she turned her thoughts in that direction she would be overcome by grief that was so intense that she could not prevent herself from dissolving into tears, wherever she might be. It had even happened once when she was in the queue at a supermarket.

She recognised that the intensity of her emotions and her inability to control them were totally foreign to the otherwise mature and confident adult that—justifiably—she felt herself to be.

Two sessions sufficed for me to learn enough about the lamentable relationships she had had all her life with the closest members of her family to cause me to feel justified in assuming that her prenatal life had been similarly wretched and that she was suffering from a placenta-transference. The effect of the explanation was dramatic. The intensity of her feelings about ending the relationship was immediately reduced to a sadness she could cope with.

A rather similar upshot occurred in the case of a married lady whose husband had only recently recovered from a grave illness. They were absolutely devoted to one another and during his illness she had suffered intense anxiety. However, he had made a remarkable recovery, and all the latest tests had had a most satisfactory result. Since it was not a condition that was liable to recur, they could expect to enjoy many happy, healthy years together. Nevertheless, this lady was in a state of perpetual dread that her husband might suddenly disappear at any moment.

The anxiety even made it almost impossible for her to sleep. She too had had a most unloving family and since her mother had often told her that she had been an unwanted child, I felt strongly that an explanation of the placenta mechanism might be appropriate. And so it proved to be. The patient immediately felt the explanation was valid, and the anxiety subsided.

Finally, a rather different problem. One could hardly describe as a patient the young woman who asked to talk to me, but she certainly had a problem. She was in love with a man whom she felt sure was her Mr Right, but she was finding his incessant demands for reassurance that she would never leave him a really serious strain. She understood that any young man might be anxious for reassurance on this score, but it certainly seemed that her friend's anxiety was excessive. She foresaw that it might continue to be a problem even after they were married. She wanted me to have a talk with him, and I agreed to do so.

It turned out that he, like the other two patients, had had a very unloving family. Interestingly, a teddy bear had been his most prized possession until he was ten, when it was given away without his knowledge. Again an account of the placenta mechanism proved very helpful.

In the next chapter we will look at some other conditions that may sometimes be referable to the prenatal state or to birth itself.

18   *Problems Stemming from Birth and Life in the Womb*

Anxiety Referable to Birth

When a person has felt sufficiently loved and secure throughout his period in the womb to become psychologically ready to be born, birth is an ordeal that he is ready, even eager to undertake. After all, during his long history he has survived the challenge on innumerable previous occasions. Moreover, he is ready to relinquish all the features peculiar to life in the womb, and he will interpret the pressures that are expelling him therefrom as benign forces that are helping him towards a wider field of existence.

Nevertheless, birth is liable to be a somewhat painful and frightening process for most of us, and for the person who is not psychologically ready to be born it is especially frightening.

To begin with, if a person has felt unwanted throughout his period in the womb, it is understandable that he may interpret the expulsive forces of labour not as benign and helping him towards a wider field of existence but as thrusting him into extinction. At all events, if only in fantasy, he tries initially to resist these forces. But the moment may come when the foetus feels his consciousness is ebbing or being withdrawn from him—a very different matter to just falling asleep—and very frightening. At the same time, if the mother is totally preoccupied with herself, and the foetus is not yet in touch with the helpers outside, it can feel it has been abandoned. It may then interpret the natural resistances of the maternal tissues as obstacles deliberately designed to prevent it from surviving. It is not surprising if birth leaves a scar upon the psyche!

Such a scar is particularly likely to result, I think, if the foetus actually loses consciousness during birth. If this happens, I believe it cannot always distinguish this loss of consciousness from extinction. At the least, it loses the possibility of seeing life after it has been born as an extension of its life before it was born, and the process of birth as merely the transition from one to the other. To my mind this makes a strong case for the use of hypnosis in childbirth whenever possible. It can render the process painless for the mother, and since she is fully conscious throughout, she can maintain psychological contact with her baby. Incidentally, I have found that a person who has an exaggerated and fear-ridden concern about dying may be projecting upon the change of state, that he knows lies ahead of him, anxiety which became ingrained into his mind during the change of state that lies behind him but which he has forgotten.

Other important changes in life are also capable of stirring up feelings that were ingrained in a person at birth.

The American psychiatrist Erik H. Erikson lists eight 'psycho-social changes'—as he calls them—when a person moves from one stage of life to the next. In my experience there are two periods of this nature when a person tends to be particularly vulnerable. The first is the onset of puberty or adolescence; the second is the arrival of the menopause in women or—occurring rather later in life—the period of retirement for men. But such events as moving from toddlerhood to childhood can do it, as can moving from one house to another or exchanging the unmarried for the married state, as well as vice versa. Finally, I am convinced that the experience of giving birth can be a powerful factor in reawakening the fears a woman experienced when she herself was being born.

Symbolical Perpetuation of Aspects of Intrauterine Life

As I have said, the foetus that has reached the ideal psychological state before being born will be ready to relinquish every aspect of life in the womb; but for the foetus who was pushed out before it felt ready to go, it is a different matter. It will have been born carrying with it one or both of two tendencies. One of these is that it will constantly be seeking to recreate the conditions of life in the womb, which, of course, it can only do in symbolical ways. The other is that the individual will *be unable to avoid* unconsciously seeing certain situations as symbolically repeating aspects of intrauterine life, and of reacting to them accordingly. Between them, these two tendencies can create a variety of problems or, at least, personal foibles.

For an instance of the first tendency, consider the business of taking in food and air. While an infant is inside his mother, his umbilical cord conveys from the placenta a ceaseless stream of food and oxygen that enters his body at the navel. Immediately after birth the cord is removed and the functions of the navel as the port of entry of food and air suddenly shift to the nose and mouth. I have not known of breathing being a problem. However, no matter how a good substitute the nipple may be for the umbilical cord, or the arms of the mother and the skin of her body for the protective wall of the womb—not to mention the all-encompassing amniotic fluid that is softer even than water, there is one respect in which they cannot help falling short.

The situation in the womb, so long as it lasts, is constant and uninterrupted. By contrast, the contacts with the breast are inevitably intermittent and limited. If the infant falls asleep at the breast, when it wakes up it is likely to find itself alone. Thus the infant who is trying to recreate the womb situation from contact with the breast is doomed to disappointment. Unless it is able to accept this reality, when the time comes for it to move on from the breast, it will try to extract from the next phase of its psychological maturation more from that stage also than it can possibly give. This train of events is continually repeated, resulting in the adult who, for instance, is still trying—unconsciously—to extract from his oral activities more satisfaction than they can give. Hence one reason for a tendency to overeat, or smoke or drink to excess.

In a different direction, without realising what he is doing, a person who feels he was pushed out of the womb before he was ready may continue to try to recreate womb-like situations in various ways throughout his life. A clear example may be provided by the way he decorates his house or apartment. He may also decline anything, such as the offer of promotion in his work, that will take him further away from where he unconsciously still wants to be: the place from which he resented being pushed out. Of course, behind the unconscious longing to be back in the womb may be the longing to be back 'Upstairs'.

Some Sexual Problems Related to Birth and the Period around It

Removal of the cord, which from the point of view of the infant was psychologically premature, may produce a problem that I will mention in the hope of bringing relief to some sufferers. It is not very unusual for a man to have needless feelings of inferiority about the size of his penis. When these feelings are not allayed by authoritative and entirely justified assurance that his equipment is perfectly normal, it is possible that the fear covers an unconscious factor of some kind. Therapy may bring the factor to light fairly readily, leading to relief of the symptom. However, when the feelings are proving unusually difficult to relieve, the fact may be that the patient's *conscious* longing for a larger model of the tube attached to his abdomen is the expression of an *unconscious* longing for the return of the original tube of which he felt he was robbed. When one considers that the umbilical cord is the original link with the beloved, whether in the sense of the placenta or the mother, it is understandable that this confusion could arise.

Since the sexual act very frequently occurs in a dimmed light, if not in darkness, and contact is of the essence, it is easy to understand that either sex may unconsciously see the sexual act as a return to the womb. For the male, the symbolism of the act is obvious. For the female it is less obvious but, by what is technically known as 'role reversal', being penetrated can have for the female the same significance as does penetrating for the male. If a person is indeed carrying in his unconscious memories of what seemed to him to be threats to his life while getting out of the womb, it is not surprising if, at an unconscious level, he—or she—is frightened of getting back into it again, if only symbolically. This fear can be one cause of conditions that make penetration virtually impossible. A male may have difficulty in maintaining an erection; the female may experience spasms of her vagina that she cannot relax. Moreover, loss of consciousness during birth may lead later to difficulties in the letting go, which is the essence of orgasm.

Does everyone who has had a somewhat unsatisfactory time in the womb and also perhaps a difficult birth, suffer from some such consequences? Most certainly not! I suspect that the prenatal period and the experience of birth often leave some mark—perhaps in the form of an idiosyncrasy such as difficulty in putting one's head under water—but in most cases any problem it causes is insignificant and its origin is unrecognised and unsought. I'm also sure that experiences in a former lifetime, such, for instance, as dying in some place one could not get out of, have rendered some people particularly sensitive to the conditions of life in the womb and to the difficulties in leaving it. This might account, at least in part, for some people being more affected than others by what would appear comparable birth experiences.

One point emerging from recognition of the reality of the soul and the problems which can arise from the prenatal period is the realisation that to risk bringing about a pregnancy unless both the potential parents genuinely want a child may be a gross unkindness to a future individual.

Let There Be Light

I will end this chapter with the story of a case that is of interest to me for more than one reason. It involves a birth trauma, but it taught me—as a therapist—not to become bogged down in that phase of a patient's history. In short, it is a case I could not have treated successfully before I had come to recognise the value of reincarnation in psychiatry.

Daphne was a married lady in her mid-twenties. Her problem was that she could not tolerate being in a dark room. She could not even turn the light off before going to sleep. If someone who did not know of her foible chanced to enter her room while she was asleep and, finding the light on, switched it off for her, she would awaken in panic. It was imperative for her that the moment she awoke she should be able to see all around her. This had not been a problem for her until she married a man who happened to be unable to sleep if there were so much as a chink of light in the room!

Daphne proved an excellent hypnotic subject and I told her that as I was counting to 'ten', something would be bubbling up to her awareness which would give us a clue to the reason that instant light was of such importance to her. Within seconds she was experiencing herself as a small girl, aged about six, playing with friends in a barn that was stacked high with bales of hay. Daphne had slipped down the narrow gap between two stacks of bales and could not get out. She was terrified.

A fear of the dark quite often has its origin in a prenatal or birth experience, and since finding herself at the bottom of what was virtually a tunnel from which she could not get out was the kind of thing that could reactivate a birth trauma, I felt that something of the sort was probably involved here. With this in mind I suggested that now Daphne would become aware of something that would help us to understand why she was so *very* frightened.

Almost at once she found herself as a much smaller girl, aged perhaps three, in bed. She could hear the grown-ups talking and laughing in the room below and she was feeling bored. So she started to cry, vigorously. This caused her sister, who was a year or two older, to arrive with a pillow that she put over Daphne's face. Whether she intended simply to muffle her bawling or to silence her on some more permanent basis never became clear because, at that moment, their mother appeared on the scene.

Though this episode might theoretically have accounted for Daphne's fear of being in a dark room, I still felt sure that the origin of that fear in fact lay still further back. I suggested, therefore, that if there were anything earlier that was relevant, she would soon find herself back in that occurrence. I was not surprised when Daphne next found herself in the womb. She was feeling cramped and wanting to get out. Quite soon labour started, and it then transpired that she was presenting as a breech, that is, backside first.

The actual birth was difficult and at one point in the course of the process she gave a cry on account of pain in her back. However, eventually the delivery was completed and all appeared to be well. I brought her back to the present day and back to normal consciousness, expecting to hear a gratifying: 'Ah! Now I understand why I hate the dark so much!' But not a bit of it. All I got was:

'Wasn't that funny about my back? My back has always hurt but somehow it feels better now.' Her fear of the dark was unaffected. At this point, had I not believed in reincarnation, I'm sure I would have spent more time fruitlessly exploring the intrauterine period. As it was, my belief in reincarnation caused me to suspect that we needed to look for something even earlier.

At the next session, therefore, I hypnotised Daphne again and, without offering any more detailed guidance, said that at the count of 'ten' she would be aware of something else that would tell us more about the reason for her fear of the dark. Gradually an extraordinary story unfolded.

It started with Daphne immediately experiencing herself as a boy, thirteen or fourteen years old, who was sitting at a table in a large room with a high vaulted ceiling. He was writing most painstakingly in a big ledger. It emerged that both his parents had died and the local squire had adopted him. Because he could read and write, the squire had taught him how to keep the accounts of the estate, and it was on these that he was working with such care. The squire came to rely more and more upon the boy, much to the jealous fury of his real son, who—for whatever reason—was illiterate.

When the boy had grown up, the squire often had him sitting with him on the magistrates' bench, and in due course, whenever the squire had to be away on other business, he would appoint the young man to deputise for him. On one of these occasions, who should appear before him but the squire's natural son, charged with rape. There was no doubt about his guilt and the young man could do no less than sentence him to a week in the stocks.

At that point I ended the session and brought Daphne back to the present day and—almost—to normal consciousness. Curiously, for about half an hour she had a foot in both camps so to speak—the present day and her life as this boy. She was able to tell me, for instance, that the boy's parents had died of the plague. They had been servants of the squire, which was why the squire had adopted their son.

I commented that a week in the stocks sounded a very light sentence for rape, but Daphne corrected me. Apparently, once in the stocks a person was not allowed out of them for any reason until his sentence had expired, and for all that period he was fair game for everyone to taunt as they wished and make his life hell. Obviously, this did nothing to endear the adopted young man to the squire's natural son.

At the next session, Daphne was soon back in the life of this young man, but at a later period. He had been desperately ill, and though he had survived he had been left totally blind, which suggests that the illness might have been meningitis. The son lost no opportunity to torment him, but there were limits to what he could do so long as the squire was alive. However, when the squire died, the situation changed—drastically. The first thing the real son did was to discharge all the servants and replace them with new ones. These he told that the blind man was subject to fits of violence. He was in fact intending to kill the adopted son and was preparing, in advance, a defence of self-defence. It was pitiful to watch Daphne as she was reliving this period. I shall never forget her saying, 'I even had to stop playing the lute so that I might hear him coming.' Eventually the day arrived when the son succeeded in approaching the blind man by stealth; and he stabbed him to death.

Now the explanation of Daphne's fear of the dark was clear. It was nothing to do with her birth or prenatal period. It arose from that life which ended by her being murdered for lack of *sight*. It is small wonder that in this life she felt an urgent need always to be able to see all around her; but since her eyes were perfect, what had become essential for Daphne was not sight but *light*!

Recovering this story effectively relieved Daphne of her terror of being in darkness.

19   *Look Again*

In this final chapter I will try to pinpoint what I should like to feel people were carrying away with them after reading this book.

Anyone considering the concept of reincarnation for the first time may find his thoughts focussing upon the past, upon the possibility that he has lived before. And of course the past is not without importance. From the study of history we may learn what might with benefit be repeated and—no less important—avoided.

Often it is only by a study of the past that we can fully understand the present, and in psychiatry a patient's problem may elude resolution until its origin is discovered in events of a former lifetime. A patient does not need to believe in reincarnation before he can experience such a healing regression. However, it is essential for the therapist to be able to accept the possibility that it is to a former lifetime that his patient has regressed. Almost the first thing I learned from Joan was that if a therapist fails to recognise such a regression for what it is, that is a reliving of a genuine experience, the therapy will get nowhere. I should add that no exploration of former lifetimes is likely to be of any help at all in resolving a problem that in fact is concerned only with affairs of the present lifetime. The past is no haven into which one can escape from problems of the present. Nor, I might add, is 'Upstairs'.

Belief in reincarnation adds new dimensions to our understanding of ourselves. For instance, it extends the timescale by which we are accustomed to consider human affairs. Cases in this book illustrate that even experiences from centuries ago can influence and shape our present lives. The more we can learn about ourselves, the better the chance we have of ordering our affairs with wisdom, as the present is undoubtedly shaping our future. Hence, belief in reincarnation bids us focus upon the here and now.

As I gained experience as a therapist, I came to realise that a patient's reaction to a circumstance could be more significant than the circumstance itself.

The reason is clear: the nature of the patient's reaction is an indication of a trait in his character and, more often than not, it is this character trait that is the basic cause of his problem. In due course, this realisation crystallised into my notions about the Power Merchant trait.

I have tried ad nauseam to explain why I see the character trait that I have called the Power Merchant as being virtually universal and *The Human Sickness*. As I suggested in the first chapter, forces that have the effect of diminishing the barriers between people could be described as positive while those that tend to increase those barriers could be described as negative. For the words positive and negative, we can surely substitute good and evil. Since the Power Merchant trait does nothing to diminish the barriers between people, it clearly belongs on the wrong side of the fence.

I have also expressed the view that a character trait, by its very nature, does not end with the end of a lifetime but may become part of the very shape, so to speak, of that which reincarnates. BUT, I have also tried to show that once a person has become aware that he harbours any particular trait, he can change it *by forming a sufficiently strong wish to do so*. It is not always easy to form such a wish, but no one has ever suggested that spiritual evolution is easy.

Belief in something that can reincarnate is inseparable from a belief in reincarnation. The Christian religion calls that something the soul, and it is convenient to stay with that term. Just as belief in reincarnation is inseparable from belief in the soul, so belief in the soul is inseparable from the belief that there are orders of reality that are not physical. Without this belief, one's interests are bound to be centred on the survival of one's physical body and somewhat confined to material realities and such values as wealth and status.

But whether one recognises it or not, the fact is that one has a soul. Of that I have not the slightest doubt. The evidence from a multitude of sources is overwhelming. Therefore, in addition to one's physical appetites one longs for things that are not physical. Paramount amongst these is the longing to love and to be loved in a sense that is not carnal.

However, if one is unaware of the true nature of these longings, as is often the case, the energy that should go into striving for what indeed would satisfy them becomes deflected into the body. We behave as though the earth is our one and only abode, and our exaggerated focus on the body at the expense of its non-physical component, reinforces the body's appetites. But since no form of physical gratification is the right food for these exaggerated longings, they are not appeased. Hence they persist. Moreover they not only persist but their intensity tends to increase, eventually becoming insatiable.

We seem to have forgotten that the physical body is not merely the vehicle that conveys the soul during those phases of its evolution which it spends on this level of reality, but that it is also the *precision instrument* through which the soul gathers experience for its evolution. We tend to pay it less of the kind of attention it really *needs* than we pay our motor car, and our efforts to satisfy the insatiable lead, all too often, to excesses of food, drink, drugs and sex. In addition, we tend to expose our body, quite needlessly, to danger of permanent damage as, for instance, by excessively loud noise or foolhardy physical exploits.

The consequences to which any of these excesses can lead may be sad enough, but even they can be dwarfed by those caused by the drive for power. On the level of interpersonal relationships this drive can cause severe distress, but on the global or international level it is ominous indeed. 'If you can devise an effective shield against any weapon we can throw at you at the moment, what response have we got but to devise a weapon still more effective?' Such seems to be one line of thinking, by no means yet abandoned. It is a relic of the jungle ethic which is surely the origin of the Power Merchant trait.

The stark reality, however, is that no form of technology can ever guarantee complete protection from attacks of any kind. As small arms become easier to procure, and weapons of mass destruction easier to produce, the situation is becoming ever more disturbing. But there is a way, just one, that would indeed guarantee immunity from attacks of any kind on any scale, from the most trivial to the most horrific. And it does not depend upon technology. This way is the universal, complete *eradication of the desire* ever to launch an attack by eradicating the Power Merchant trait. It would come about by the complete change of the ethic by which we live. Does such a project appear totally unrealistic? I readily concede that, at first sight, it does.

But look again.

Does it appear more unrealistic than the assumption that our planet and life upon it can survive indefinitely unless some such project is undertaken?

It is surely no accident that the world's great religions enjoin their followers to 'Do unto others as you would they would do unto you' or, in slightly different words, 'Love your neighbour as yourself'. The founders of these religions could not have failed to recognise that if we continued to live—as to a large extent we were and still are living—by the jungle ethic of 'Survival of the Fittest', we would inevitably end by destroying our planet and every living thing upon it. And those founders would not have asked of their followers something that was impossible.

Mind-boggling and awe-inspiring as this project may seem, it is essentially only an expansion of the philosophy that has been the basis of my approach to psychotherapy for many years. I believe that I am not overstating the case if I say that this approach has helped a considerable number of individuals—and through them, their families—to find happiness, sometimes even within a single, or at most two sessions, when years of therapy along more usual lines had not helped.

I do not recall just when it began, but quite early in my career I became accustomed to starting a day of psychotherapy with a brief prayer. I would ask for the right feelings in my heart, the right thoughts in my head and the right words in my mouth to deal with each situation as it arose. When Ray went 'Upstairs', I usually addressed specific requests to her. I am certain that I received a constant flow of help from 'Upstairs' and that such successes as I had were mainly due to this help.

However, working with a single individual and sometimes turning his approach to life upside down is one thing, especially if he is actively seeking help. It is obviously a vastly different matter to persuading the population of a planet to adopt a new ethic, especially when many of its individuals will be vigorously resistant to the very idea. Can it possibly be done? I am sure the correct answer, in one word, is 'YES'.

The magnitude of the task is indeed awe-inspiring. Nevertheless, I am certain God could bring it about and would bring it about if enough of us, while we are down here, were to ask Him, with sufficient energy in our request, to help us undertake the job. We need to ask for His help to come to grips with the Power Merchant within ourselves, and thus inspire those around us to do the same. With His help, I am sure the project is not unrealistic but can and will be realized. Perhaps it will happen through some cataclysmic event, or perhaps step by step. I believe it was no less a sage than Lao Tsu who observed that the longest journey begins by putting one foot in front of the other.

In conclusion, let me reiterate: my experience over forty years as a psychiatrist has convinced me that, whether one believes in reincarnation or not, eradicating the Power Merchant trait by doing as you would be done by is the only ethic compatible with the sustained health of the individual and of the community.

At present, our planet is not, on the whole, an inviting place. The concept of reincarnation teaches us that it is not only our children who will inherit the world we leave behind. There are lessons we have to learn that have to be learnt 'down here'. Until we have learned them, we shall have to come back ourselves.

Bibliography

Friel, J.P., editor (1974) *Dorland's Illustrated Medical Dictionary*, 25th edition. Philadelphia, W.B. Saunders.

Grant, Joan (1937) *Winged Pharaoh*. London, Arthur Barker.

Grant, Joan (1956) *Time Out of Mind*. London, Arthur Barker.

Grant, Joan (1962) *A Lot to Remember*. London, Robert Hale.

Grant, Joan & Kelsey, Denys (1967) *Many Lifetimes*. New York, Doubleday.

Reber, A.S. & Reber, E.S. (2001) *The Penguin Dictionary of Psychology*. London, Penguin Books.

Verney, Thomas & Kelly, John (1988) *The Secret Life of The Unborn Child*. New York, Time Warner.

"Have you remembrances, the glimmering arches that span the summits of the mind?" Kahlil Gibran.

Each Life—Each Day

Each life I keep on being born anew.
All trials I must know;
not one may I pass by.
And when I die –
into my being I shall take
the essence of my every mistake,
to mould me into the creature
I shall be once more.
The sum of all
my virtues and my vices,
deeply contained within the core.

And likewise, too, each day
I'll keep on being born anew,
if I dare die
to what I really thought I knew.
My weakest spot is
what I thought my strength to be.
If I should really know myself
– one day –
I shall be free –
a god I'll be.

From *Glimmering Arches* by Renée van Tuyll. Wassenaar, Servire (1974)